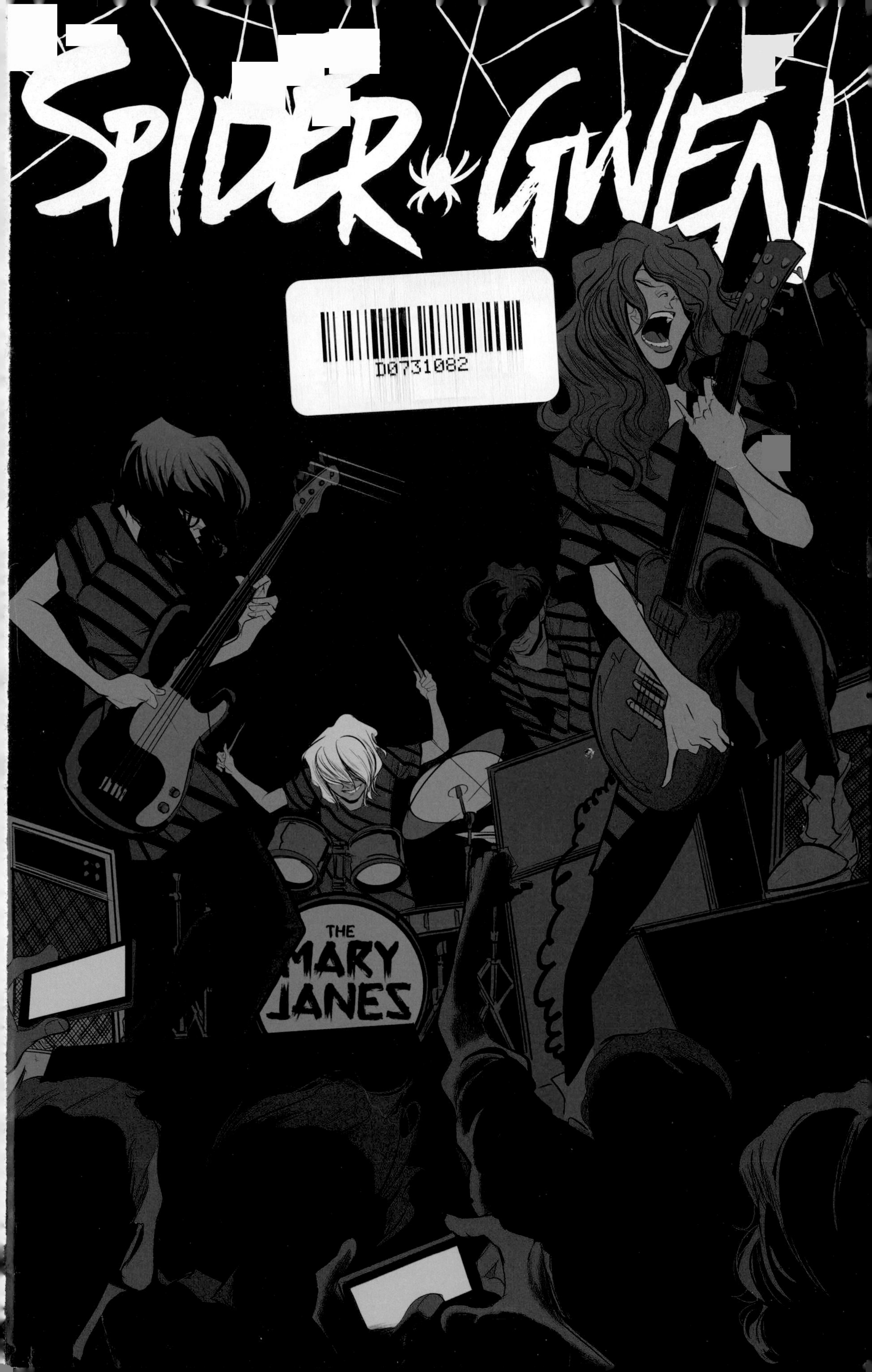
SPIDER GWEN
THE
MARY
JANES

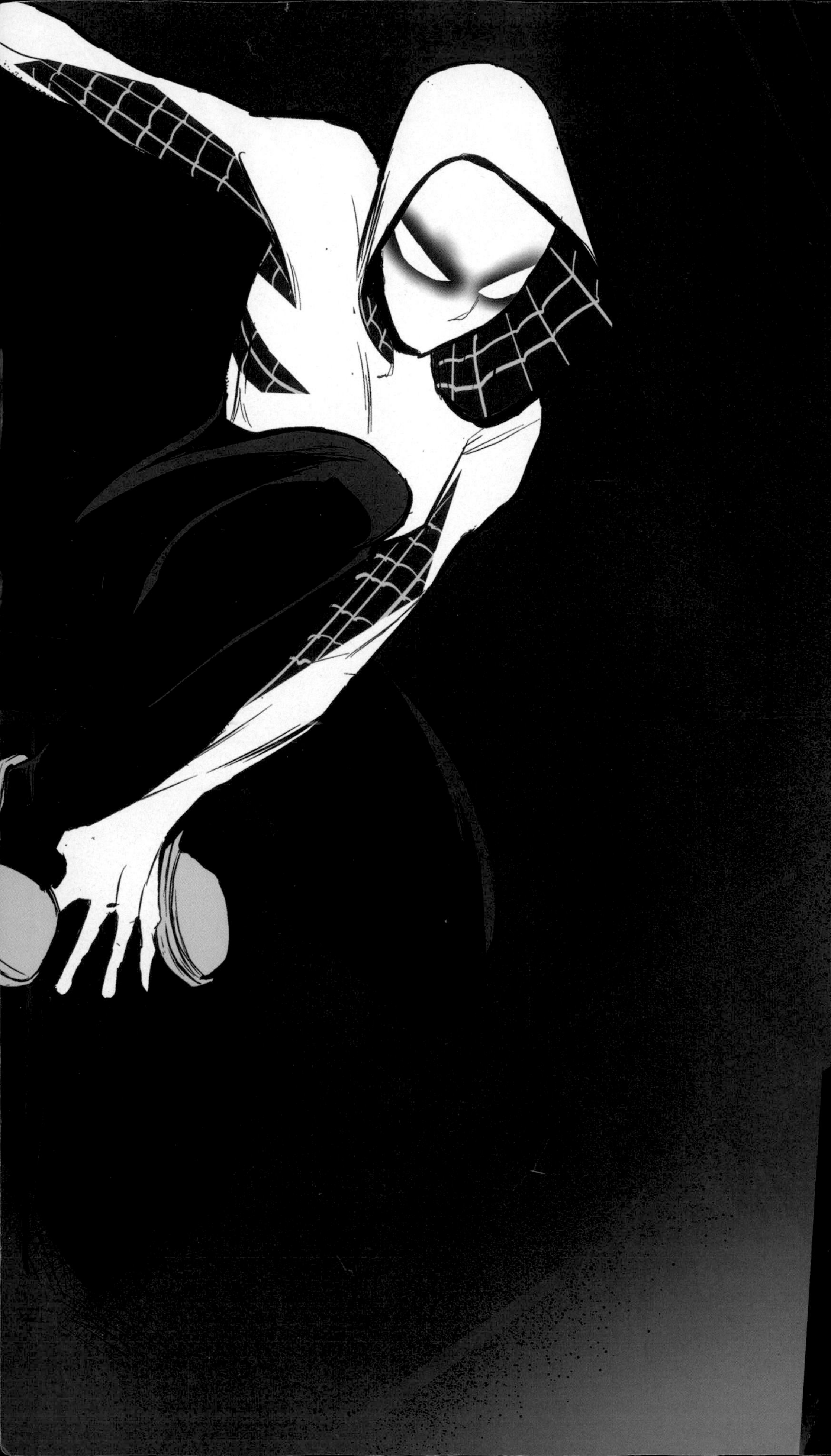

# SPIDER-GWEN

## MOST WANTED?

JASON LATOUR
WRITER

ROBBI RODRIGUEZ
ARTIST

RICO RENZI
COLOR ARTIST

VC'S CLAYTON COWLES
LETTERER

ROBBI RODRIGUEZ
COVER ART

ELLIE PYLE
ASSOCIATE EDITOR

DEVIN LEWIS
ASSISTANT EDITOR

NICK LOWE
EDITOR

JENNIFER GRÜNWALD
COLLECTION EDITOR

SARAH BRUNSTAD
ASSISTANT EDITOR

ALEX STARBUCK
ASSOCIATE MANAGING EDITOR

MARK D. BEAZLEY
EDITOR, SPECIAL PROJECTS

JEFF YOUNGQUIST
SENIOR EDITOR, SPECIAL PROJECTS

DAVID GABRIEL
SVP PRINT, SALES & MARKETING

JAY BOWEN
BOOK DESIGNER

AXEL ALONSO
EDITOR IN CHIEF

JOE QUESADA
CHIEF CREATIVE OFFICER

DAN BUCKLEY
PUBLISHER

ALAN FINE
EXECUTIVE PRODUCER



**SPIDER-GWEN VOL. 0: MOST WANTED?** Contains material originally published in magazine form as EDGE OF SPIDER-VERSE #2 and SPIDER-GWEN #1-5. First printing 2015. ISBN# 978-0-7851-9773-7. Published by MARVEL WORLDWIDE, INC., a subsidiary of MARVEL ENTERTAINMENT, LLC. OFFICE OF PUBLICATION: 135 West 50th Street, New York, NY 10020. Copyright © 2015 MARVEL No similarity between any of the names, characters, persons, and/or institutions in this magazine with those of any living or dead person or institution is intended, and any such similarity which may exist is purely coincidental. **Printed in Canada.** ALAN FINE, President, Marvel Entertainment; DAN BUCKLEY, President, TV, Publishing and Brand Management; JOE QUESADA, Chief Creative Officer; TOM BREVOORT, SVP of Publishing; DAVID BOGART, SVP of Operations & Procurement, Publishing; C.B. CEBULSKI, VP of International Development & Brand Management; DAVID GABRIEL, SVP Print, Sales & Marketing; JIM O'KEEFE, VP of Operations & Logistics; DAN CARR, Executive Director of Publishing Technology; SUSAN CRESPI, Editorial Operations Manager; ALEX MORALES, Publishing Operations Manager; STAN LEE, Chairman Emeritus. For information regarding advertising in Marvel Comics or on Marvel.com, please contact Jonathan Rheingold, VP of Custom Solutions & Ad Sales, at jrheingold@marvel.com. For Marvel subscription inquiries, please call 800-217-9158. **Manufactured between 10/2/2015 and 11/9/2015 by SOLISCO PRINTERS, SCOTT, QC, CANADA.**

10 9 8 7 6 5 4 3 2 1

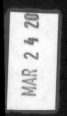

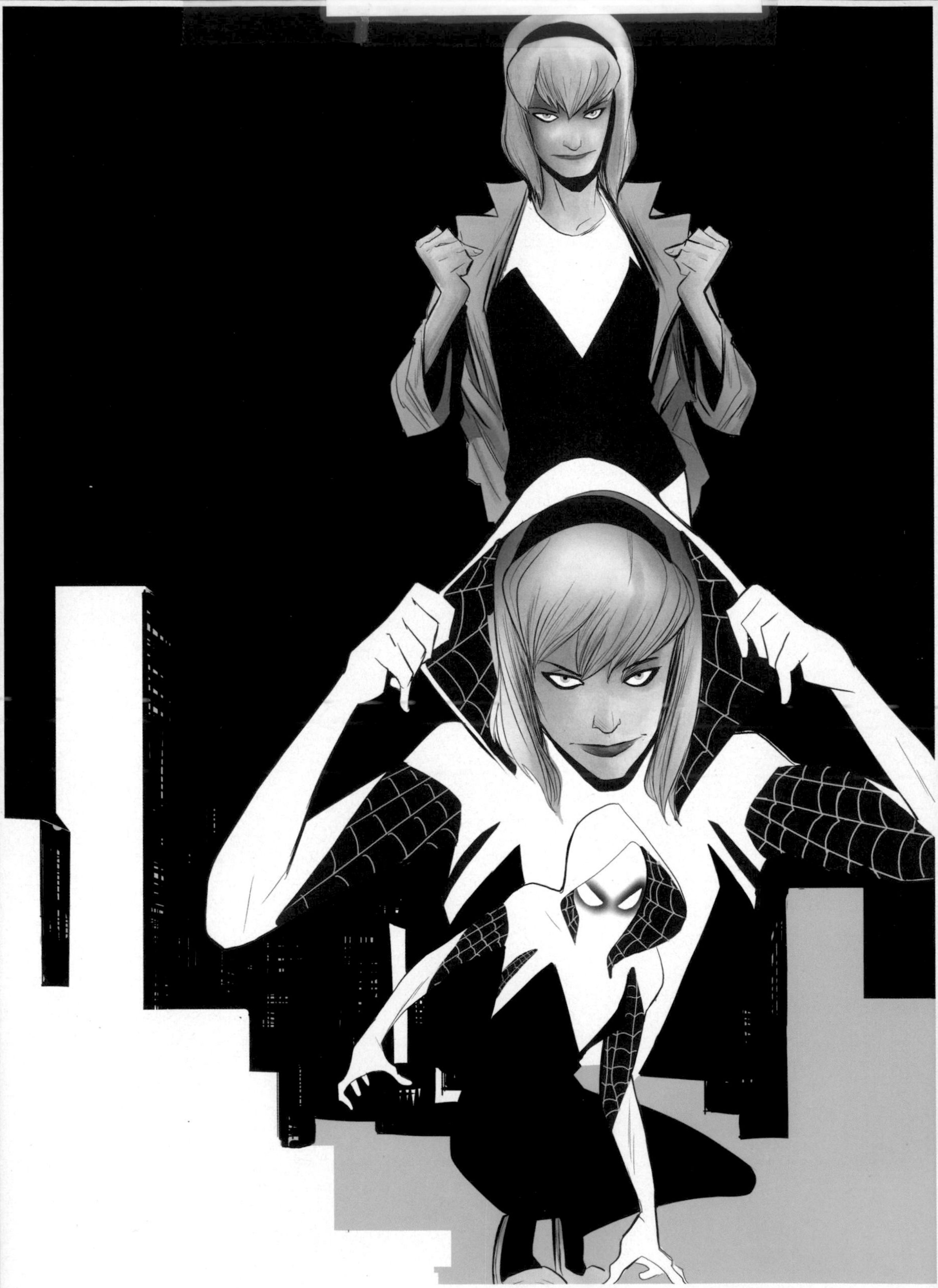

EDGE OF SPIDER-VERSE #2

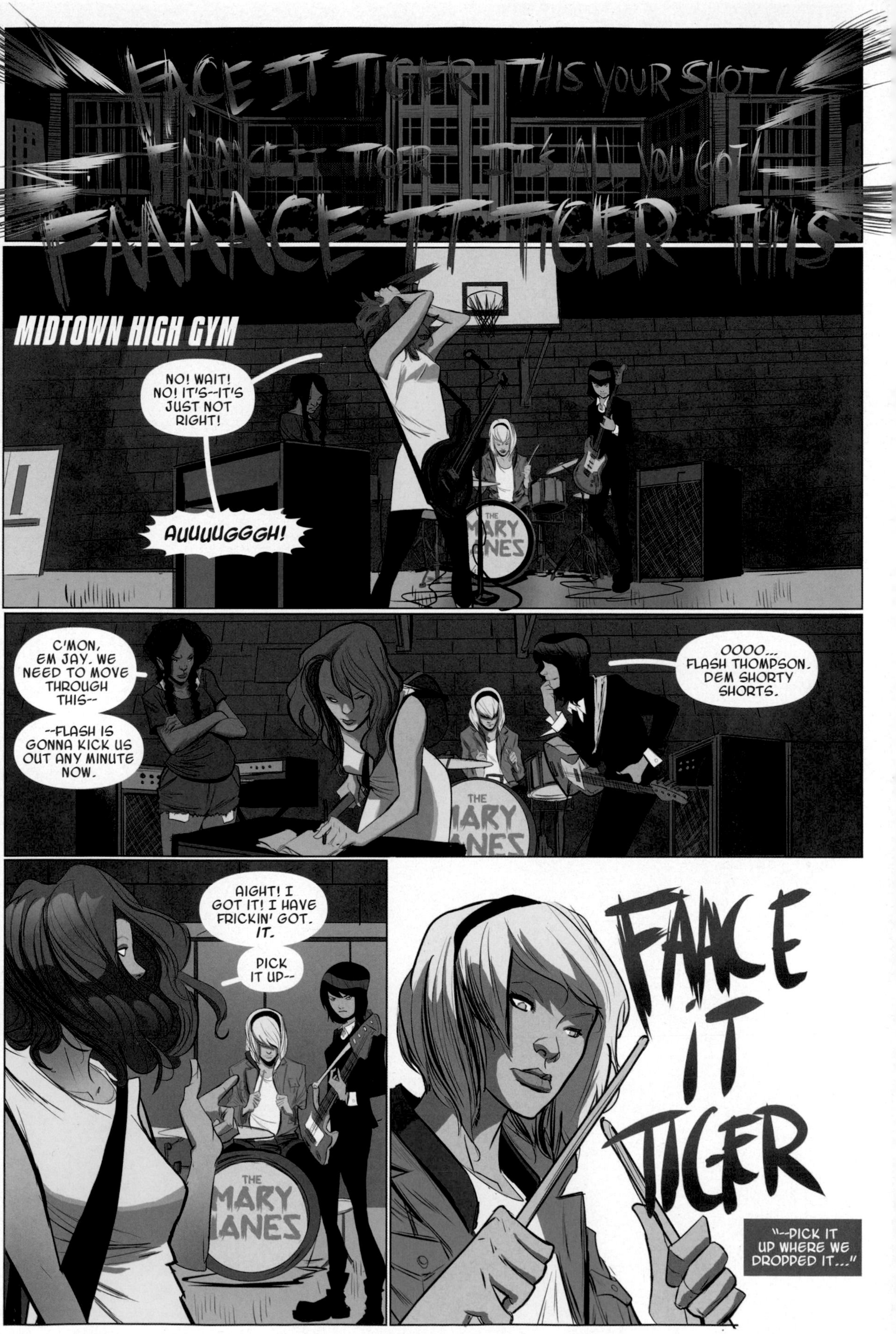
FAACE IT TIGER THIS YOUR SHOT!
FAAACE IT TIGER IT'S ALL YOU GOT!
FAAACE IT TIGER THIS
MIDTOWN HIGH GYM
NO! WAIT! NO! IT'S--IT'S JUST NOT RIGHT!
AUUUUGGGH!
THE MARY JANES
C'MON, EM JAY. WE NEED TO MOVE THROUGH THIS--
--FLASH IS GONNA KICK US OUT ANY MINUTE NOW.
OOOO... FLASH THOMPSON. DEM SHORTY SHORTS.
AIGHT! I GOT IT! I HAVE FRICKIN' GOT. IT.
PICK IT UP--
FAACE IT TIGER
"--PICK IT UP WHERE WE DROPPED IT..."

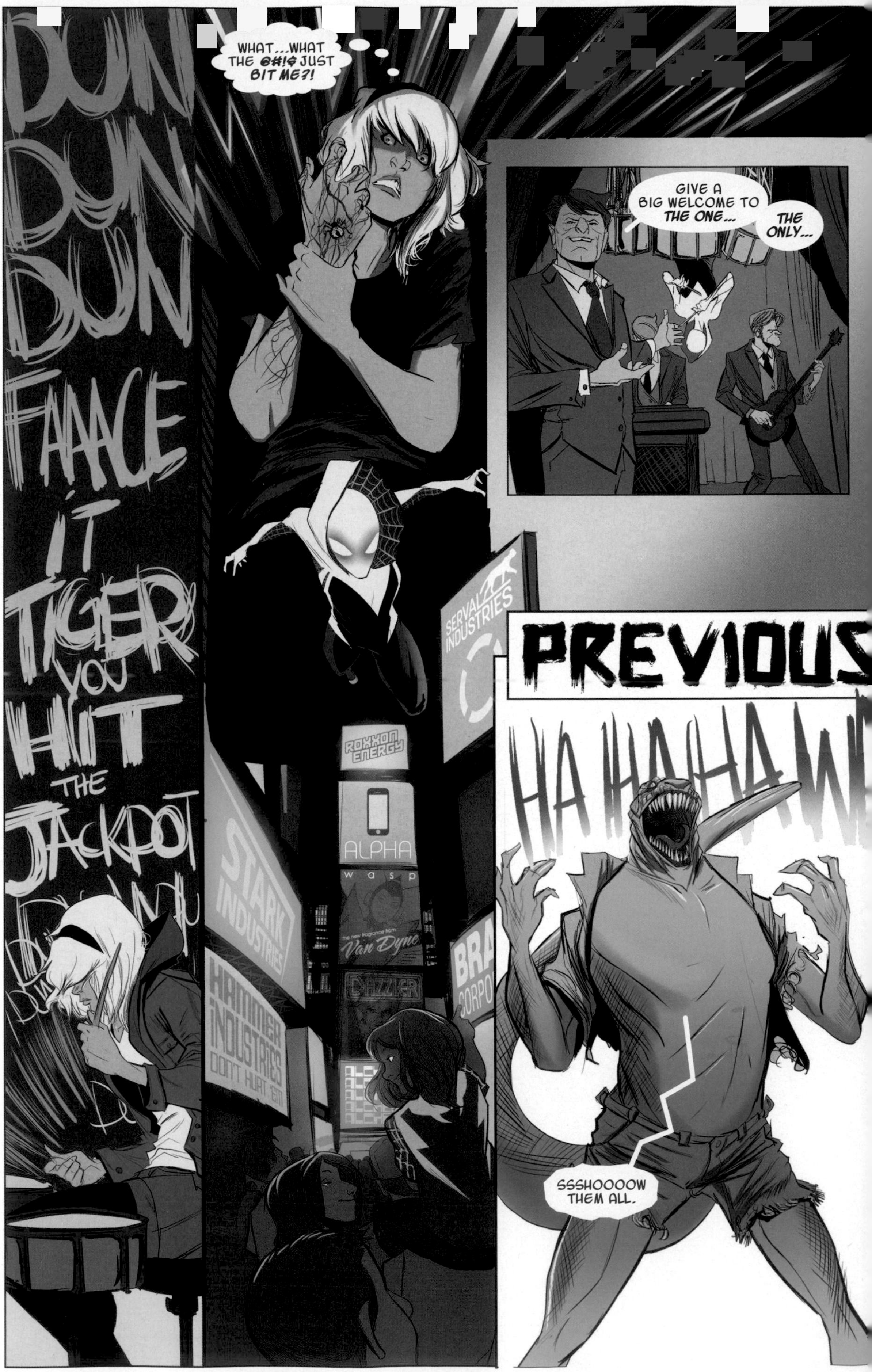
DUN DUN DUN DUN
FAAACE IT TIGER YOU HIT THE JACKPOT
WHAT...WHAT THE @#!$ JUST BIT ME?!
SERVAL INDUSTRIES
ROXXON ENERGY
ALPHA
wasp
The new fragrance from Van Dyne
STARK INDUSTRIES
HAMMER INDUSTRIES DON'T HURT 'EM
DAZZLER
GIVE A BIG WELCOME TO THE ONE...
THE ONLY...
PREVIOUS
HAHAHAW
SSSHOOOOW THEM ALL.

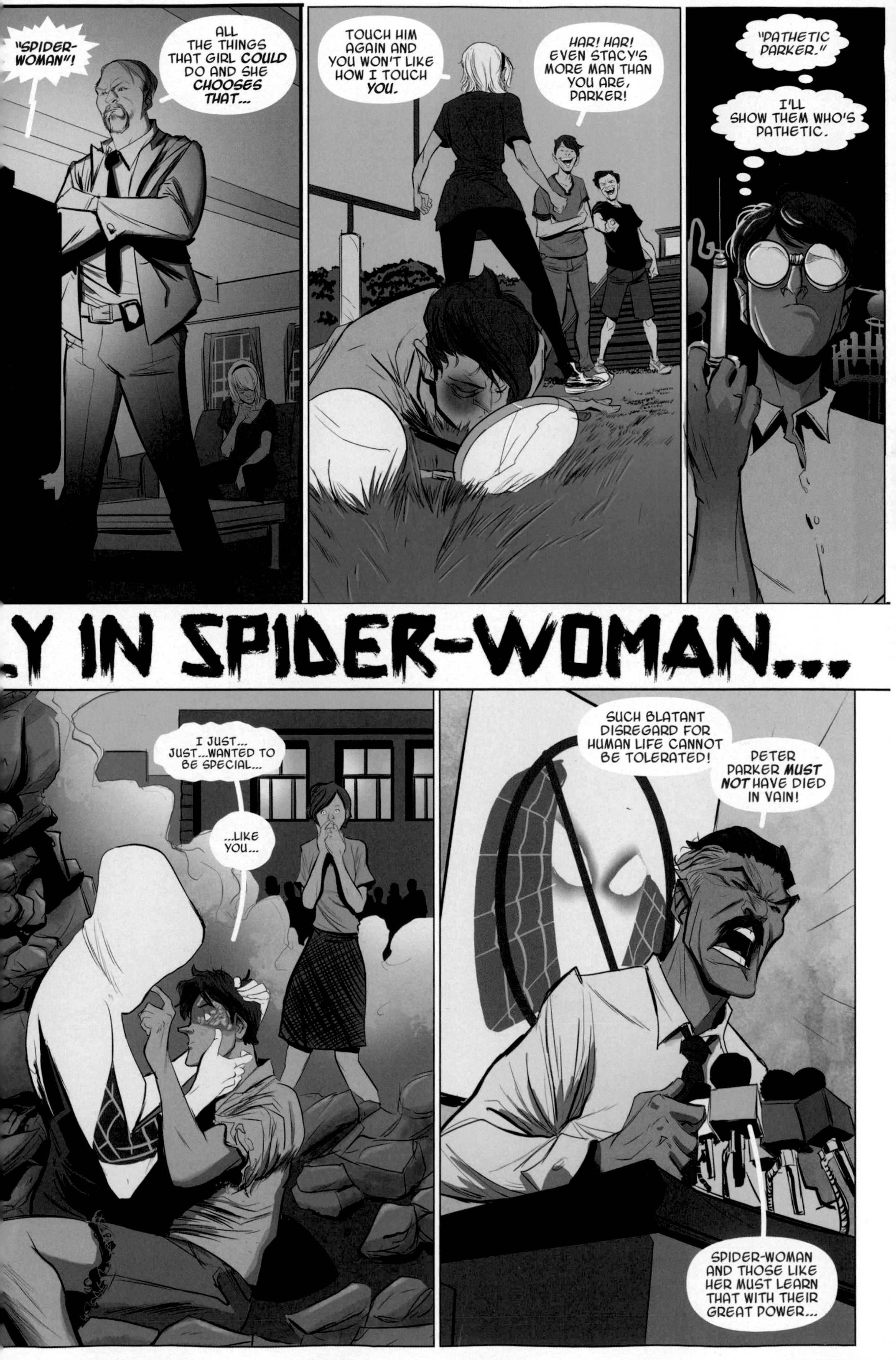
"SPIDER-WOMAN"!
ALL THE THINGS THAT GIRL COULD DO AND SHE CHOOSES THAT...
TOUCH HIM AGAIN AND YOU WON'T LIKE HOW I TOUCH YOU.
HAR! HAR! EVEN STACY'S MORE MAN THAN YOU ARE, PARKER!
"PATHETIC PARKER."
I'LL SHOW THEM WHO'S PATHETIC.
..Y IN SPIDER-WOMAN...
I JUST... JUST...WANTED TO BE SPECIAL...
...LIKE YOU...
SUCH BLATANT DISREGARD FOR HUMAN LIFE CANNOT BE TOLERATED!
PETER PARKER MUST NOT HAVE DIED IN VAIN!
SPIDER-WOMAN AND THOSE LIKE HER MUST LEARN THAT WITH THEIR GREAT POWER...

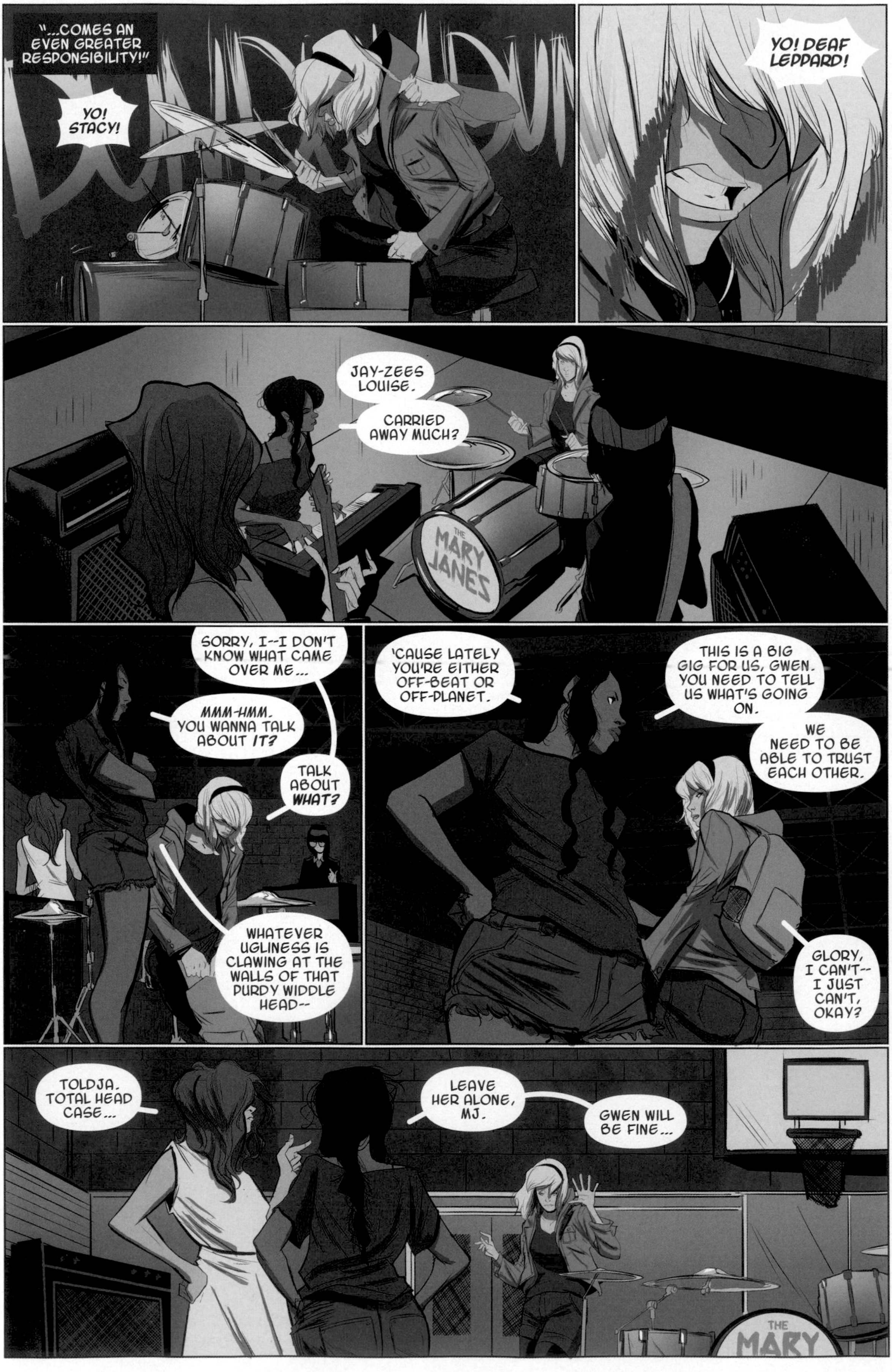
"...COMES AN EVEN GREATER RESPONSIBILITY!"
YO! STACY!
YO! DEAF LEPPARD!
JAY-ZEES LOUISE.
CARRIED AWAY MUCH?
THE MARY JANES
SORRY, I--I DON'T KNOW WHAT CAME OVER ME...
MMM-HMM. YOU WANNA TALK ABOUT IT?
TALK ABOUT WHAT?
WHATEVER UGLINESS IS CLAWING AT THE WALLS OF THAT PURDY WIDDLE HEAD--
'CAUSE LATELY YOU'RE EITHER OFF-BEAT OR OFF-PLANET.
THIS IS A BIG GIG FOR US, GWEN. YOU NEED TO TELL US WHAT'S GOING ON.
WE NEED TO BE ABLE TO TRUST EACH OTHER.
GLORY, I CAN'T-- I JUST CAN'T, OKAY?
TOLDJA. TOTAL HEAD CASE...
LEAVE HER ALONE, MJ.
GWEN WILL BE FINE...
THE MARY

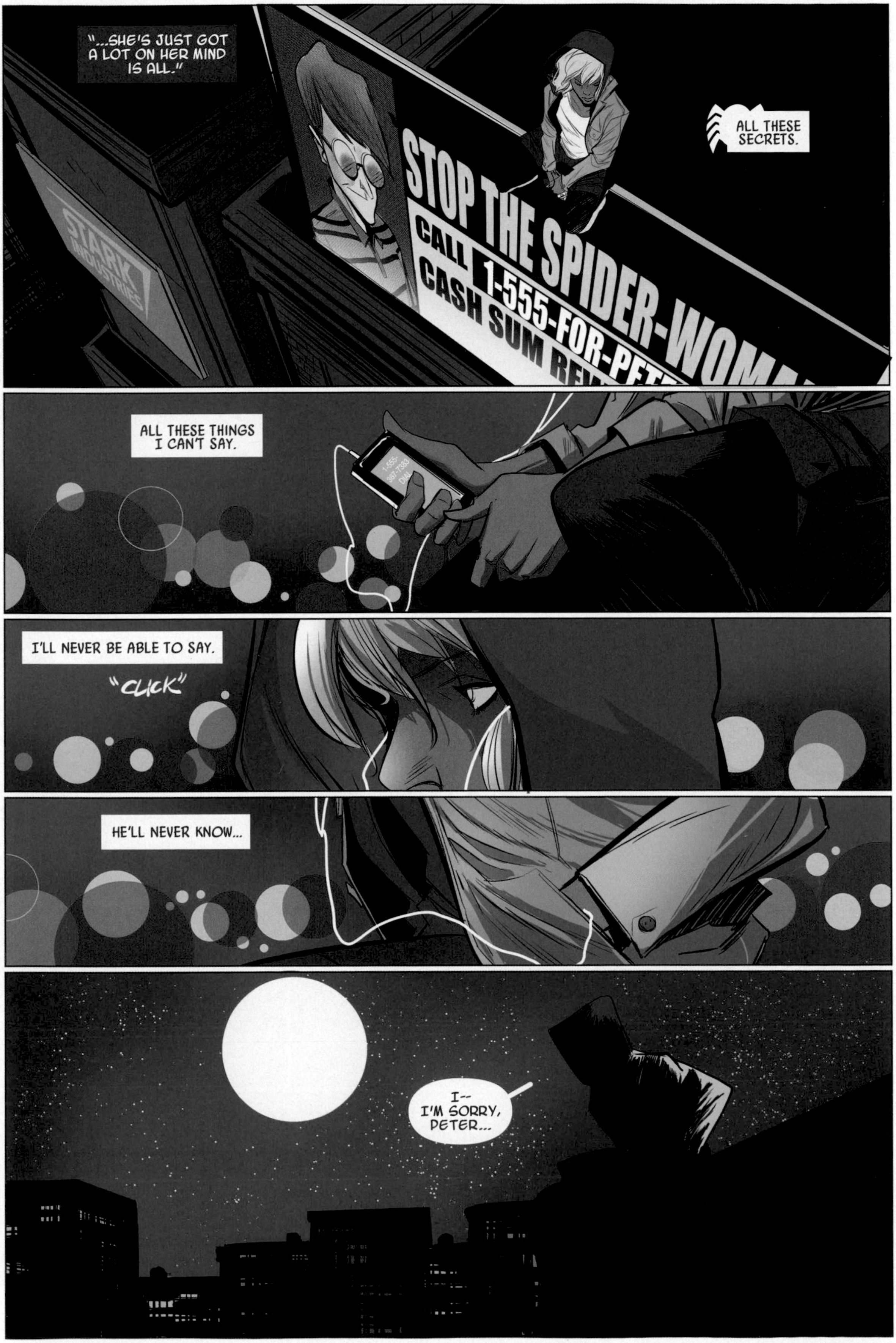

"...SHE'S JUST GOT A LOT ON HER MIND IS ALL."
STOP THE SPIDER-WOMA
CALL 1-555-FOR-PETE
CASH SUM RE
STARK INDUSTRIES
ALL THESE SECRETS.
ALL THESE THINGS I CAN'T SAY.
I'LL NEVER BE ABLE TO SAY.
"CLICK"
HE'LL NEVER KNOW...
I-- I'M SORRY, PETER...

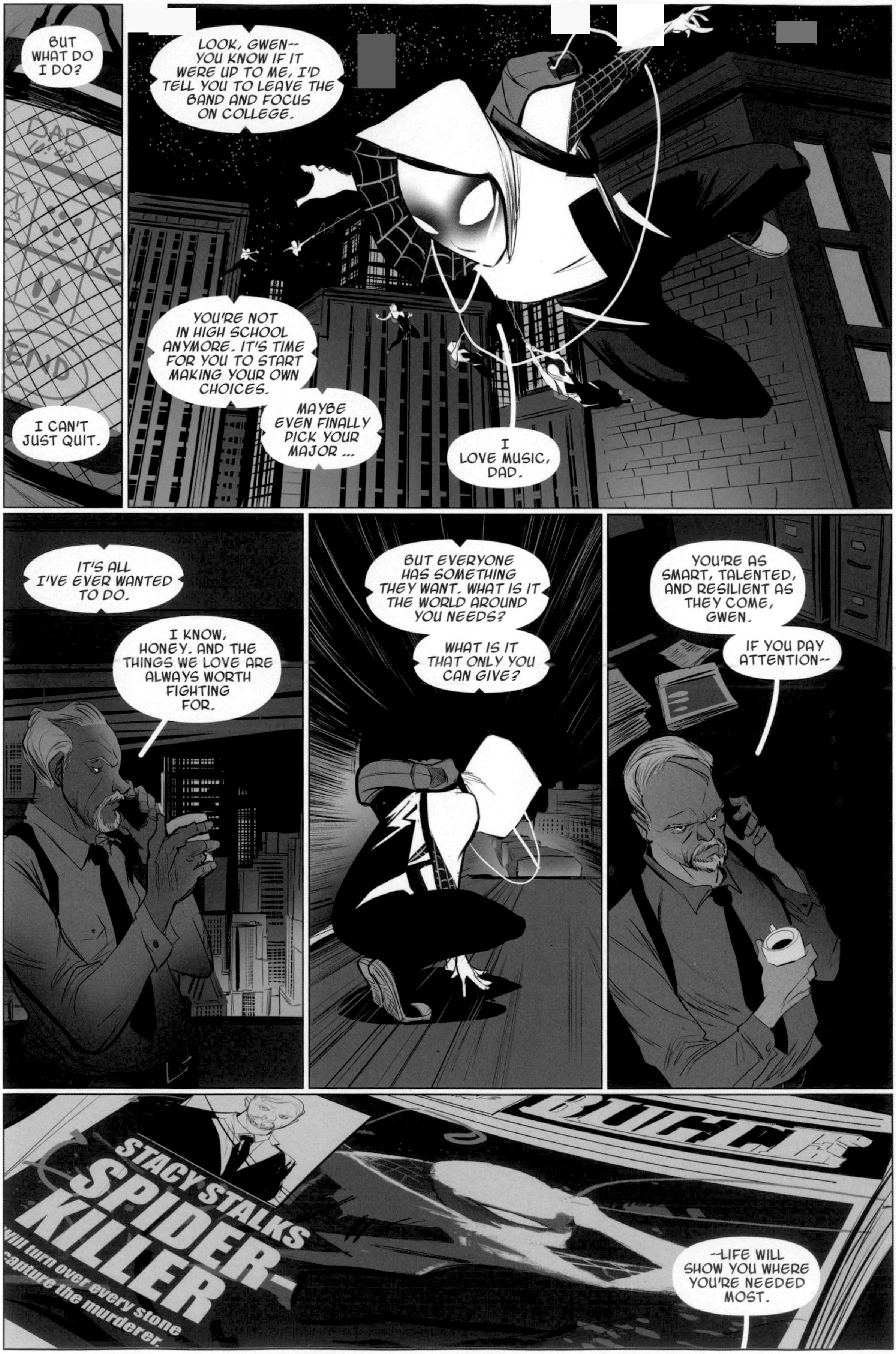
BUT WHAT DO I DO?
LOOK, GWEN-- YOU KNOW IF IT WERE UP TO ME, I'D TELL YOU TO LEAVE THE BAND AND FOCUS ON COLLEGE.
YOU'RE NOT IN HIGH SCHOOL ANYMORE. IT'S TIME FOR YOU TO START MAKING YOUR OWN CHOICES.
MAYBE EVEN FINALLY PICK YOUR MAJOR ...
I CAN'T JUST QUIT.
I LOVE MUSIC, DAD.
IT'S ALL I'VE EVER WANTED TO DO.
I KNOW, HONEY. AND THE THINGS WE LOVE ARE ALWAYS WORTH FIGHTING FOR.
BUT EVERYONE HAS SOMETHING THEY WANT. WHAT IS IT THE WORLD AROUND YOU NEEDS?
WHAT IS IT THAT ONLY YOU CAN GIVE?
YOU'RE AS SMART, TALENTED, AND RESILIENT AS THEY COME, GWEN.
IF YOU PAY ATTENTION--
STACY STALKS SPIDER-KILLER
will turn over every stone
capture the murderer.
--LIFE WILL SHOW YOU WHERE YOU'RE NEEDED MOST.

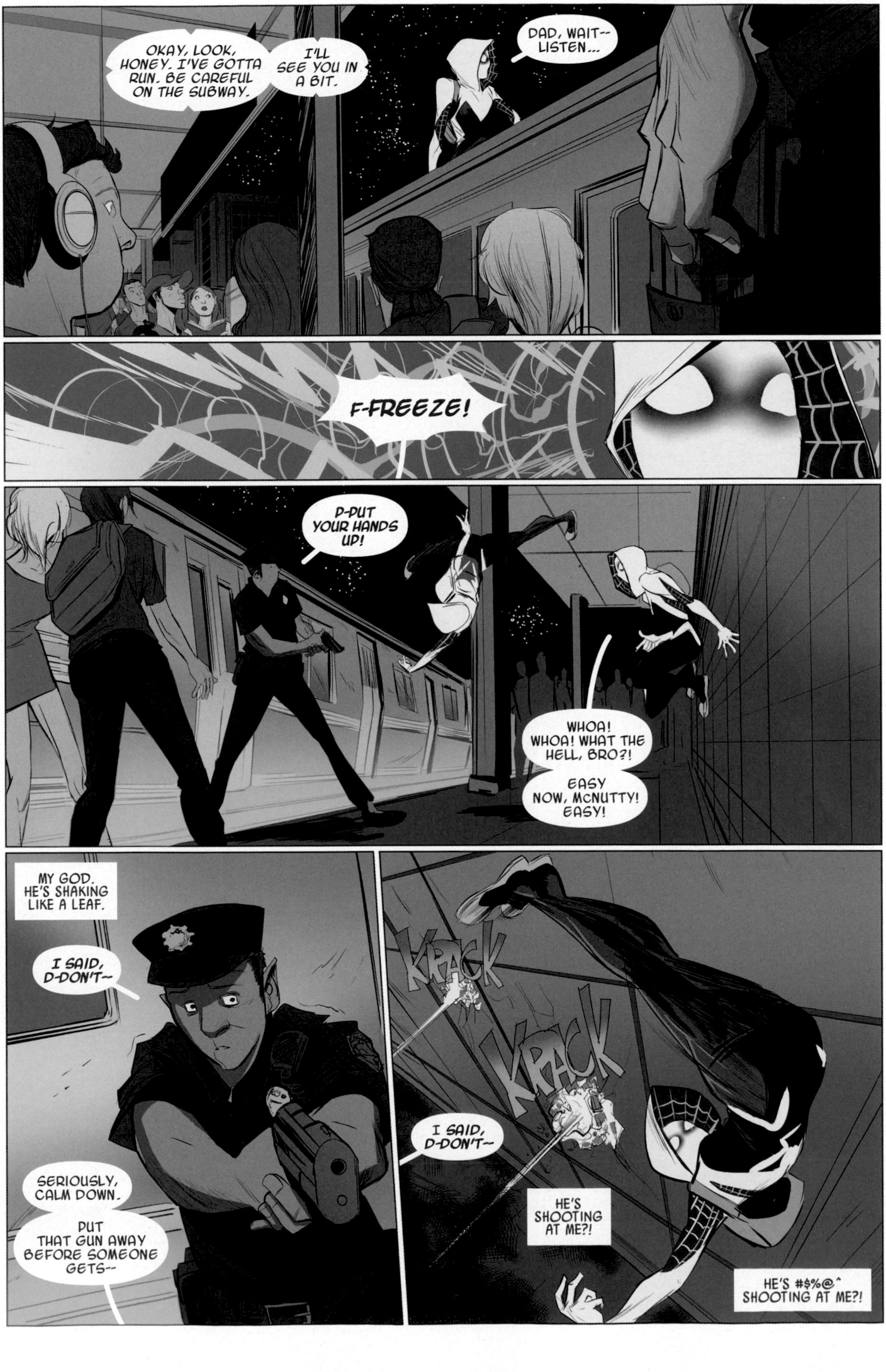
OKAY, LOOK, HONEY. I'VE GOTTA RUN. BE CAREFUL ON THE SUBWAY.
I'LL SEE YOU IN A BIT.
DAD, WAIT-- LISTEN...
F-FREEZE!
D-PUT YOUR HANDS UP!
WHOA! WHOA! WHAT THE HELL, BRO?!
EASY NOW, MCNUTTY! EASY!
MY GOD. HE'S SHAKING LIKE A LEAF.
I SAID, D-DON'T--
SERIOUSLY, CALM DOWN.
PUT THAT GUN AWAY BEFORE SOMEONE GETS--
KRACK
KRACK
I SAID, D-DON'T--
HE'S SHOOTING AT ME?!
HE'S #$%@^ SHOOTING AT ME?!

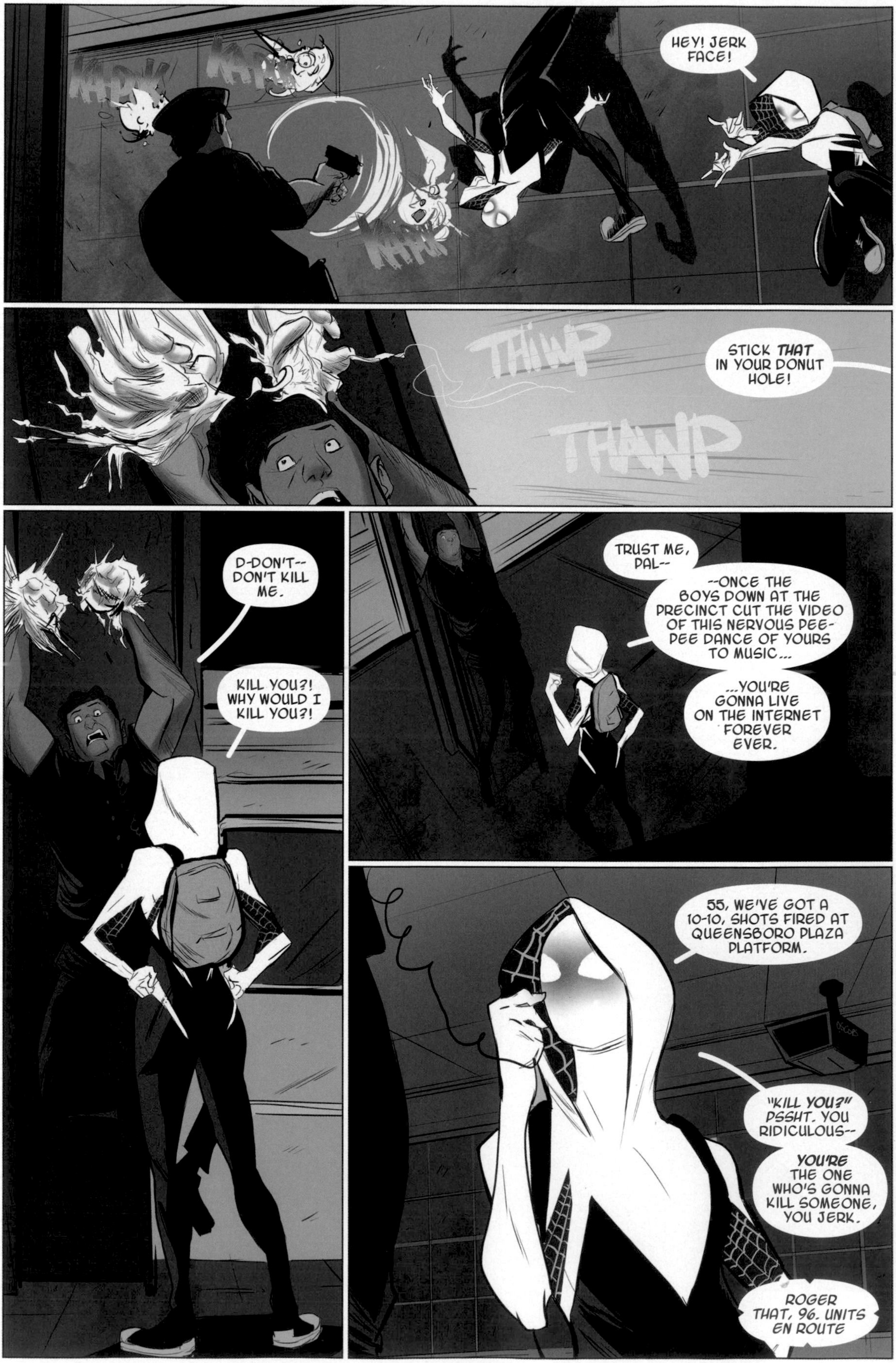

KAPOW
KAPOW
HEY! JERK FACE!
KAPOW
THWIP
STICK THAT IN YOUR DONUT HOLE!
THAWP
D-DON'T-- DON'T KILL ME.
KILL YOU?! WHY WOULD I KILL YOU?!
TRUST ME, PAL--
--ONCE THE BOYS DOWN AT THE PRECINCT CUT THE VIDEO OF THIS NERVOUS PEE-PEE DANCE OF YOURS TO MUSIC...
...YOU'RE GONNA LIVE ON THE INTERNET FOREVER EVER.
55, WE'VE GOT A 10-10, SHOTS FIRED AT QUEENSBORO PLAZA PLATFORM.
"KILL YOU?" PSSHT. YOU RIDICULOUS--
YOU'RE THE ONE WHO'S GONNA KILL SOMEONE, YOU JERK.
ROGER THAT, 96. UNITS EN ROUTE

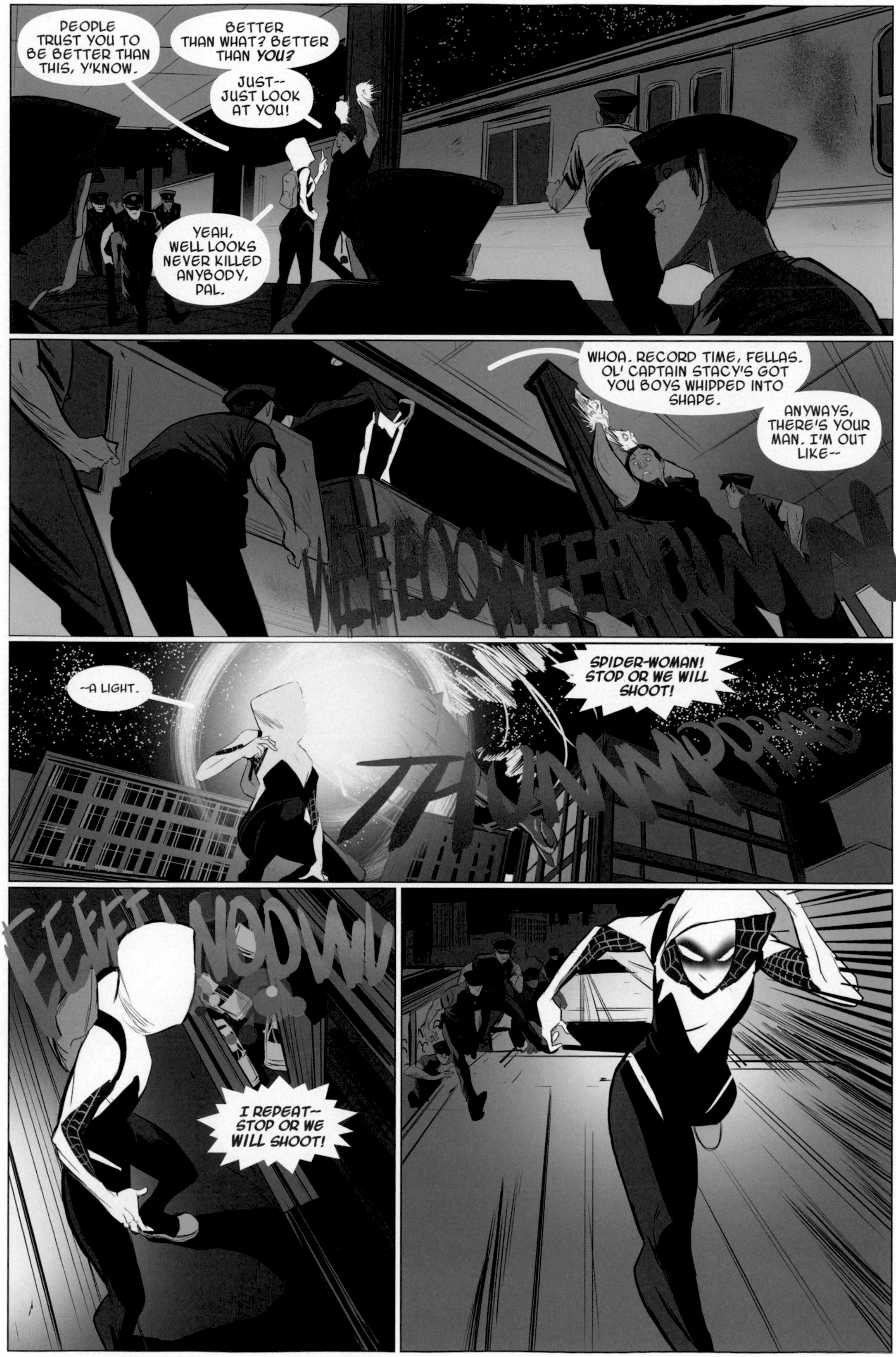
PEOPLE TRUST YOU TO BE BETTER THAN THIS, Y'KNOW.
BETTER THAN WHAT? BETTER THAN *YOU?*
JUST-- JUST LOOK AT YOU!
YEAH, WELL LOOKS NEVER KILLED ANYBODY, PAL.
WHOA. RECORD TIME, FELLAS. OL' CAPTAIN STACY'S GOT YOU BOYS WHIPPED INTO SHAPE.
ANYWAYS, THERE'S YOUR MAN. I'M OUT LIKE--
--A LIGHT.
SPIDER-WOMAN! STOP OR WE WILL SHOOT!
I REPEAT-- STOP OR WE **WILL** SHOOT!

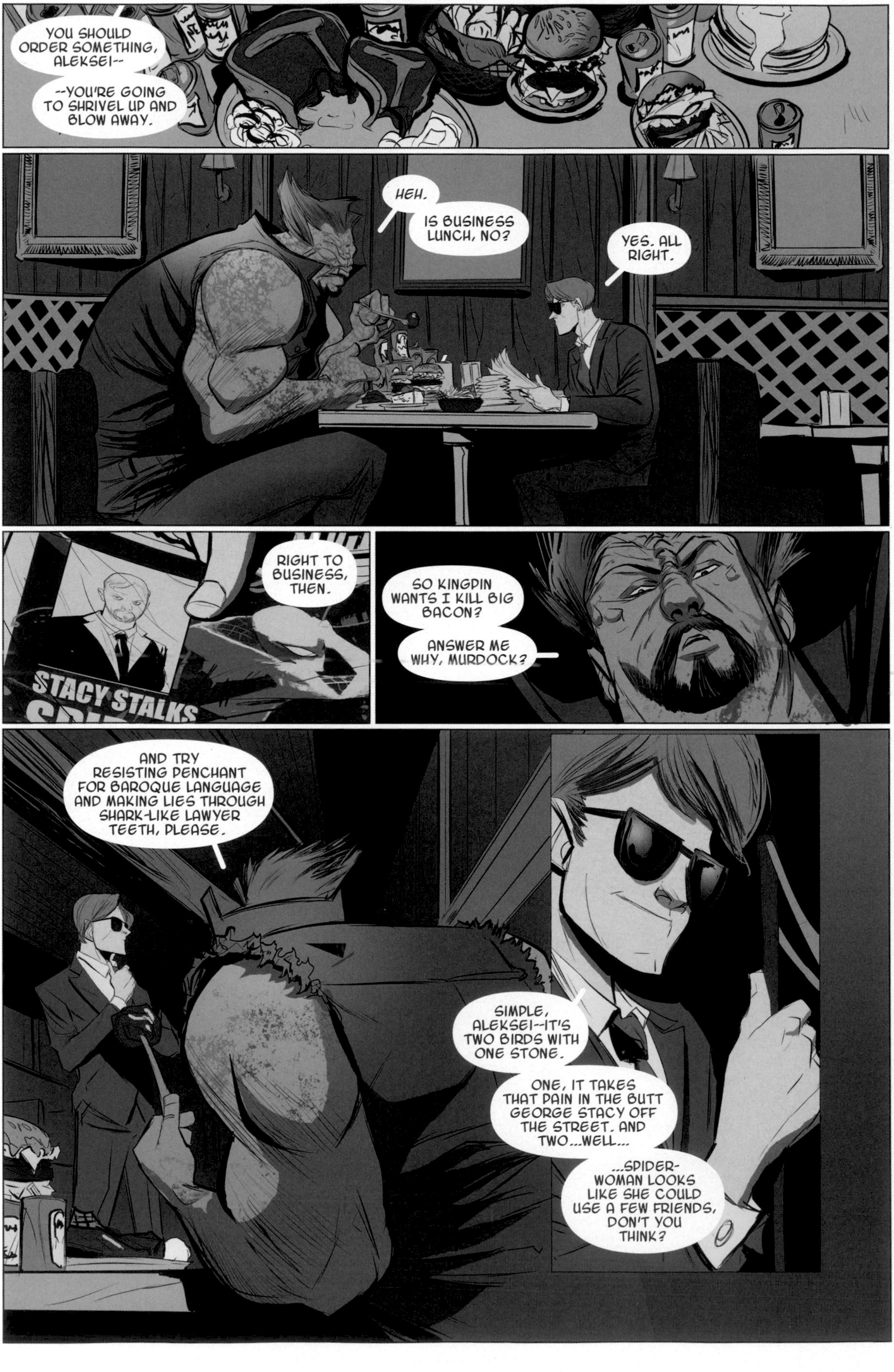
YOU SHOULD ORDER SOMETHING, ALEKSEI--
--YOU'RE GOING TO SHRIVEL UP AND BLOW AWAY.
HEH.
IS BUSINESS LUNCH, NO?
YES. ALL RIGHT.
RIGHT TO BUSINESS, THEN.
STACY STALKS
SO KINGPIN WANTS I KILL BIG BACON?
ANSWER ME WHY, MURDOCK?
AND TRY RESISTING PENCHANT FOR BAROQUE LANGUAGE AND MAKING LIES THROUGH SHARK-LIKE LAWYER TEETH, PLEASE.
SIMPLE, ALEKSEI--IT'S TWO BIRDS WITH ONE STONE.
ONE, IT TAKES THAT PAIN IN THE BUTT GEORGE STACY OFF THE STREET. AND TWO...WELL...
...SPIDER-WOMAN LOOKS LIKE SHE COULD USE A FEW FRIENDS, DON'T YOU THINK?

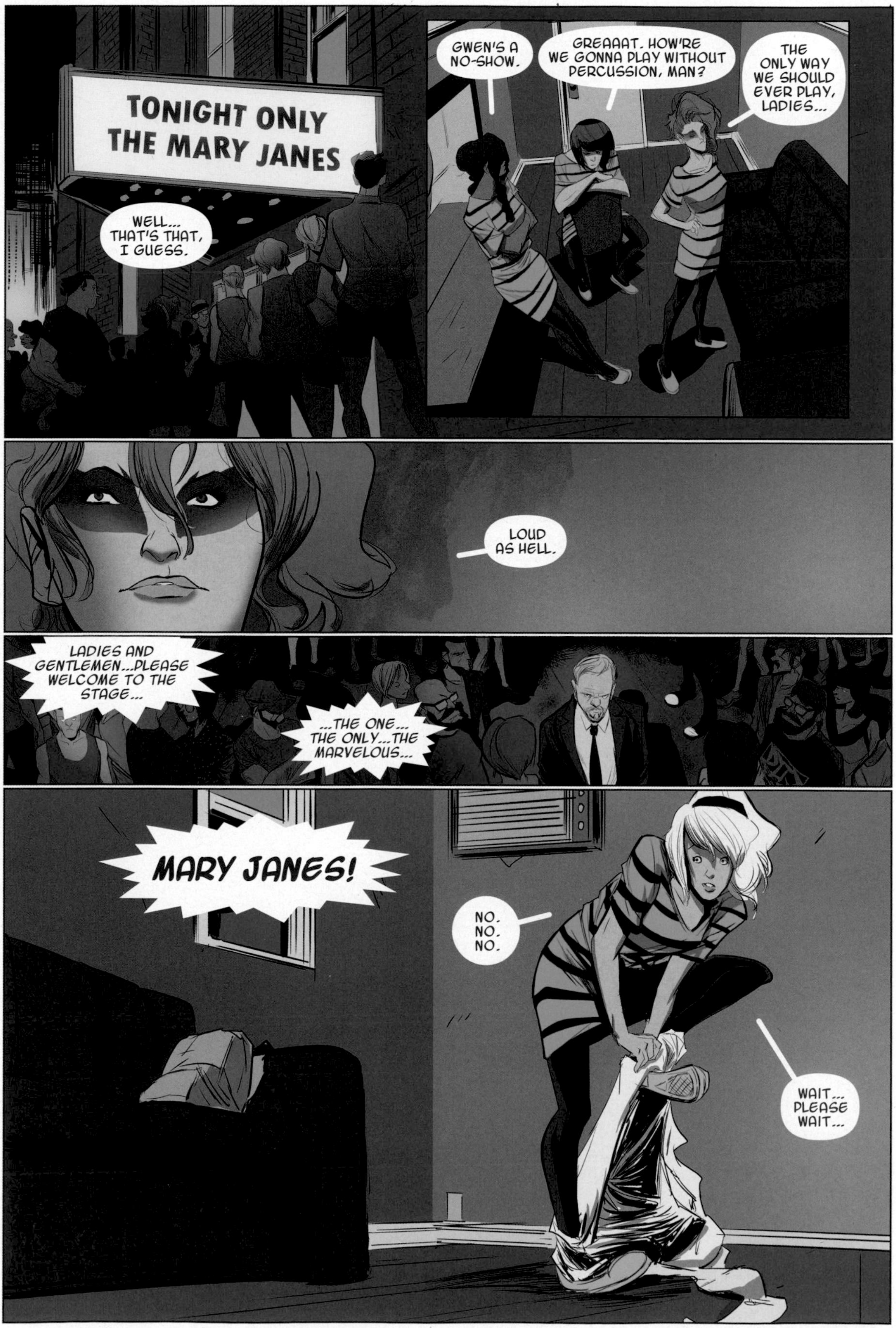
TONIGHT ONLY THE MARY JANES
WELL... THAT'S THAT, I GUESS.
GWEN'S A NO-SHOW.
GREAAAT. HOW'RE WE GONNA PLAY WITHOUT PERCUSSION, MAN?
THE ONLY WAY WE SHOULD EVER PLAY, LADIES...
LOUD AS HELL.
LADIES AND GENTLEMEN...PLEASE WELCOME TO THE STAGE...
...THE ONE... THE ONLY...THE MARVELOUS...
MARY JANES!
NO. NO. NO.
WAIT... PLEASE WAIT...

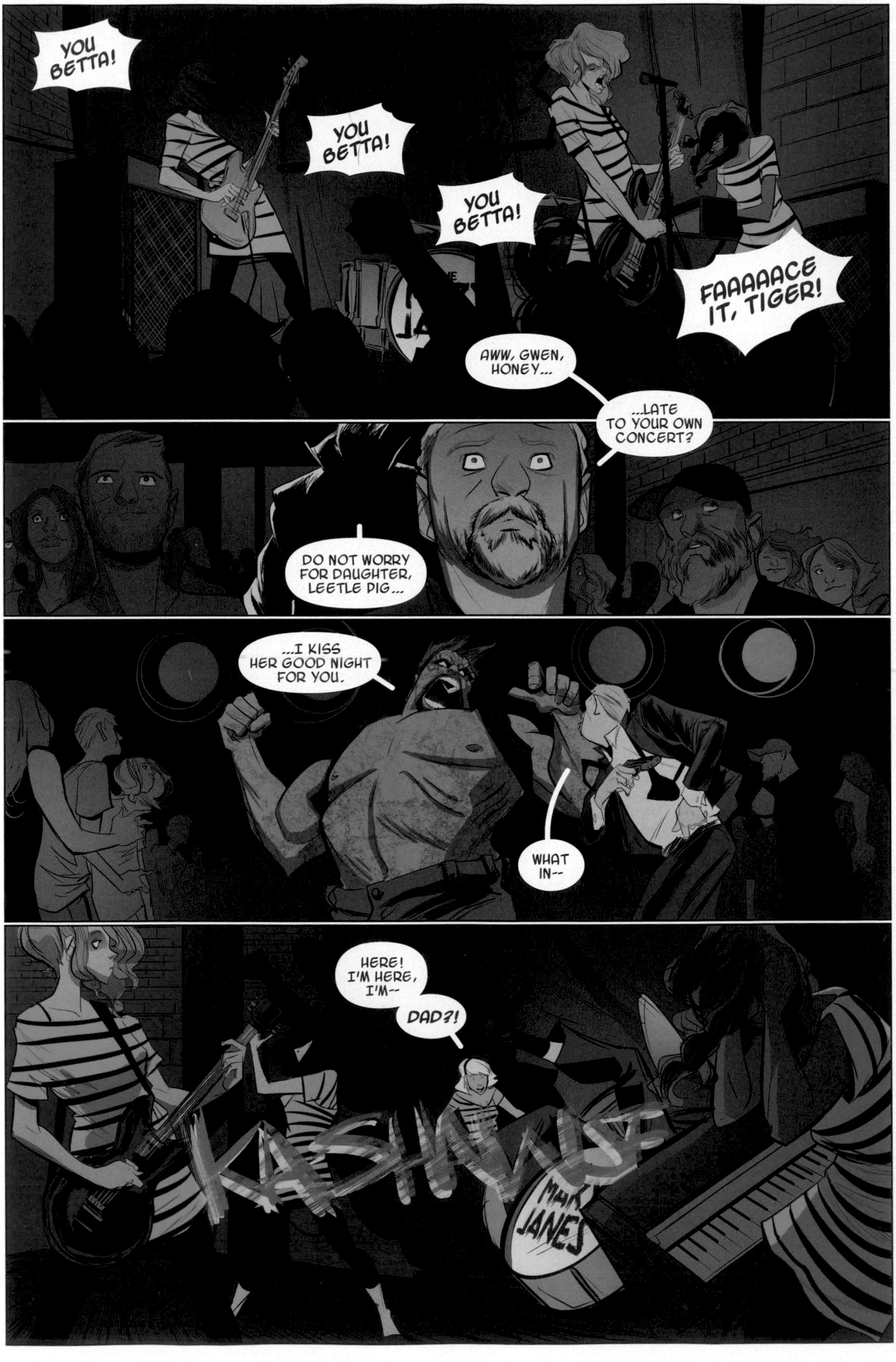
YOU BETTA!
YOU BETTA!
YOU BETTA!
FAAAAACE IT, TIGER!
AWW, GWEN, HONEY...
...LATE TO YOUR OWN CONCERT?
DO NOT WORRY FOR DAUGHTER, LEETLE PIG...
...I KISS HER GOOD NIGHT FOR YOU.
WHAT IN--
HERE! I'M HERE, I'M--
DAD?!
KASHWSH
MARY JANES

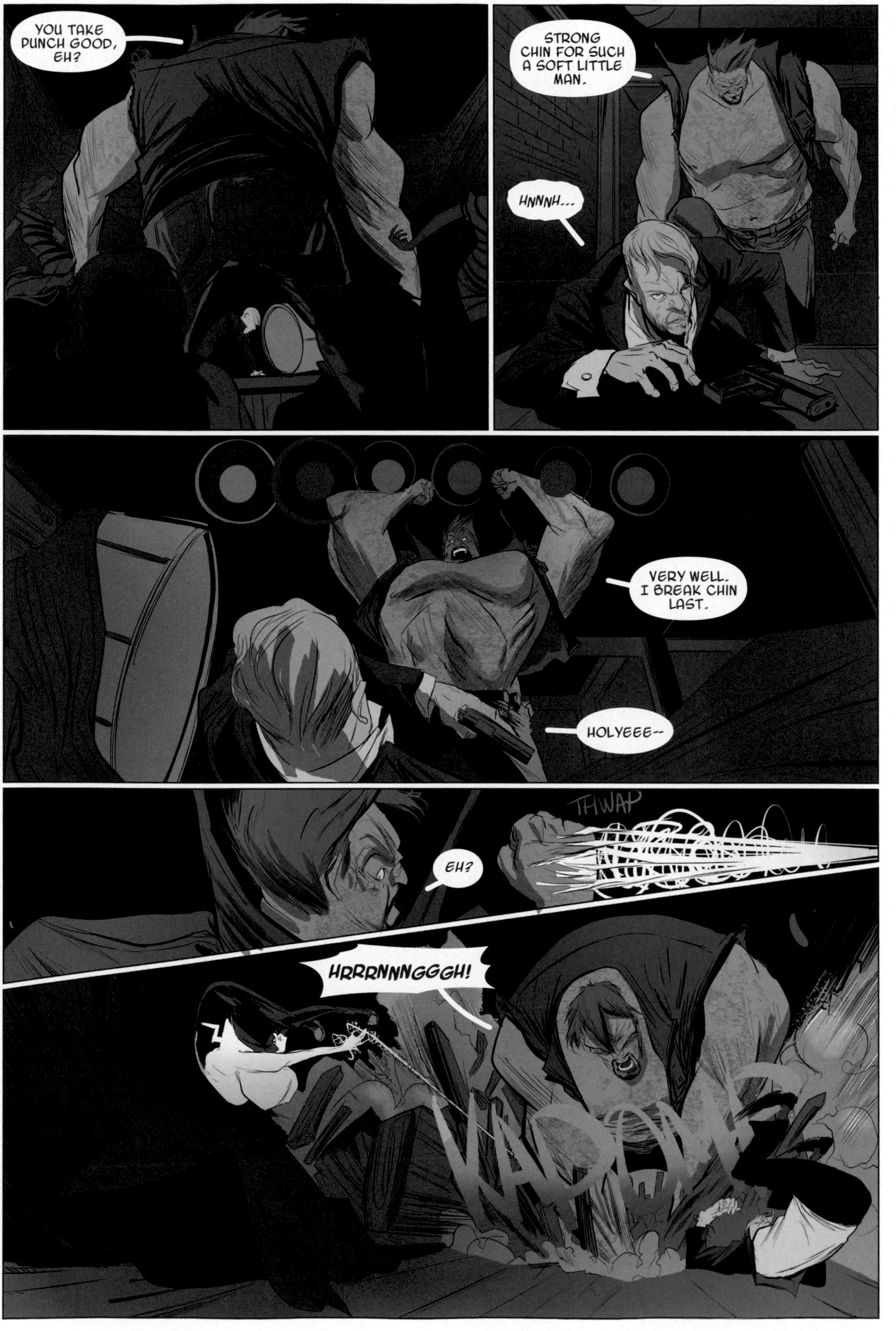
YOU TAKE PUNCH GOOD, EH?
STRONG CHIN FOR SUCH A SOFT LITTLE MAN.
HNNNH...
VERY WELL. I BREAK CHIN LAST.
HOLYEEE--
THWAP
EH?
HRRRNNNGGGH!

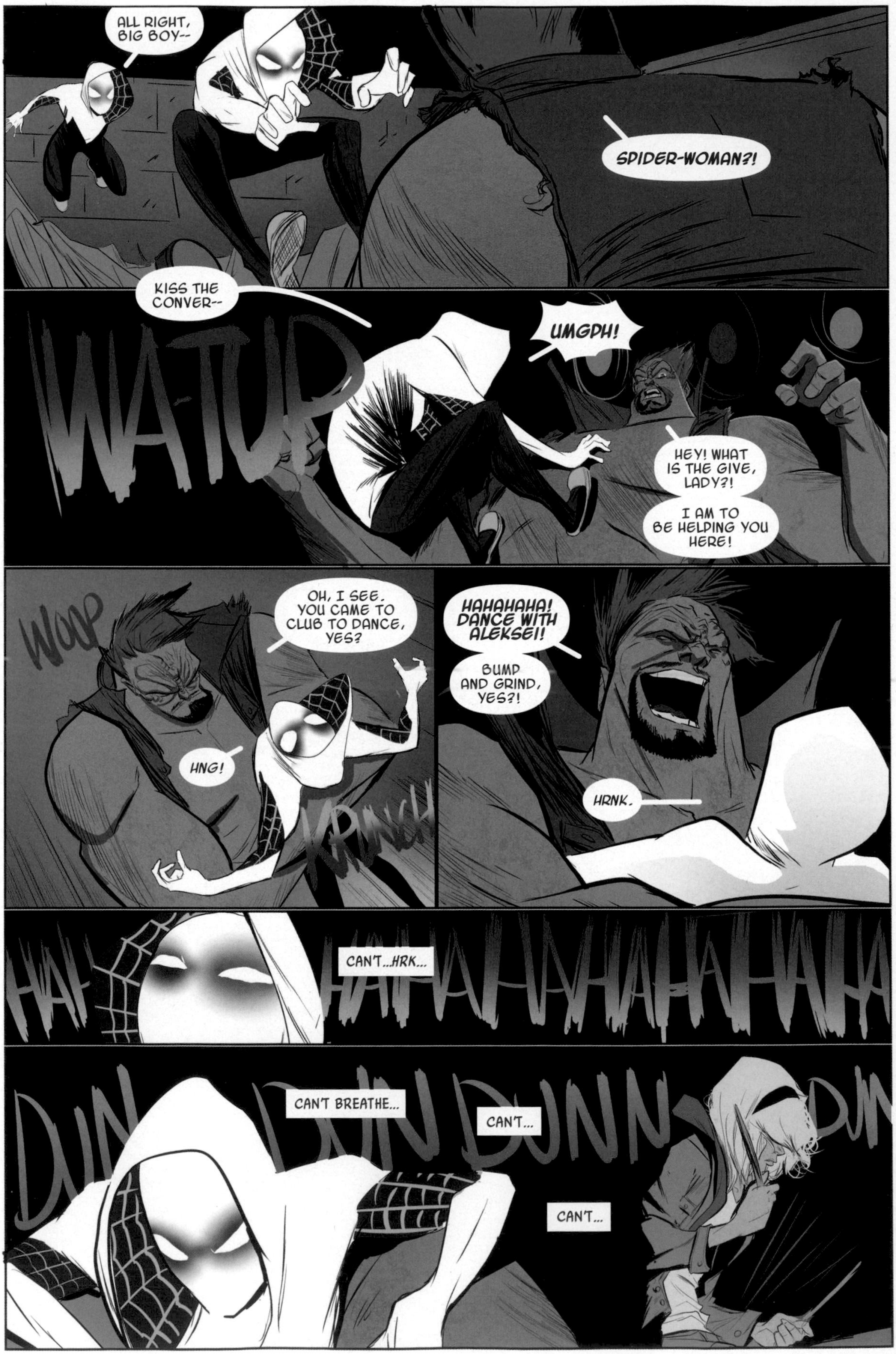
ALL RIGHT, BIG BOY--
SPIDER-WOMAN?!
KISS THE CONVER--
WATUP
UMGPH!
HEY! WHAT IS THE GIVE, LADY?!
I AM TO BE HELPING YOU HERE!
WOOP
OH, I SEE. YOU CAME TO CLUB TO DANCE, YES?
HNG!
KRUNCH
HAHAHAHA! DANCE WITH ALEKSEI!
BUMP AND GRIND, YES?!
HRNK.
CAN'T...HRK...
CAN'T BREATHE...
CAN'T...
CAN'T...

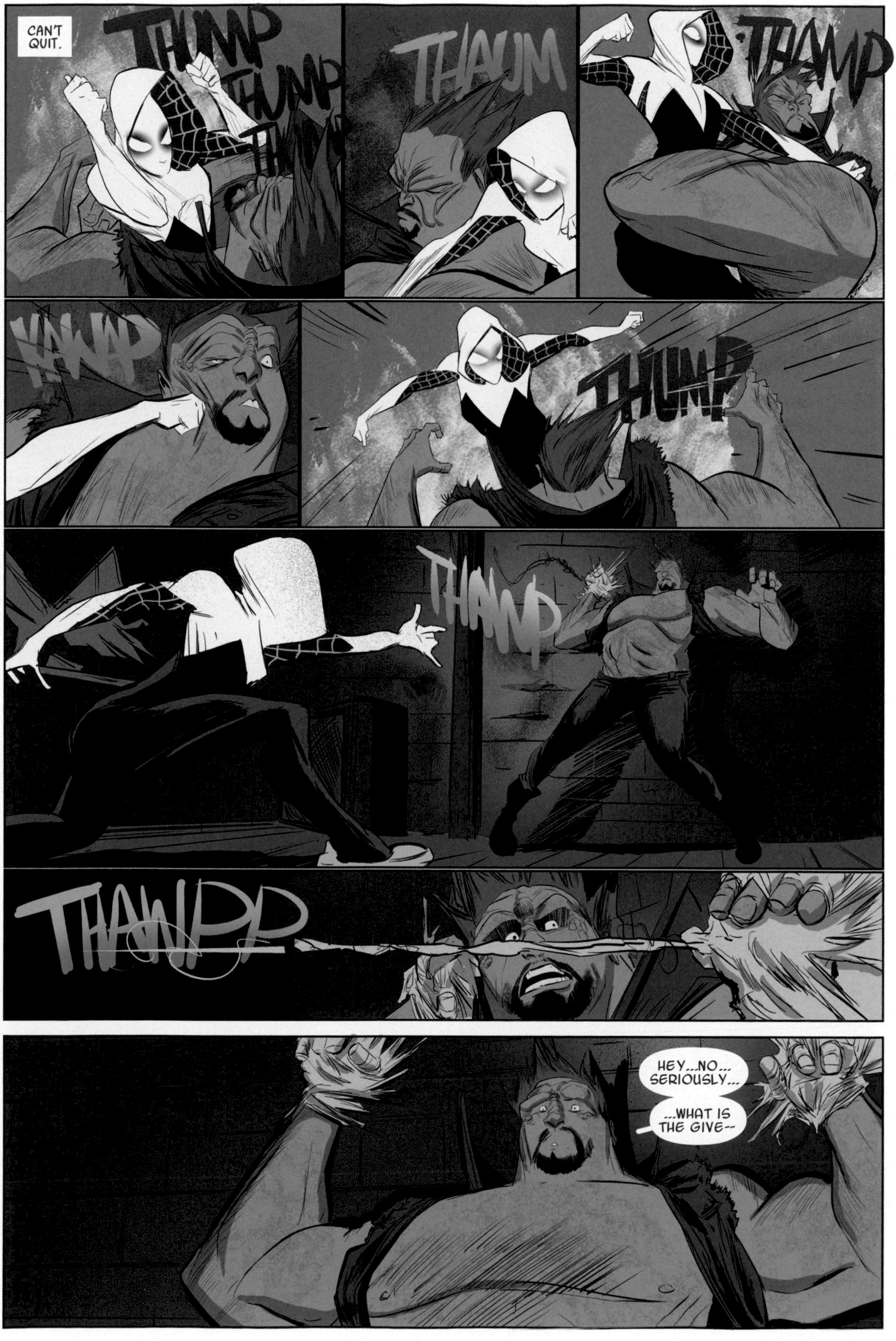

CAN'T QUIT.
THUMP
THUMP
THUMP
THAUM
THAMP
WAMP
THUMP
THAMP
THAWPP
HEY...NO... SERIOUSLY...
...WHAT IS THE GIVE--

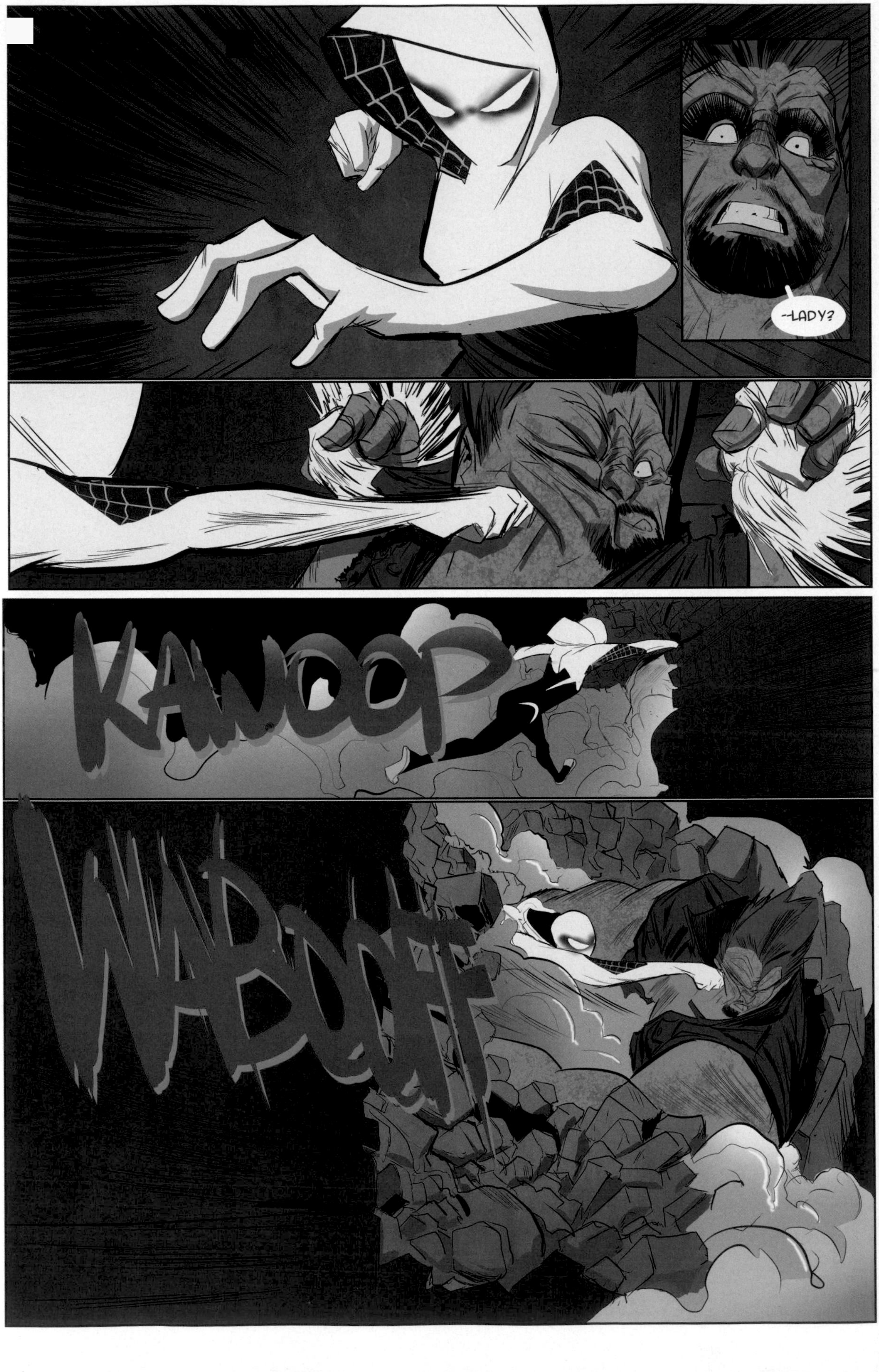
--LADY?
KAWOOP
WABOOFF

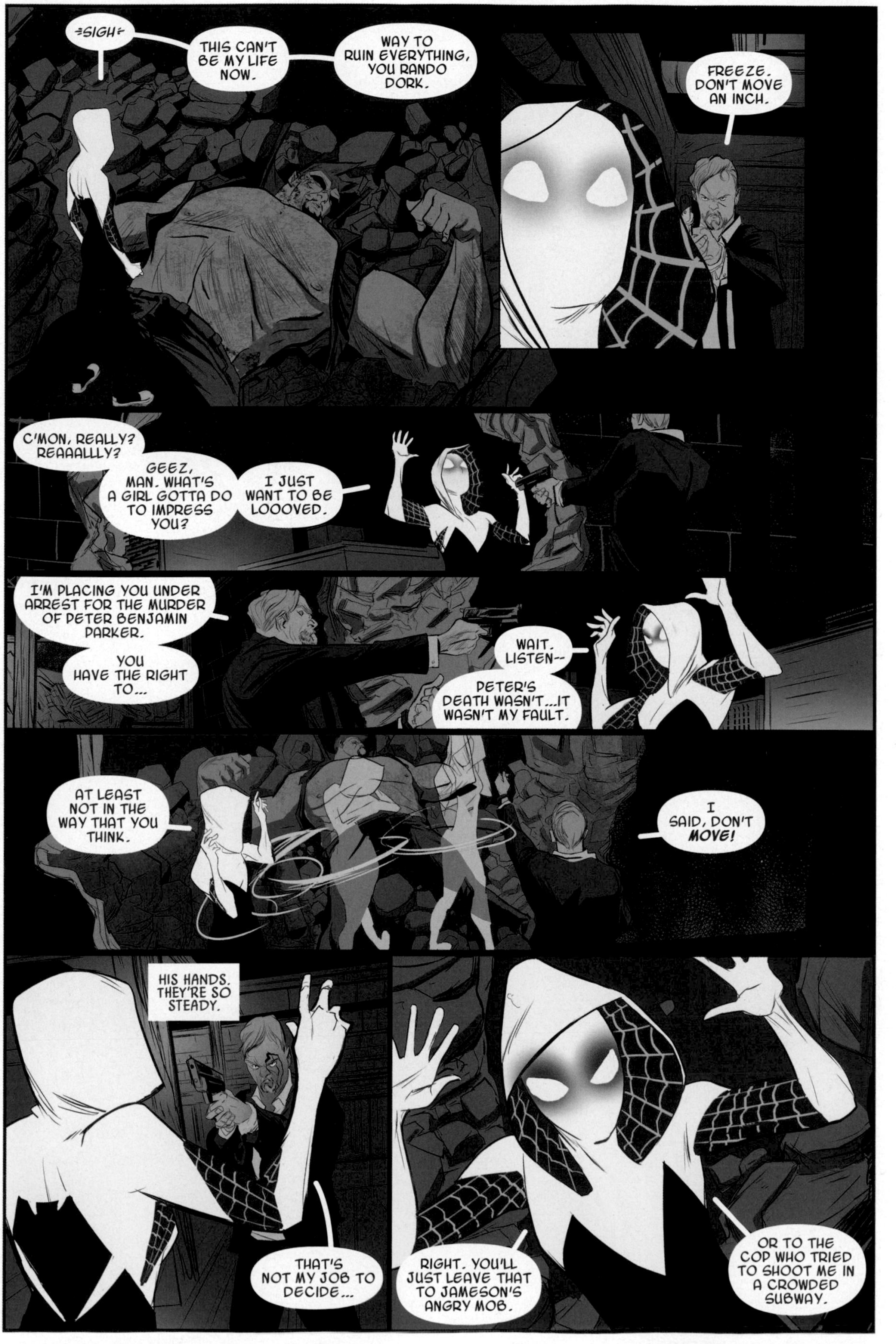

=SIGH=
THIS CAN'T BE MY LIFE NOW.
WAY TO RUIN EVERYTHING, YOU RANDO DORK.
FREEZE. DON'T MOVE AN INCH.
C'MON, REALLY? REAAALLLY?
GEEZ, MAN. WHAT'S A GIRL GOTTA DO TO IMPRESS YOU?
I JUST WANT TO BE LOOOVED.
I'M PLACING YOU UNDER ARREST FOR THE MURDER OF PETER BENJAMIN PARKER.
YOU HAVE THE RIGHT TO...
WAIT. LISTEN--
PETER'S DEATH WASN'T...IT WASN'T MY FAULT.
AT LEAST NOT IN THE WAY THAT YOU THINK.
I SAID, DON'T MOVE!
HIS HANDS. THEY'RE SO STEADY.
THAT'S NOT MY JOB TO DECIDE...
RIGHT. YOU'LL JUST LEAVE THAT TO JAMESON'S ANGRY MOB.
OR TO THE COP WHO TRIED TO SHOOT ME IN A CROWDED SUBWAY.

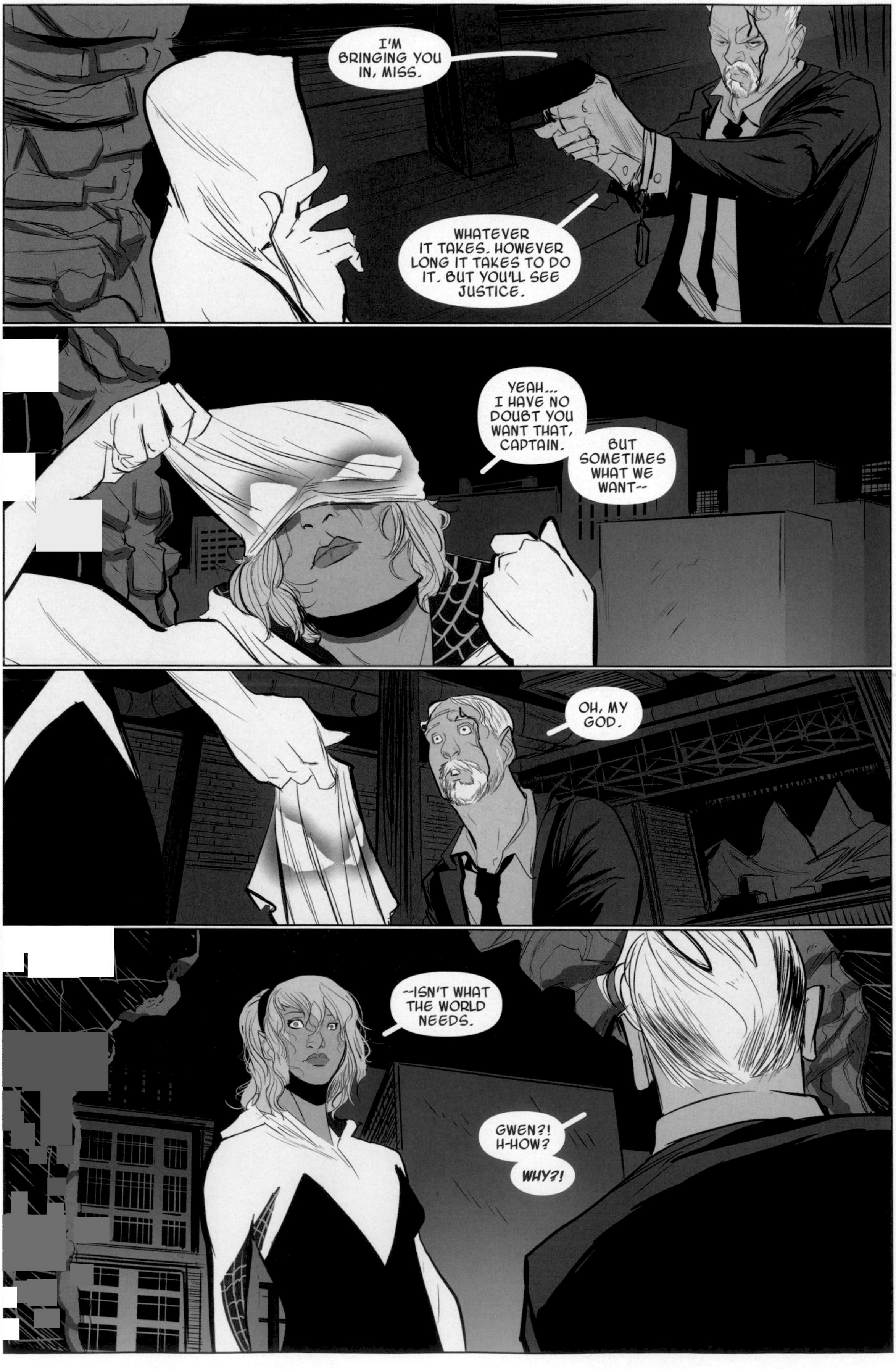
I'M BRINGING YOU IN, MISS.
WHATEVER IT TAKES. HOWEVER LONG IT TAKES TO DO IT. BUT YOU'LL SEE JUSTICE.
YEAH... I HAVE NO DOUBT YOU WANT THAT, CAPTAIN.
BUT SOMETIMES WHAT WE WANT--
OH, MY GOD.
--ISN'T WHAT THE WORLD NEEDS.
GWEN?! H-HOW?
WHY?!

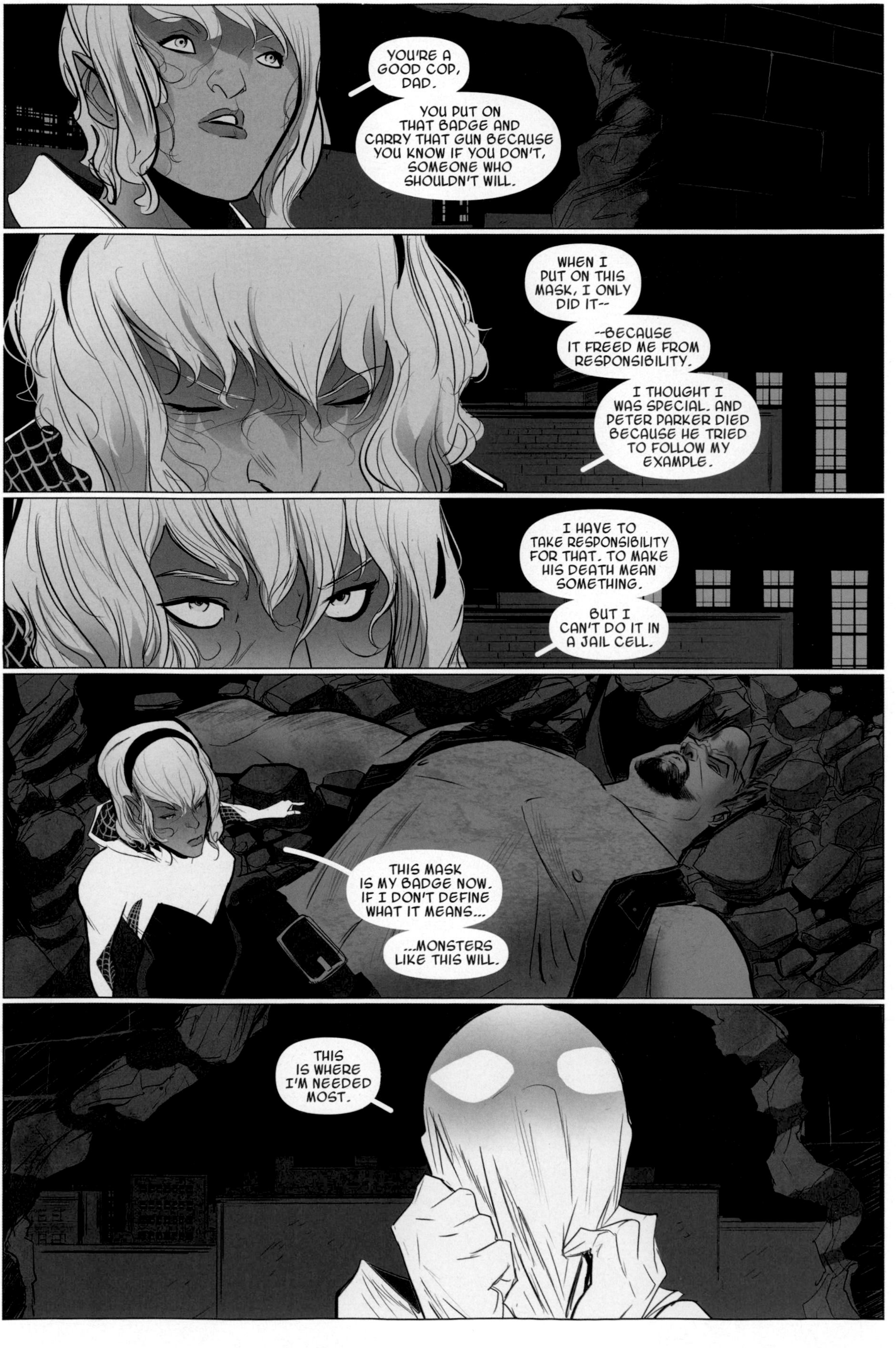
YOU'RE A GOOD COP, DAD.
YOU PUT ON THAT BADGE AND CARRY THAT GUN BECAUSE YOU KNOW IF YOU DON'T, SOMEONE WHO SHOULDN'T WILL.
WHEN I PUT ON THIS MASK, I ONLY DID IT--
--BECAUSE IT FREED ME FROM RESPONSIBILITY.
I THOUGHT I WAS SPECIAL. AND PETER PARKER DIED BECAUSE HE TRIED TO FOLLOW MY EXAMPLE.
I HAVE TO TAKE RESPONSIBILITY FOR THAT. TO MAKE HIS DEATH MEAN SOMETHING.
BUT I CAN'T DO IT IN A JAIL CELL.
THIS MASK IS MY BADGE NOW. IF I DON'T DEFINE WHAT IT MEANS...
...MONSTERS LIKE THIS WILL.
THIS IS WHERE I'M NEEDED MOST.

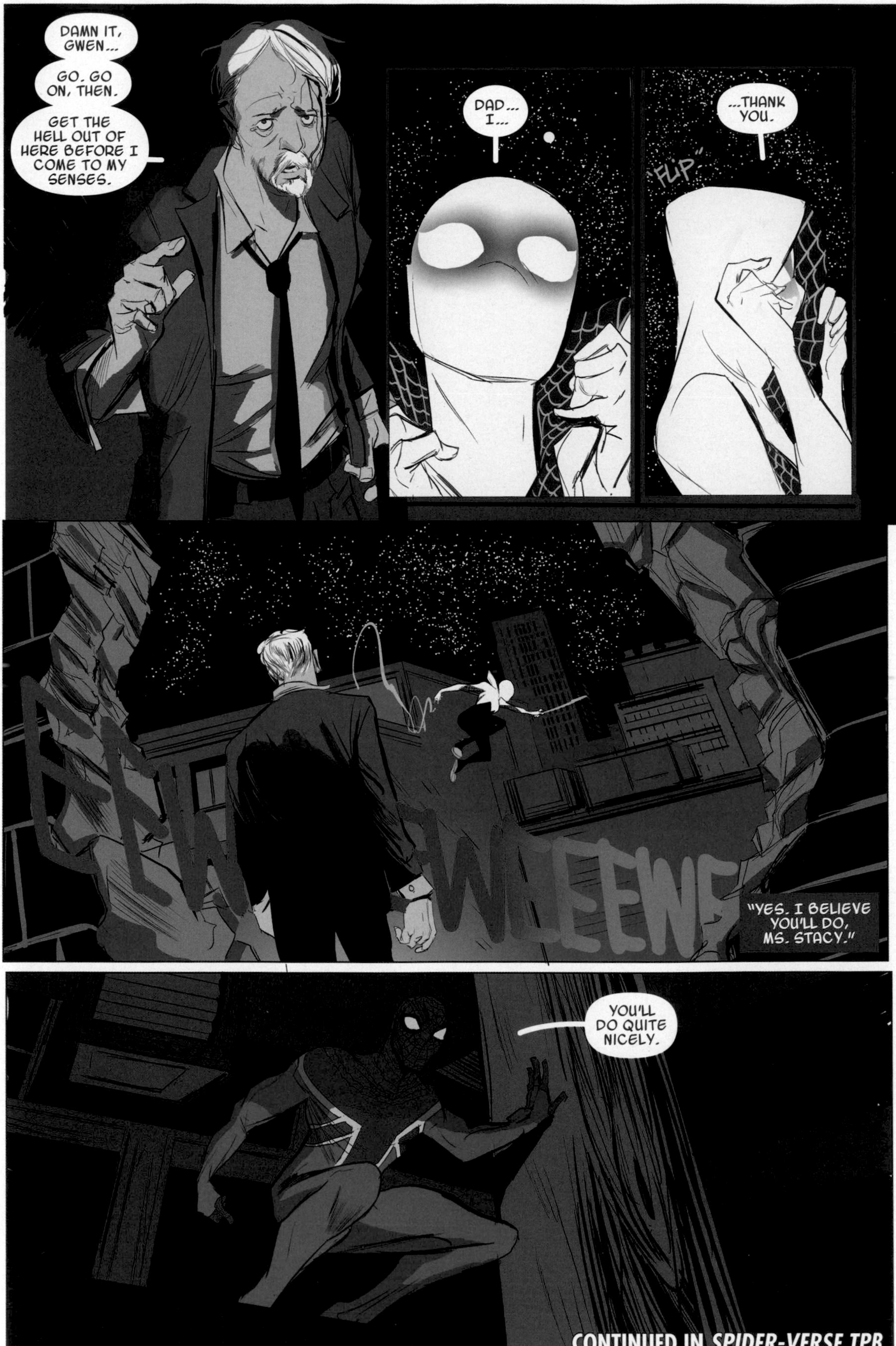
DAMN IT, GWEN...
GO. GO ON, THEN.
GET THE HELL OUT OF HERE BEFORE I COME TO MY SENSES.
DAD... I...
...THANK YOU.
FLIP
"YES. I BELIEVE YOU'LL DO, MS. STACY."
YOU'LL DO QUITE NICELY.
CONTINUED IN *SPIDER-VERSE TPB*

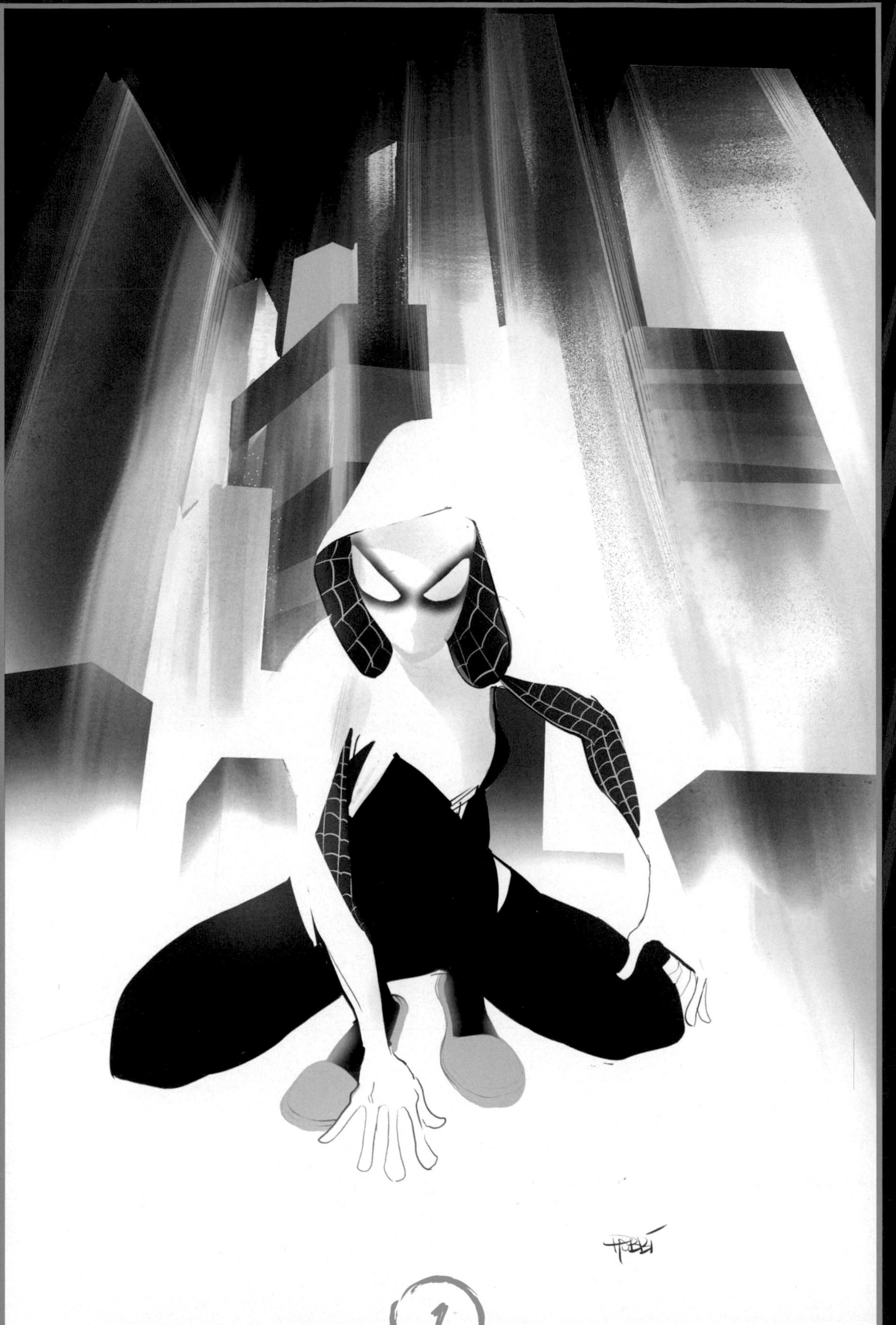

1

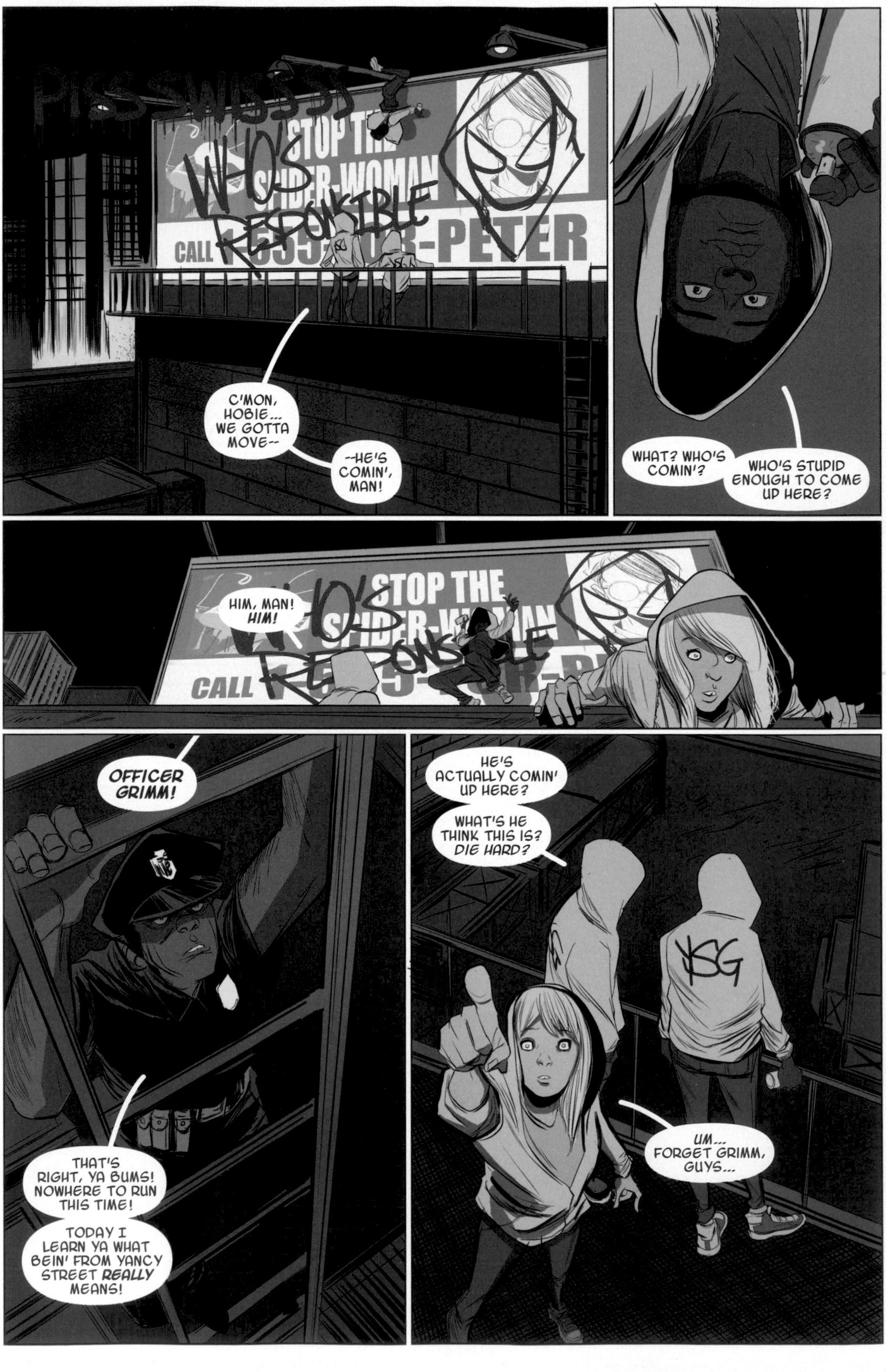
PISS SWISSSS
STOP THE SPIDER-WOMAN
CALL 1-555-[?]03-PETER
WHO'S RESPONSIBLE
C'MON, HOBIE... WE GOTTA MOVE--
--HE'S COMIN', MAN!
WHAT? WHO'S COMIN'?
WHO'S STUPID ENOUGH TO COME UP HERE?
STOP THE SPIDER-WOMAN
HIM, MAN! HIM!
OFFICER GRIMM!
THAT'S RIGHT, YA BUMS! NOWHERE TO RUN THIS TIME!
TODAY I LEARN YA WHAT BEIN' FROM YANCY STREET REALLY MEANS!
HE'S ACTUALLY COMIN' UP HERE?
WHAT'S HE THINK THIS IS? DIE HARD?
YSG
UM... FORGET GRIMM, GUYS...

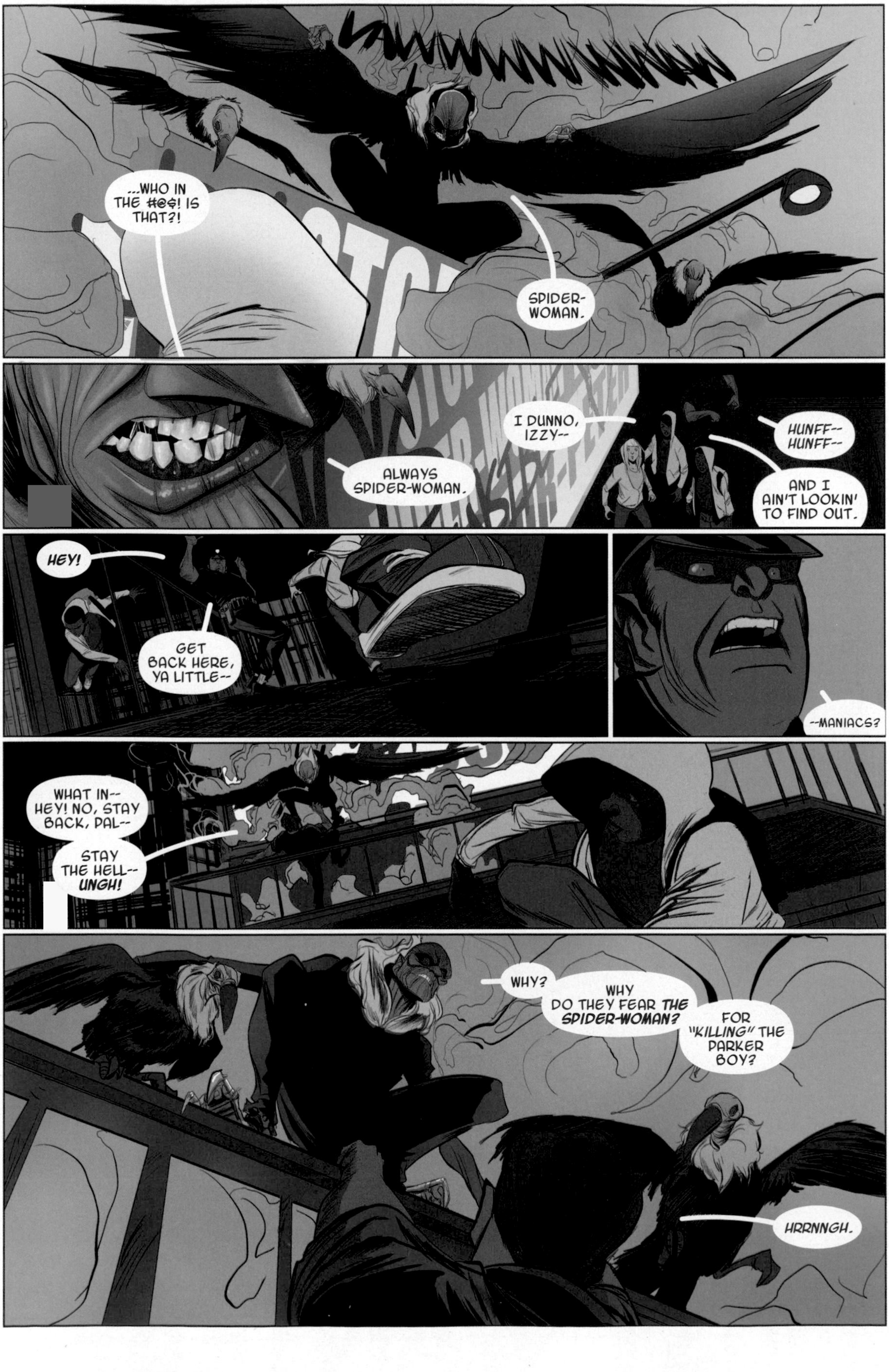

...WHO IN THE #@$! IS THAT?!
SPIDER-WOMAN.
ALWAYS SPIDER-WOMAN.
I DUNNO, IZZY--
HUNFF-- HUNFF--
AND I AIN'T LOOKIN' TO FIND OUT.
HEY!
GET BACK HERE, YA LITTLE--
--MANIACS?
WHAT IN-- HEY! NO, STAY BACK, PAL--
STAY THE HELL-- UNGH!
WHY?
WHY DO THEY FEAR THE SPIDER-WOMAN?
FOR "KILLING" THE PARKER BOY?
HRRNNGH.

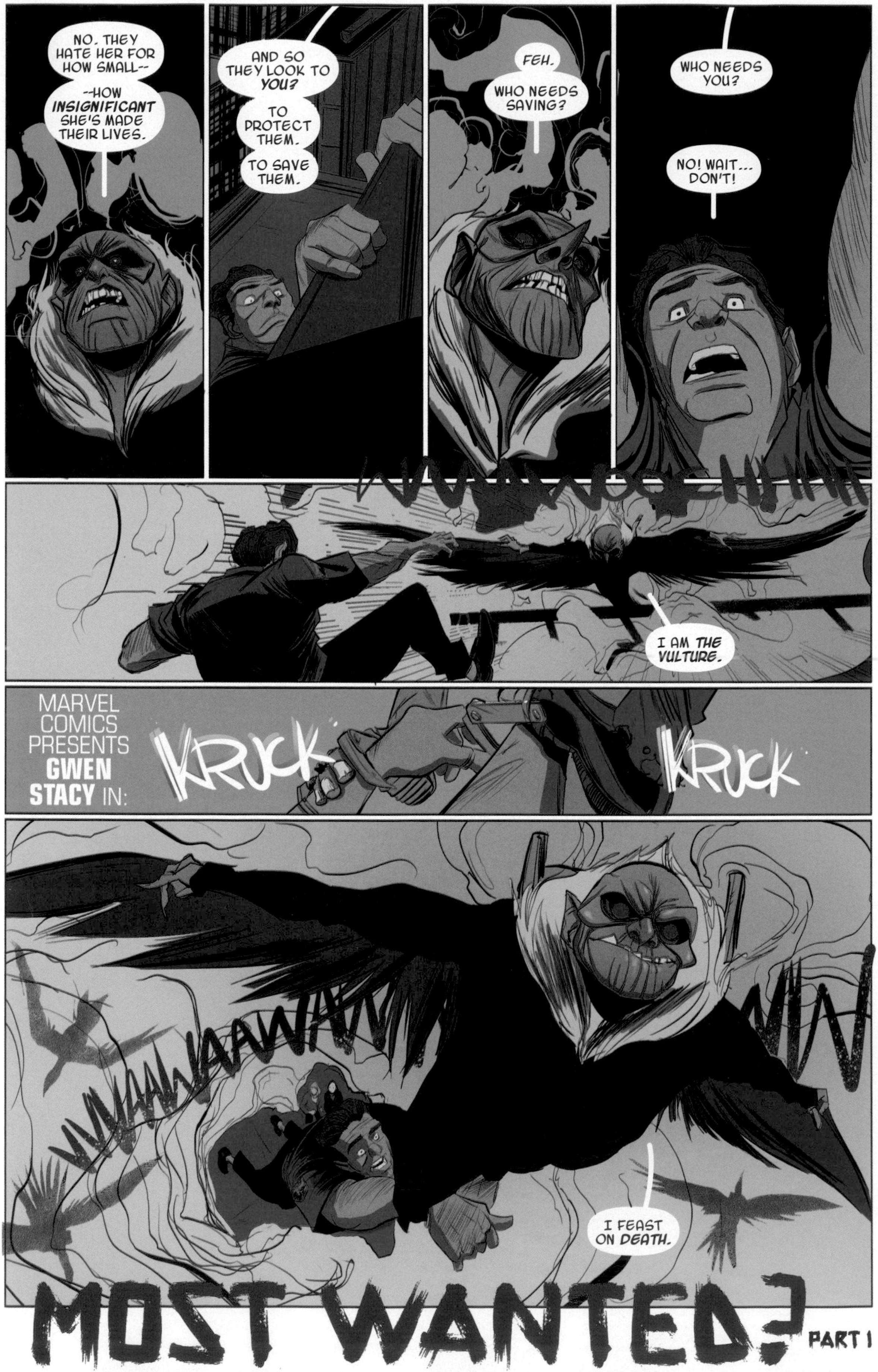

NO. THEY HATE HER FOR HOW SMALL--
--HOW INSIGNIFICANT SHE'S MADE THEIR LIVES.
AND SO THEY LOOK TO YOU?
TO PROTECT THEM.
TO SAVE THEM.
FEH.
WHO NEEDS SAVING?
WHO NEEDS YOU?
NO! WAIT... DON'T!
WWWWOOSHHHH
I AM THE VULTURE.
MARVEL COMICS PRESENTS GWEN STACY IN:
KRUCK
KRUCK
WWAAAWAAAWW
I FEAST ON DEATH.
MOST WANTED? PART 1

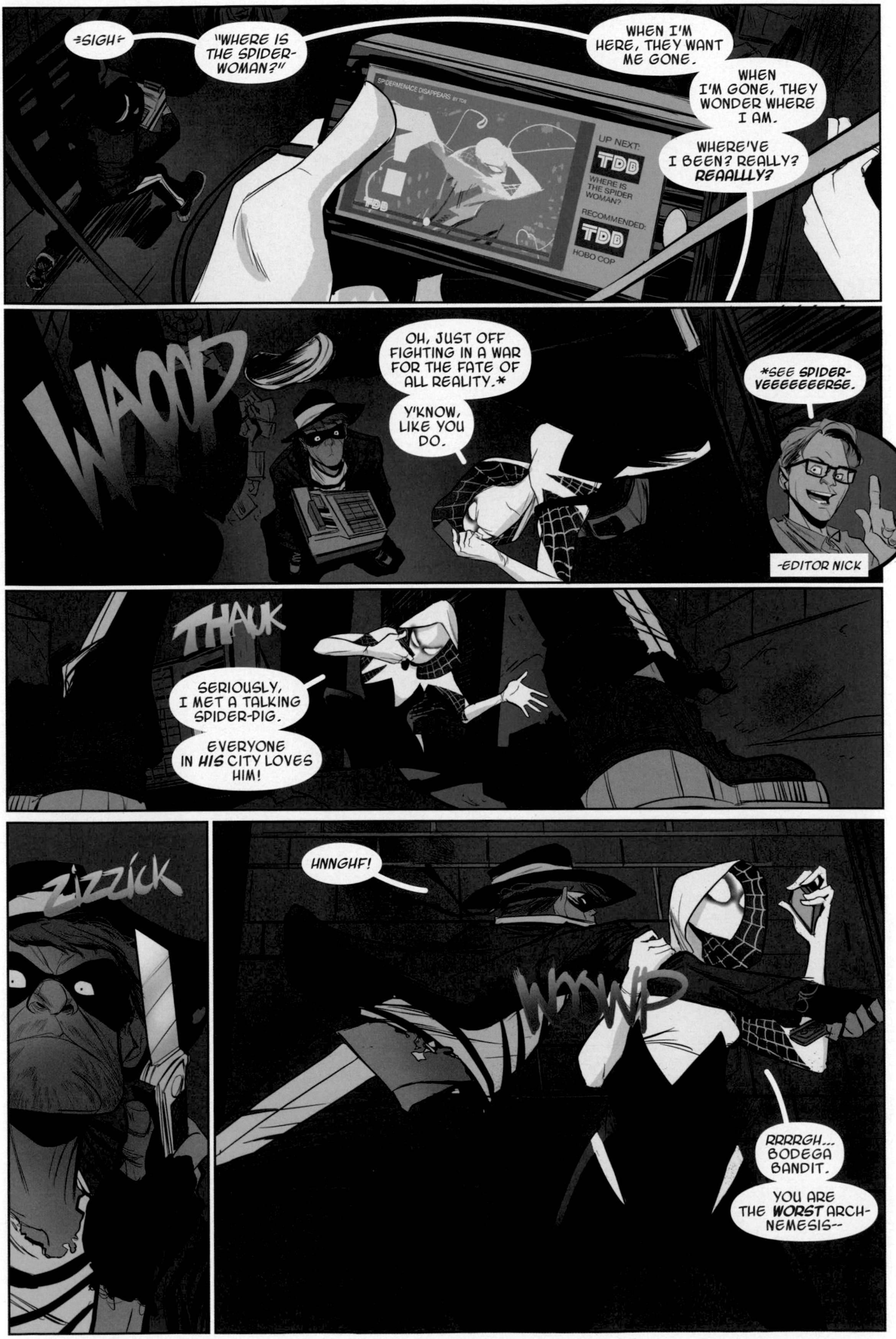

-SIGH-
"WHERE IS THE SPIDER-WOMAN?"
WHEN I'M HERE, THEY WANT ME GONE.
WHEN I'M GONE, THEY WONDER WHERE I AM.
WHERE'VE I BEEN? REALLY? **REAALLLY?**
SPIDERMENACE DISAPPEARS BY TDB
TDB
UP NEXT:
TDB
WHERE IS THE SPIDER WOMAN?
RECOMMENDED:
TDB
HOBO COP
WAOOD
OH, JUST OFF FIGHTING IN A WAR FOR THE FATE OF ALL REALITY.*
Y'KNOW, LIKE YOU DO.
*SEE **SPIDER-VEEEEEEERSE.**
-EDITOR NICK
THAUK
SERIOUSLY, I MET A TALKING SPIDER-PIG.
EVERYONE IN **HIS** CITY LOVES HIM!
ZIZZICK
HNNGHF!
WYWP
RRRRGH... BODEGA BANDIT.
YOU ARE THE **WORST** ARCH-NEMESIS--

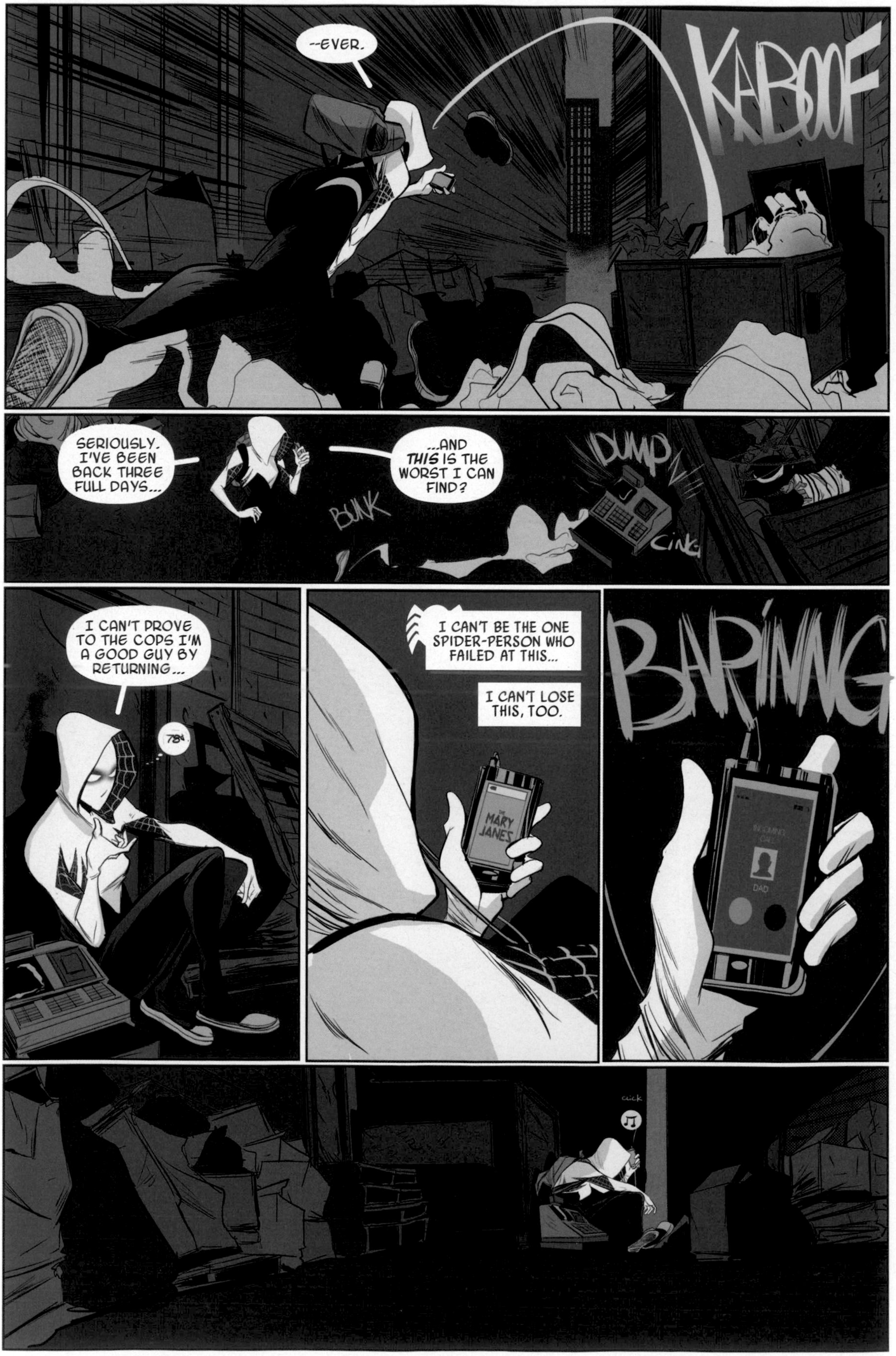
--EVER.
KABOOF
SERIOUSLY. I'VE BEEN BACK THREE FULL DAYS...
...AND THIS IS THE WORST I CAN FIND?
DUMP
BUNK
CINK
I CAN'T PROVE TO THE COPS I'M A GOOD GUY BY RETURNING...
I CAN'T BE THE ONE SPIDER-PERSON WHO FAILED AT THIS...
I CAN'T LOSE THIS, TOO.
BARING
DAD
CLICK

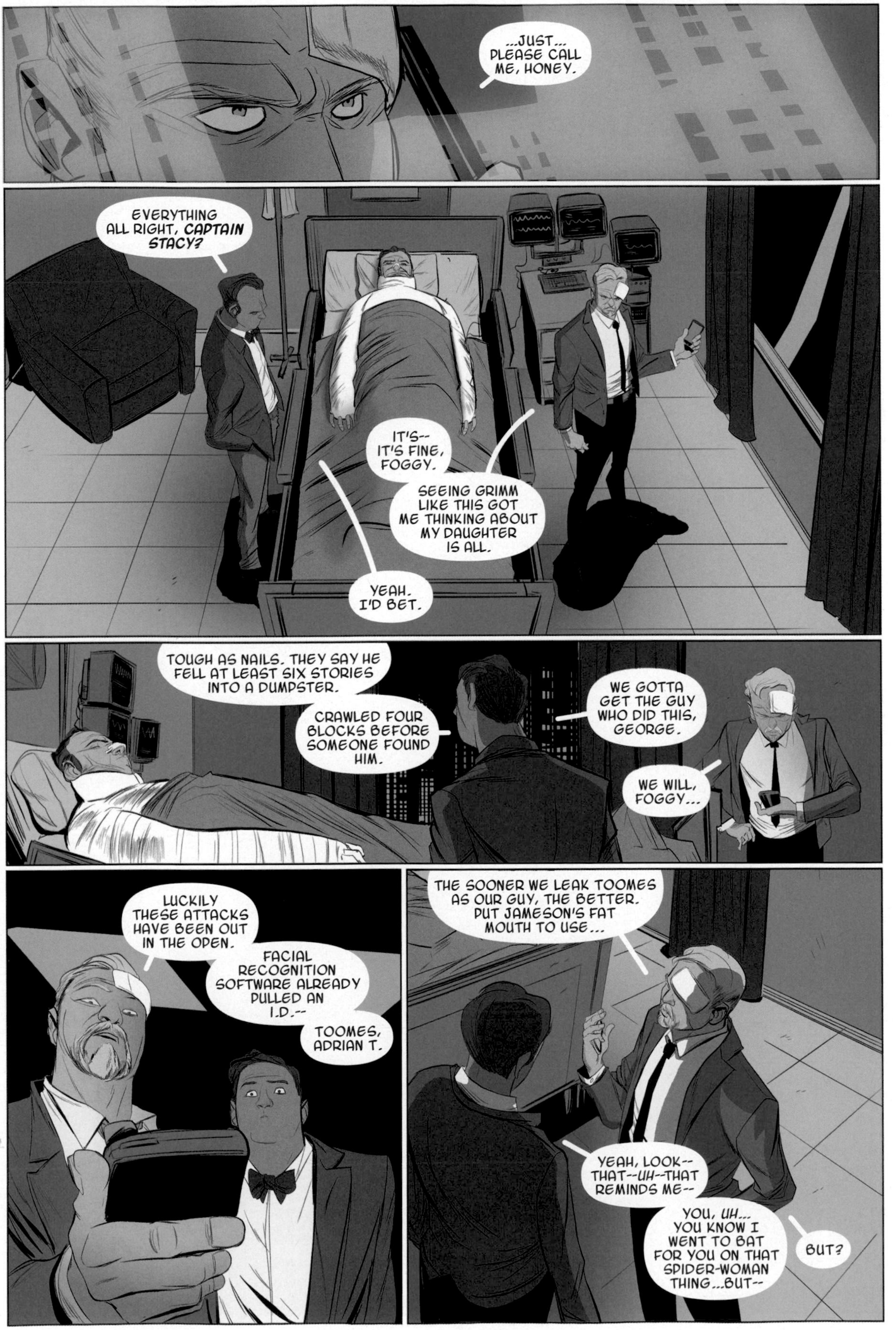
...JUST... PLEASE CALL ME, HONEY.
EVERYTHING ALL RIGHT, CAPTAIN STACY?
IT'S-- IT'S FINE, FOGGY.
SEEING GRIMM LIKE THIS GOT ME THINKING ABOUT MY DAUGHTER IS ALL.
YEAH. I'D BET.
TOUGH AS NAILS. THEY SAY HE FELL AT LEAST SIX STORIES INTO A DUMPSTER.
CRAWLED FOUR BLOCKS BEFORE SOMEONE FOUND HIM.
WE GOTTA GET THE GUY WHO DID THIS, GEORGE.
WE WILL, FOGGY...
LUCKILY THESE ATTACKS HAVE BEEN OUT IN THE OPEN.
FACIAL RECOGNITION SOFTWARE ALREADY PULLED AN I.D.--
TOOMES, ADRIAN T.
THE SOONER WE LEAK TOOMES AS OUR GUY, THE BETTER. PUT JAMESON'S FAT MOUTH TO USE...
YEAH, LOOK-- THAT--UH--THAT REMINDS ME--
YOU, UH... YOU KNOW I WENT TO BAT FOR YOU ON THAT SPIDER-WOMAN THING...BUT--
BUT?

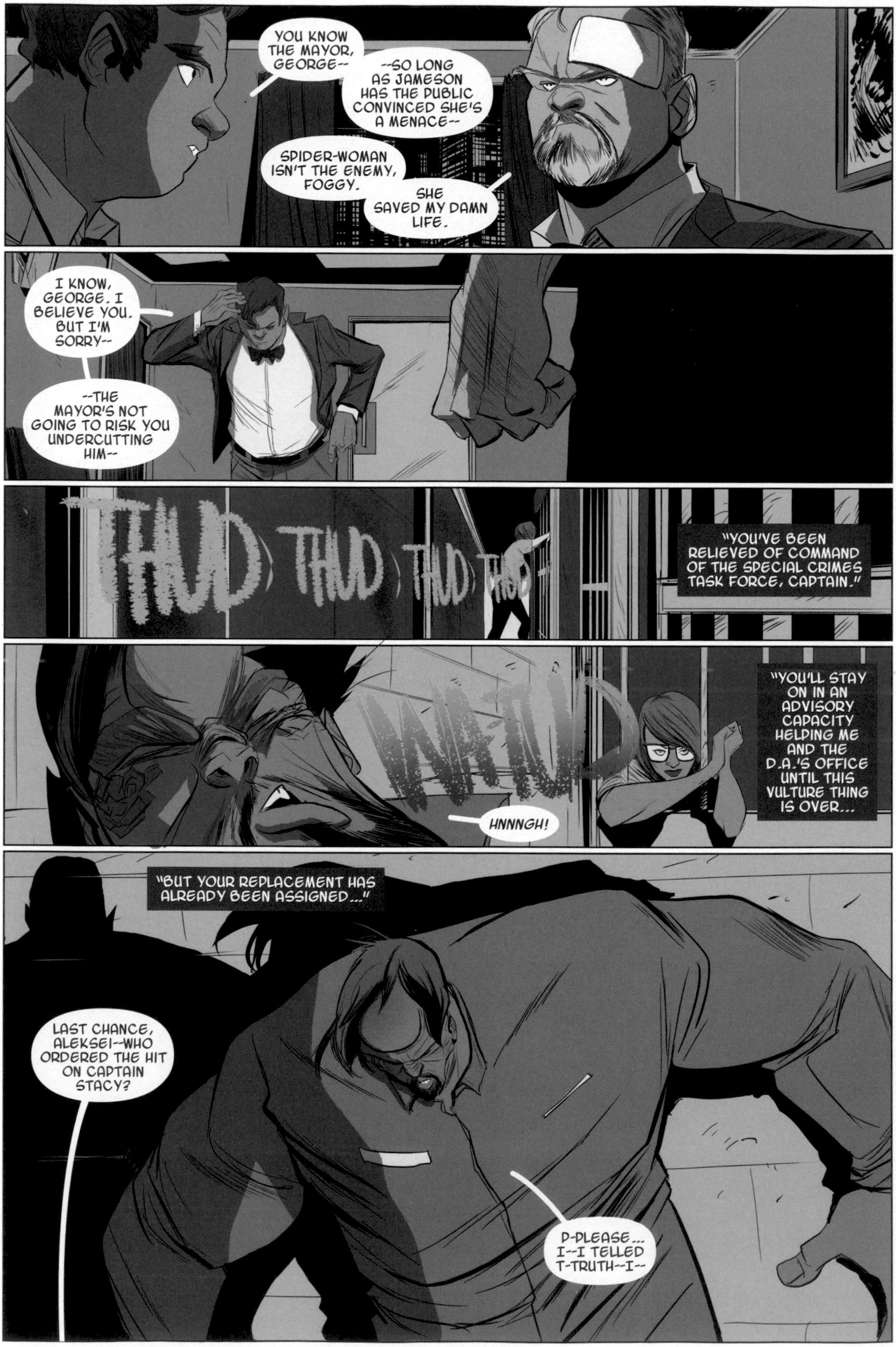
YOU KNOW THE MAYOR, GEORGE--
--SO LONG AS JAMESON HAS THE PUBLIC CONVINCED SHE'S A MENACE--
SPIDER-WOMAN ISN'T THE ENEMY, FOGGY.
SHE SAVED MY DAMN LIFE.
I KNOW, GEORGE. I BELIEVE YOU. BUT I'M SORRY--
--THE MAYOR'S NOT GOING TO RISK YOU UNDERCUTTING HIM--
THUD THUD THUD THUD
"YOU'VE BEEN RELIEVED OF COMMAND OF THE SPECIAL CRIMES TASK FORCE, CAPTAIN."
"YOU'LL STAY ON IN AN ADVISORY CAPACITY HELPING ME AND THE D.A.'S OFFICE UNTIL THIS VULTURE THING IS OVER...
HNNNGH!
"BUT YOUR REPLACEMENT HAS ALREADY BEEN ASSIGNED..."
LAST CHANCE, ALEKSEI--WHO ORDERED THE HIT ON CAPTAIN STACY?
P-PLEASE... I--I TELLED T-TRUTH--I--

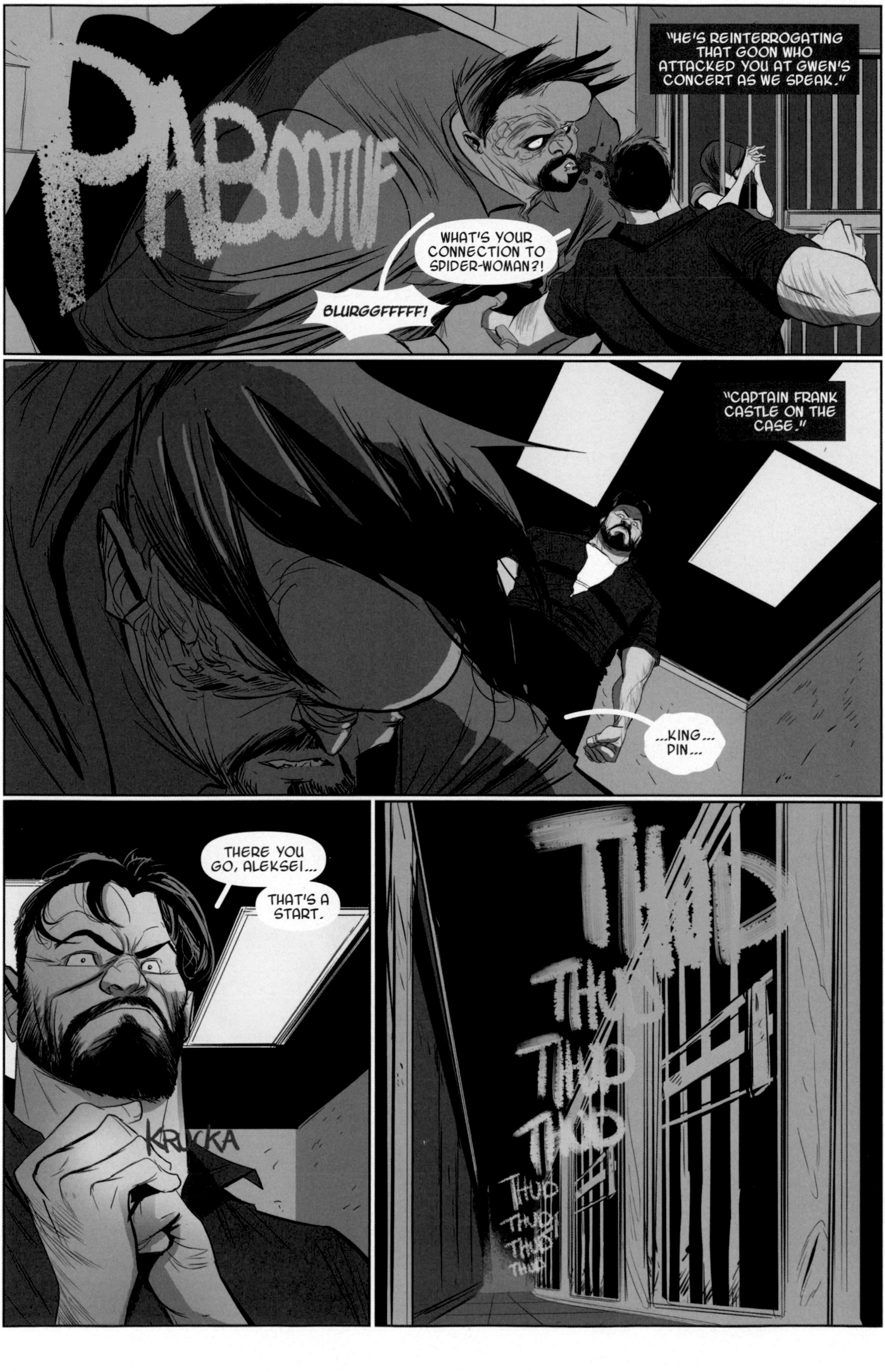
"HE'S REINTERROGATING THAT GOON WHO ATTACKED YOU AT GWEN'S CONCERT AS WE SPEAK."
PABOOTUF
WHAT'S YOUR CONNECTION TO SPIDER-WOMAN?!
BLURGGFFFFF!
"CAPTAIN FRANK CASTLE ON THE CASE."
...KING... PIN...
THERE YOU GO, ALEKSEI...
THAT'S A START.
KRUCKA
THUD
THUD
THUD
THUD
THUD
THUD
THUD
THUD

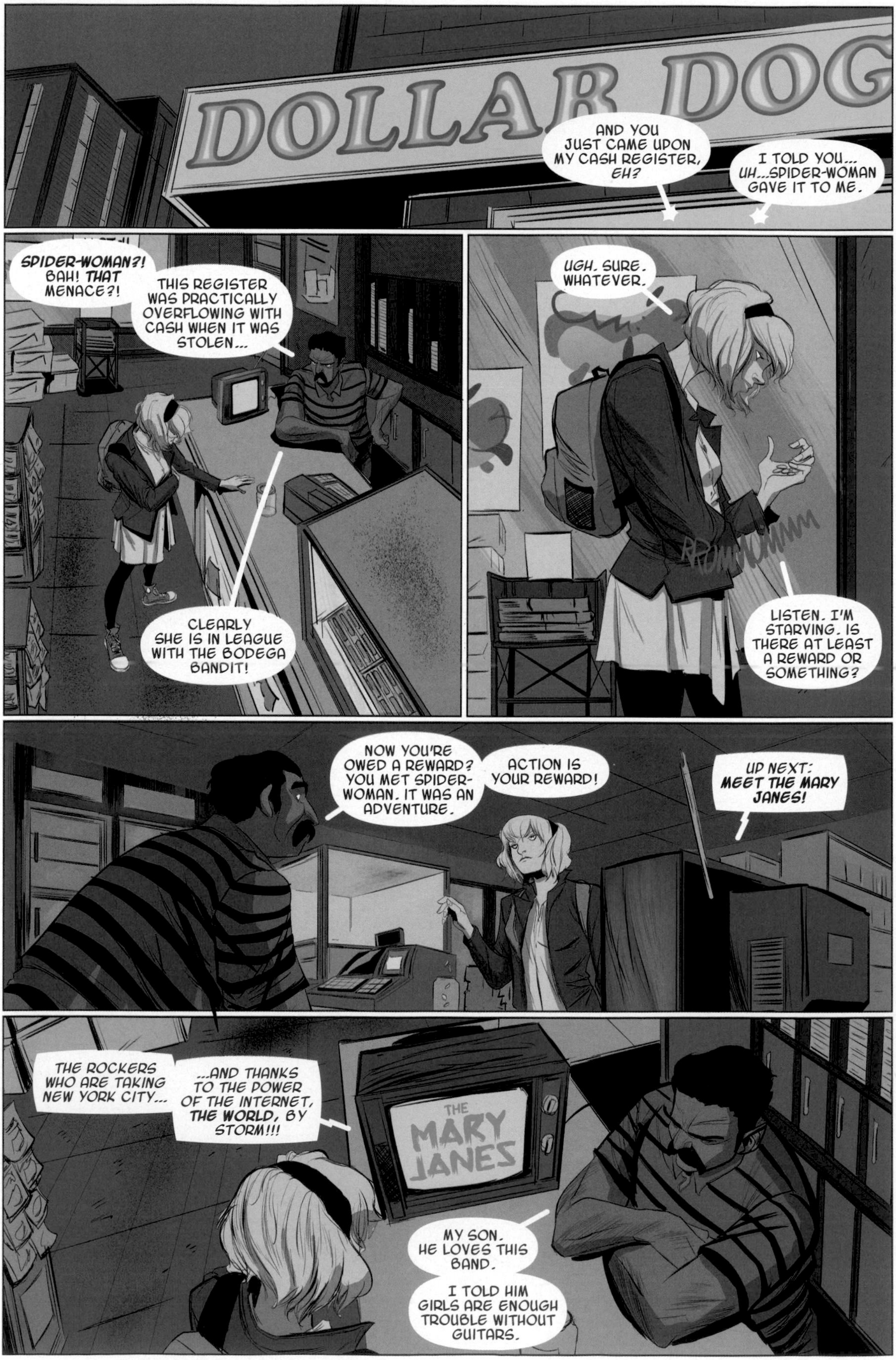
DOLLAR DOG
AND YOU JUST CAME UPON MY CASH REGISTER, EH?
I TOLD YOU... UH...SPIDER-WOMAN GAVE IT TO ME.
SPIDER-WOMAN?! BAH! THAT MENACE?!
THIS REGISTER WAS PRACTICALLY OVERFLOWING WITH CASH WHEN IT WAS STOLEN...
CLEARLY SHE IS IN LEAGUE WITH THE BODEGA BANDIT!
UGH. SURE. WHATEVER.
RROMMMMMMM
LISTEN. I'M STARVING. IS THERE AT LEAST A REWARD OR SOMETHING?
NOW YOU'RE OWED A REWARD? YOU MET SPIDER-WOMAN. IT WAS AN ADVENTURE.
ACTION IS YOUR REWARD!
UP NEXT: MEET THE MARY JANES!
THE ROCKERS WHO ARE TAKING NEW YORK CITY...
...AND THANKS TO THE POWER OF THE INTERNET, THE WORLD, BY STORM!!!
THE MARY JANES
MY SON. HE LOVES THIS BAND.
I TOLD HIM GIRLS ARE ENOUGH TROUBLE WITHOUT GUITARS.

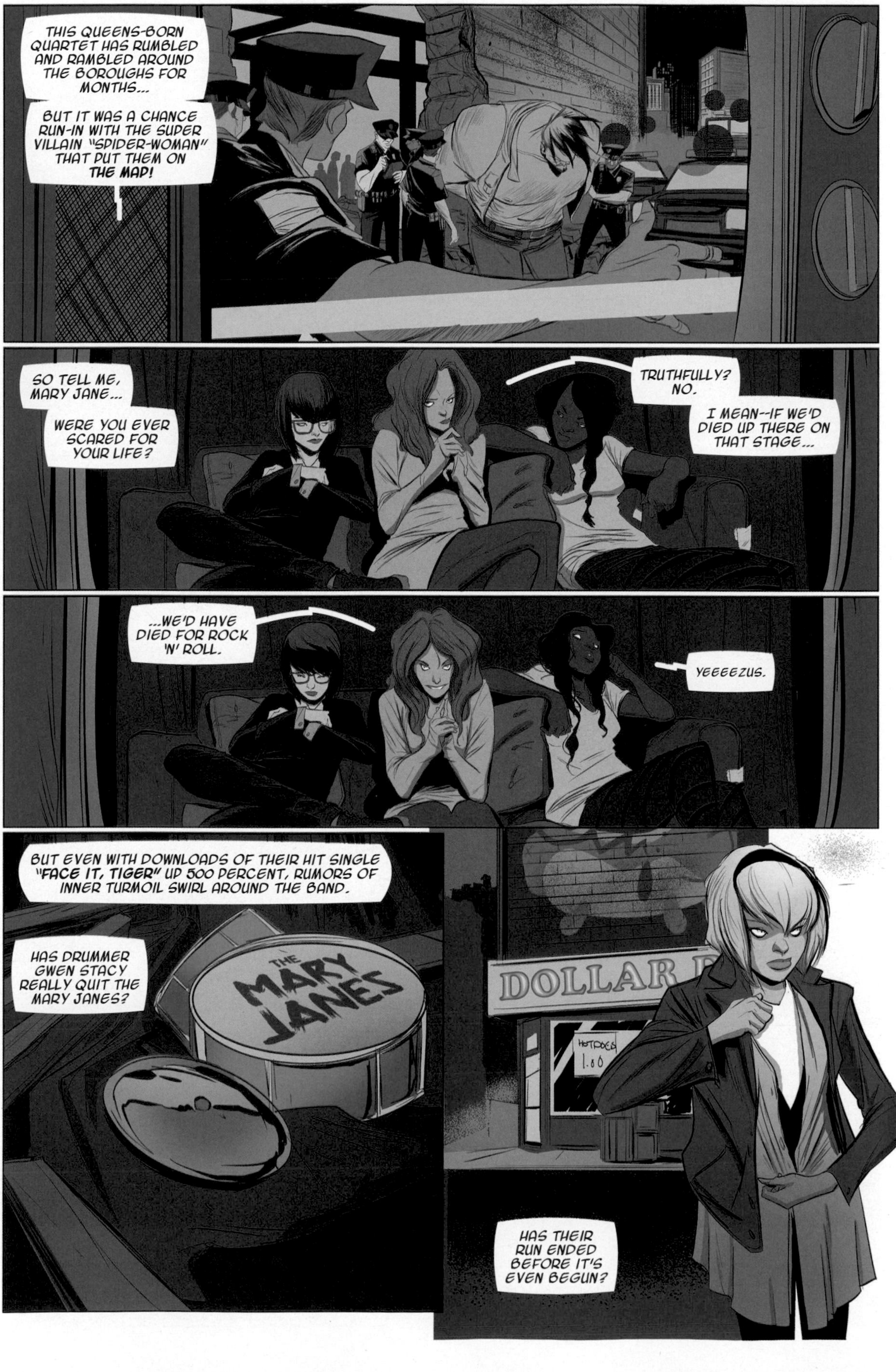
THIS QUEENS-BORN QUARTET HAS RUMBLED AND RAMBLED AROUND THE BOROUGHS FOR MONTHS...
BUT IT WAS A CHANCE RUN-IN WITH THE SUPER VILLAIN "SPIDER-WOMAN" THAT PUT THEM ON THE MAP!
SO TELL ME, MARY JANE...
WERE YOU EVER SCARED FOR YOUR LIFE?
TRUTHFULLY? NO.
I MEAN--IF WE'D DIED UP THERE ON THAT STAGE...
...WE'D HAVE DIED FOR ROCK 'N' ROLL.
YEEEEZUS.
BUT EVEN WITH DOWNLOADS OF THEIR HIT SINGLE "FACE IT, TIGER" UP 500 PERCENT, RUMORS OF INNER TURMOIL SWIRL AROUND THE BAND.
HAS DRUMMER GWEN STACY REALLY QUIT THE MARY JANES?
THE MARY JANES
DOLLAR
1.00
HAS THEIR RUN ENDED BEFORE IT'S EVEN BEGUN?

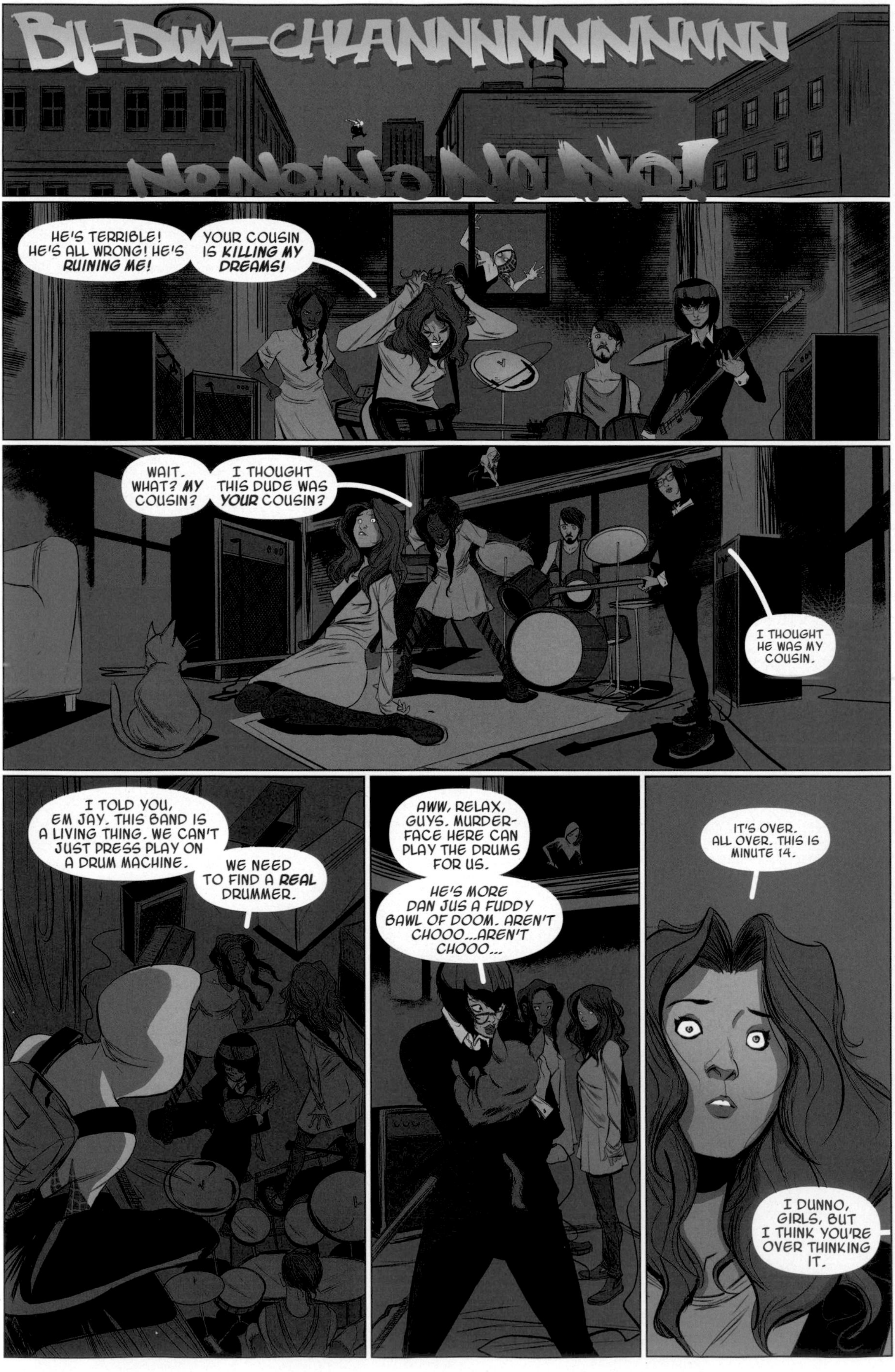
BU-DUM-CHLANNNNNNNNNNN
NONONONO NO NO NO!
HE'S TERRIBLE! HE'S ALL WRONG! HE'S RUINING ME!
YOUR COUSIN IS KILLING MY DREAMS!
WAIT. WHAT? MY COUSIN?
I THOUGHT THIS DUDE WAS YOUR COUSIN?
I THOUGHT HE WAS MY COUSIN.
I TOLD YOU, EM JAY. THIS BAND IS A LIVING THING. WE CAN'T JUST PRESS PLAY ON A DRUM MACHINE.
WE NEED TO FIND A REAL DRUMMER.
AWW, RELAX, GUYS. MURDER-FACE HERE CAN PLAY THE DRUMS FOR US.
HE'S MORE DAN JUS A FUDDY BAWL OF DOOM. AREN'T CHOOO...AREN'T CHOOO...
IT'S OVER. ALL OVER. THIS IS MINUTE 14.
I DUNNO, GIRLS, BUT I THINK YOU'RE OVER THINKING IT.

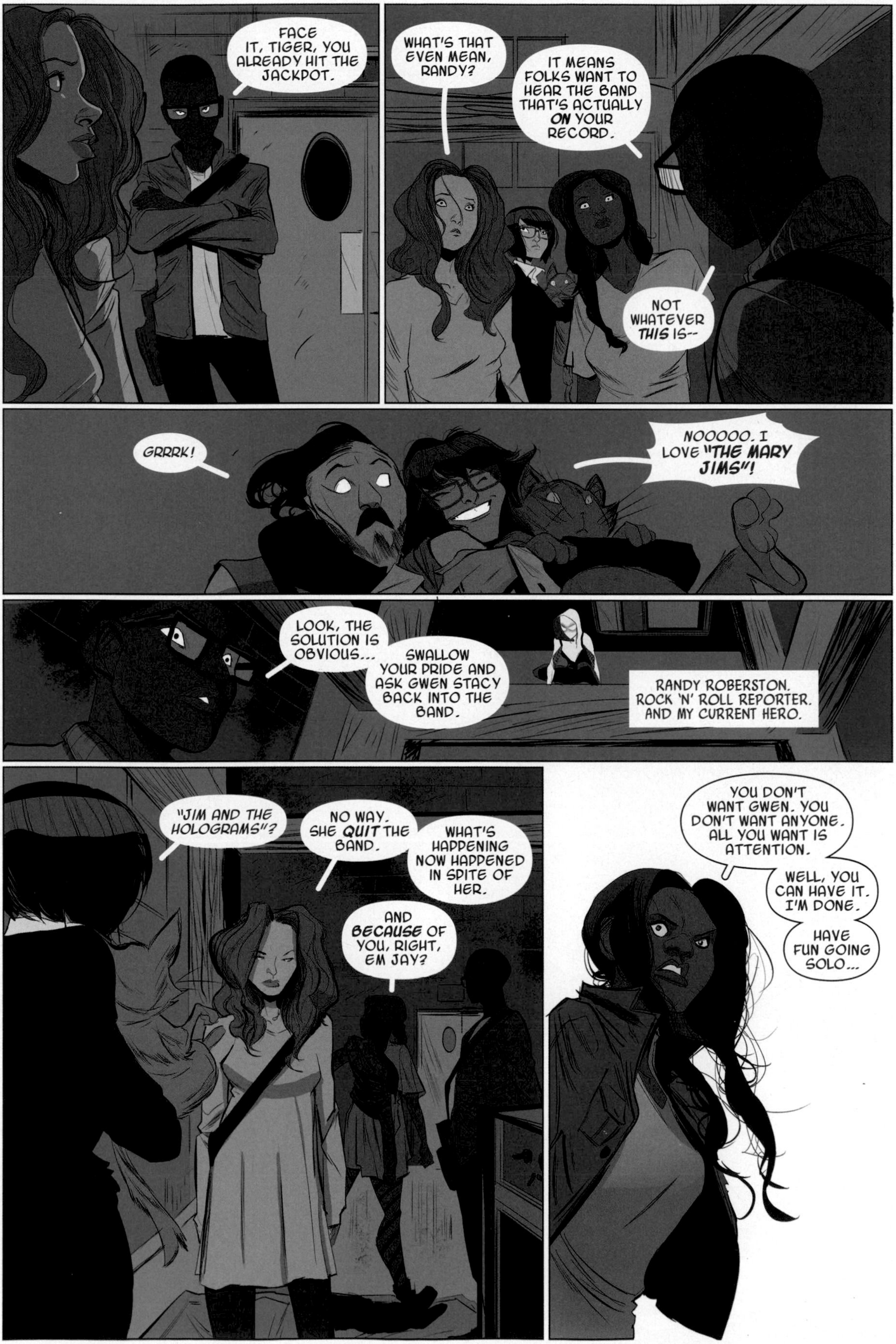
FACE IT, TIGER, YOU ALREADY HIT THE JACKPOT.
WHAT'S THAT EVEN MEAN, RANDY?
IT MEANS FOLKS WANT TO HEAR THE BAND THAT'S ACTUALLY **ON** YOUR RECORD.
NOT WHATEVER **THIS** IS--
GRRRK!
NOOOOO. I LOVE **"THE MARY JIMS"**!
LOOK, THE SOLUTION IS OBVIOUS...
SWALLOW YOUR PRIDE AND ASK GWEN STACY BACK INTO THE BAND.
RANDY ROBERSTON. ROCK 'N' ROLL REPORTER. AND MY CURRENT HERO.
"JIM AND THE HOLOGRAMS"?
NO WAY. SHE **QUIT** THE BAND.
WHAT'S HAPPENING NOW HAPPENED IN SPITE OF HER.
AND **BECAUSE** OF YOU, RIGHT, EM JAY?
YOU DON'T WANT GWEN. YOU DON'T WANT ANYONE. ALL YOU WANT IS ATTENTION.
WELL, YOU CAN HAVE IT. I'M DONE.
HAVE FUN GOING SOLO...

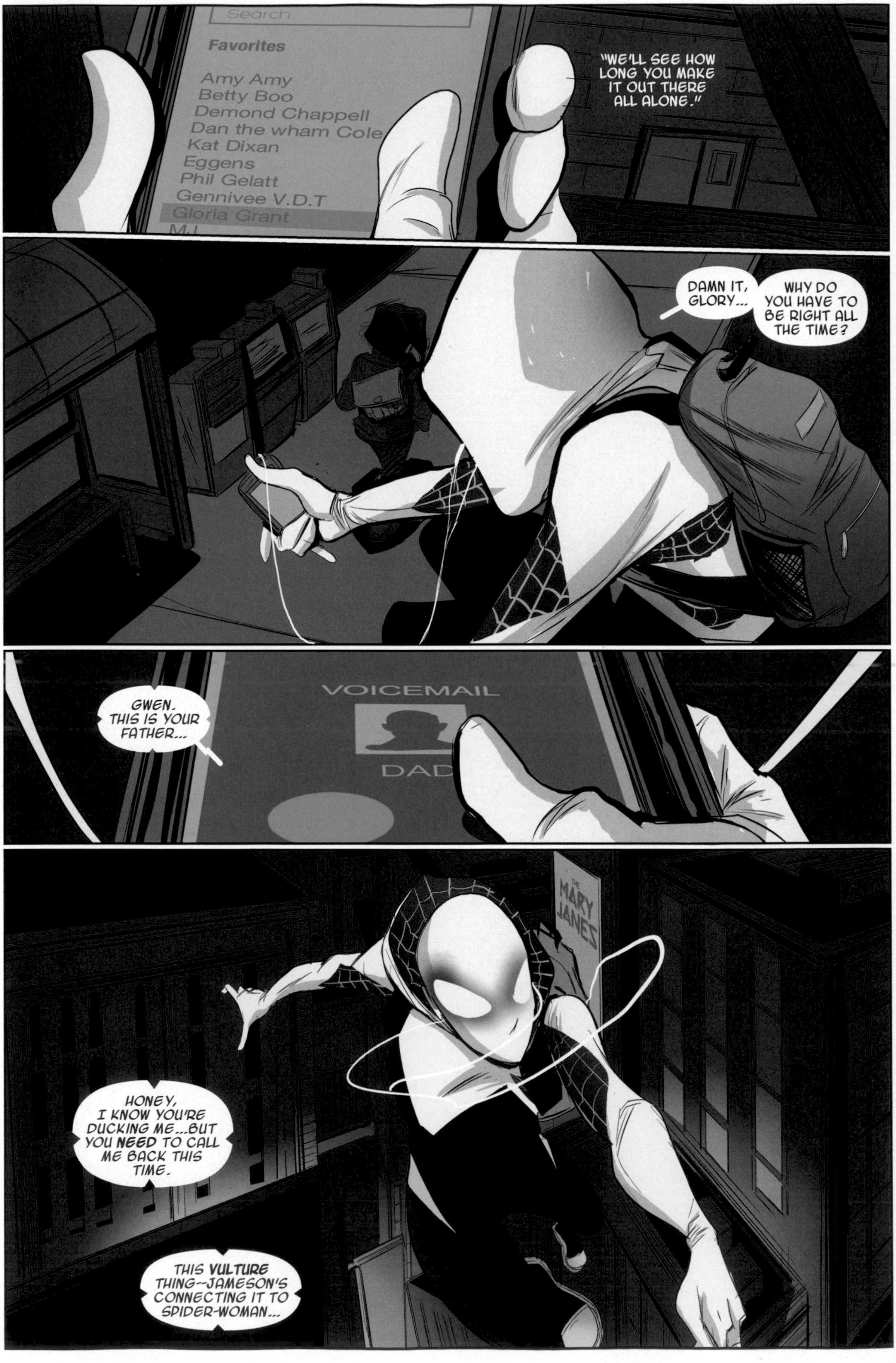
Search
Favorites
Amy Amy
Betty Boo
Demond Chappell
Dan the wham Cole
Kat Dixan
Eggens
Phil Gelatt
Gennivee V.D.T
Gloria Grant
"WE'LL SEE HOW LONG YOU MAKE IT OUT THERE ALL ALONE."
DAMN IT, GLORY...
WHY DO YOU HAVE TO BE RIGHT ALL THE TIME?
VOICEMAIL
GWEN. THIS IS YOUR FATHER...
HONEY, I KNOW YOU'RE DUCKING ME...BUT YOU NEED TO CALL ME BACK THIS TIME.
THIS VULTURE THING--JAMESON'S CONNECTING IT TO SPIDER-WOMAN...
THE MARY JANES

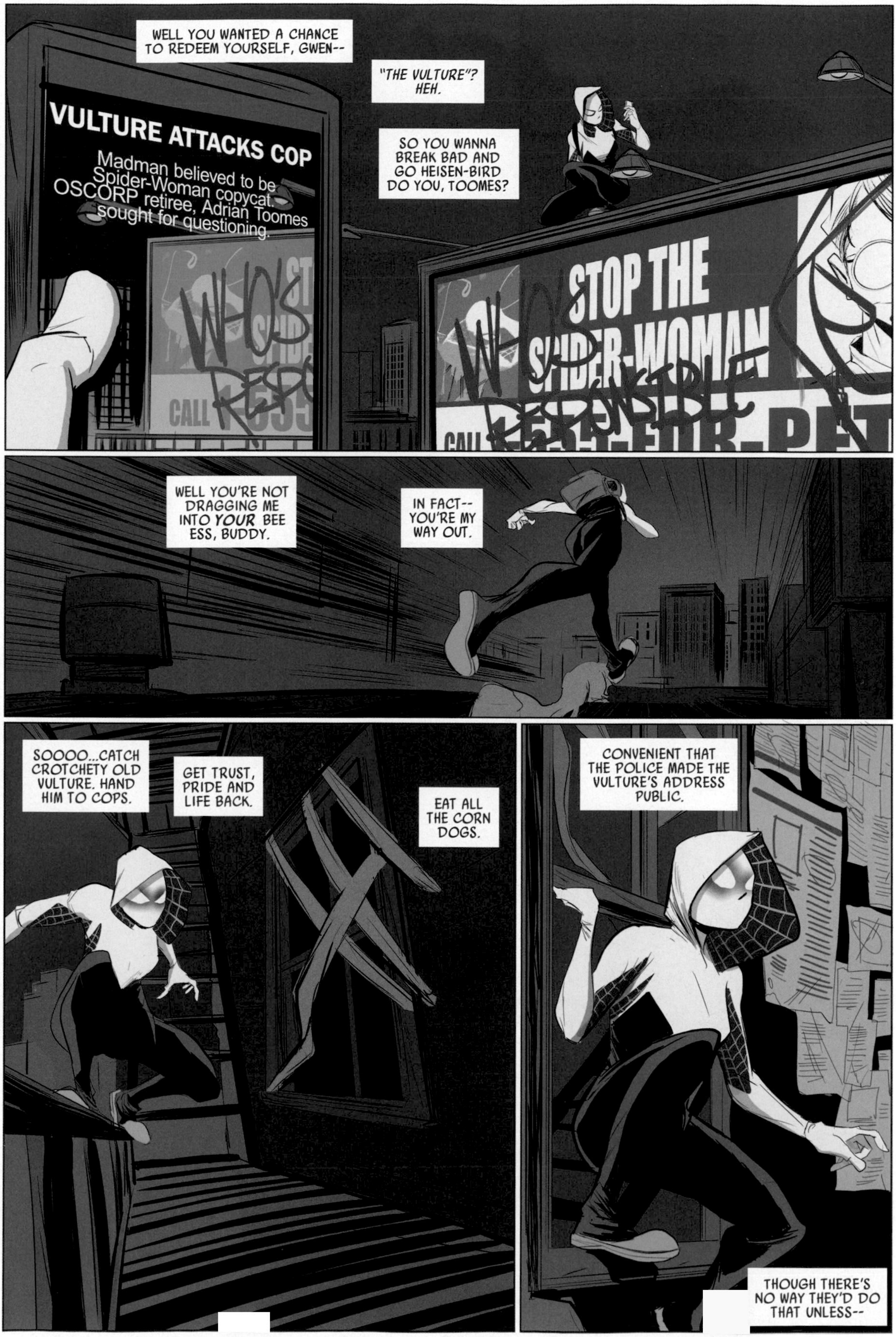
WELL YOU WANTED A CHANCE TO REDEEM YOURSELF, GWEN--
VULTURE ATTACKS COP
Madman believed to be Spider-Woman copycat. OSCORP retiree, Adrian Toomes sought for questioning.
"THE VULTURE"? HEH.
SO YOU WANNA BREAK BAD AND GO HEISEN-BIRD DO YOU, TOOMES?
STOP THE SPIDER-WOMAN
WHO'S RESPONSIBLE
WELL YOU'RE NOT DRAGGING ME INTO *YOUR* BEE ESS, BUDDY.
IN FACT-- YOU'RE MY WAY OUT.
SOOOO...CATCH CROTCHETY OLD VULTURE. HAND HIM TO COPS.
GET TRUST, PRIDE AND LIFE BACK.
EAT ALL THE CORN DOGS.
CONVENIENT THAT THE POLICE MADE THE VULTURE'S ADDRESS PUBLIC.
THOUGH THERE'S NO WAY THEY'D DO THAT UNLESS--

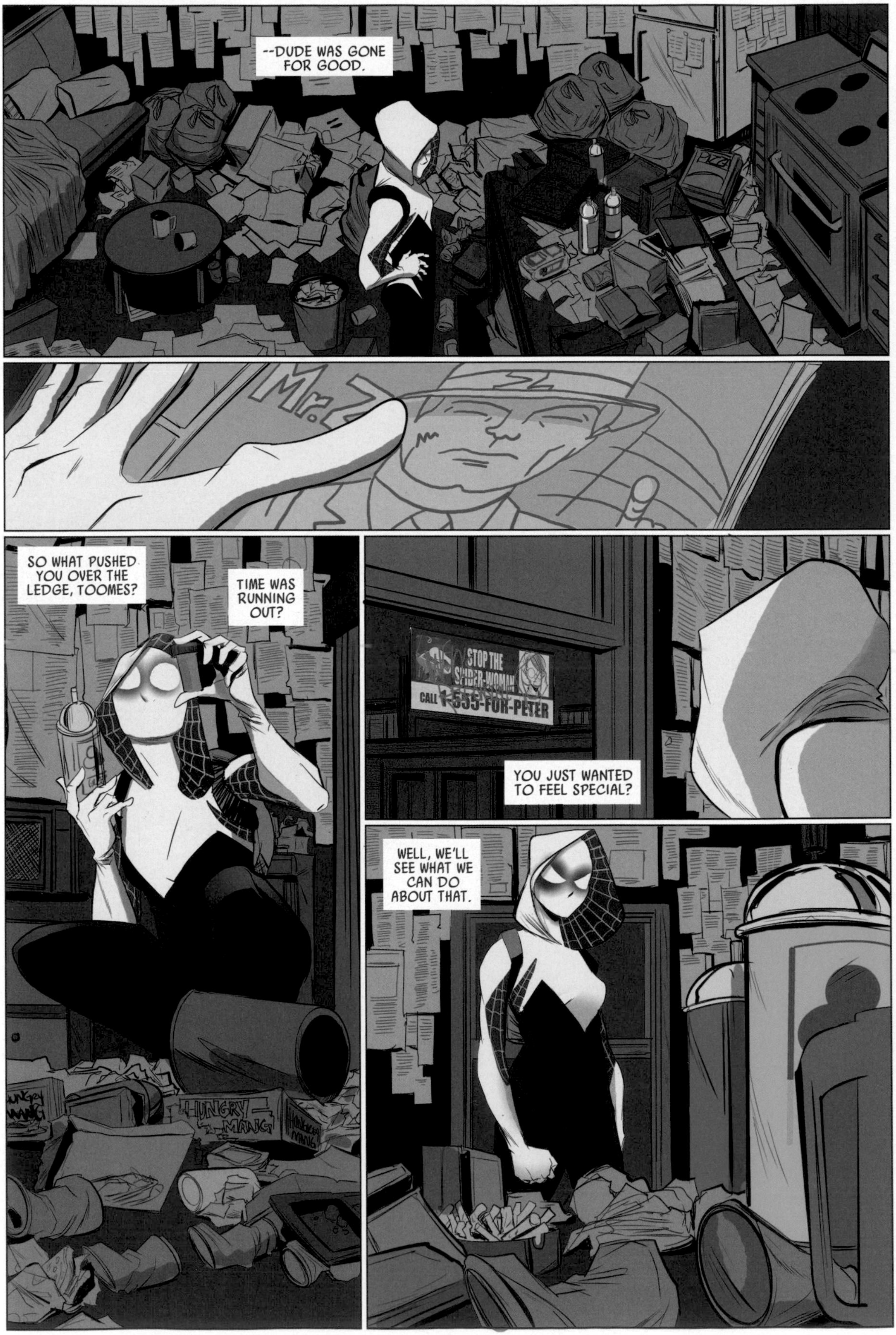
--DUDE WAS GONE FOR GOOD.
Mr. Z
SO WHAT PUSHED YOU OVER THE LEDGE, TOOMES?
TIME WAS RUNNING OUT?
STOP THE SPIDER-WOMAN
CALL 1-555-FOR-PETER
YOU JUST WANTED TO FEEL SPECIAL?
WELL, WE'LL SEE WHAT WE CAN DO ABOUT THAT.
HUNGRY MANG

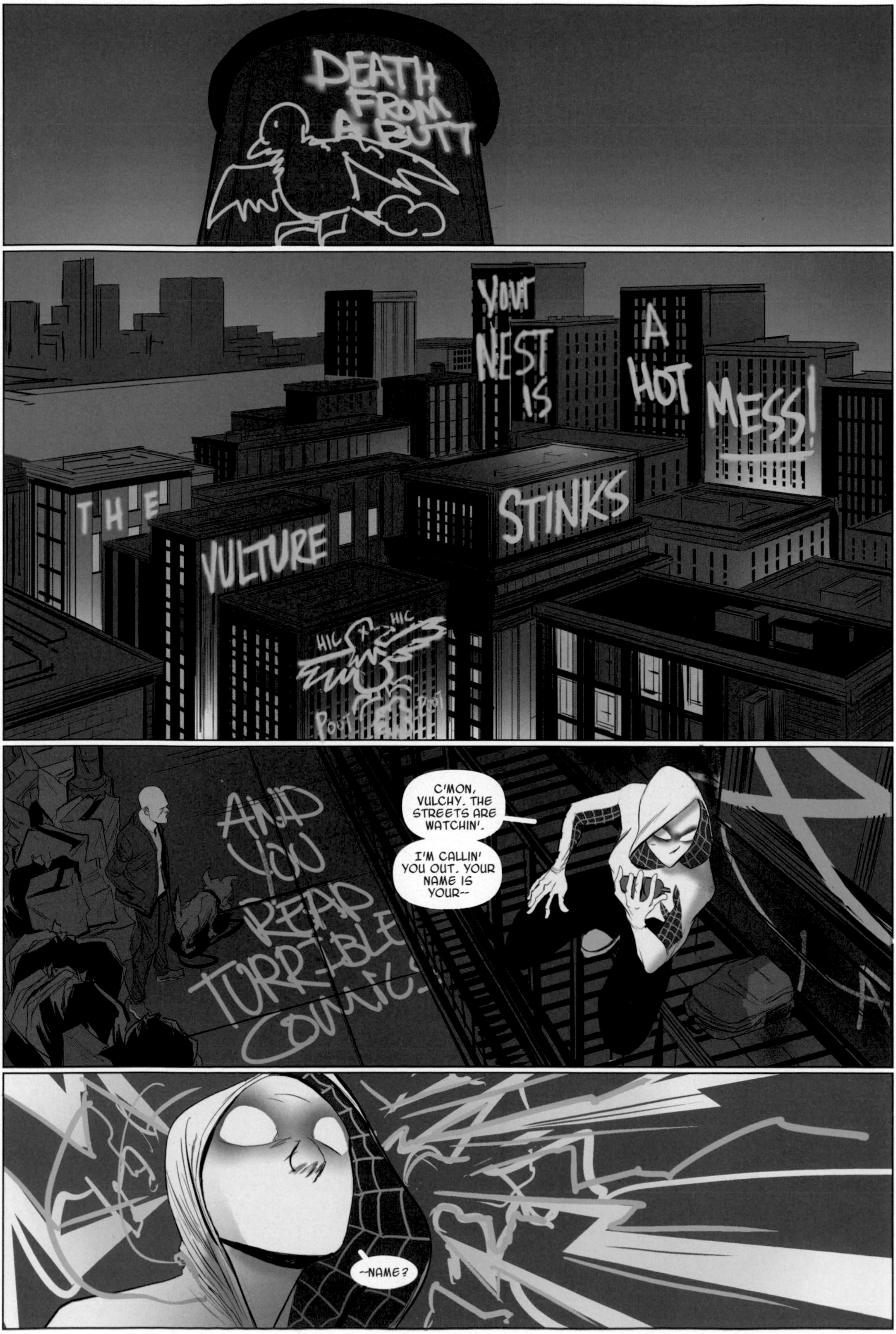
DEATH FROM A BUTT
YOUR NEST IS A HOT MESS!
THE VULTURE STINKS
HIC HIC
POOT POOT
AND YOU READ TURR-IBLE COMICS
C'MON, VULCHY. THE STREETS ARE WATCHIN'.
I'M CALLIN' YOU OUT. YOUR NAME IS YOUR--
--NAME?

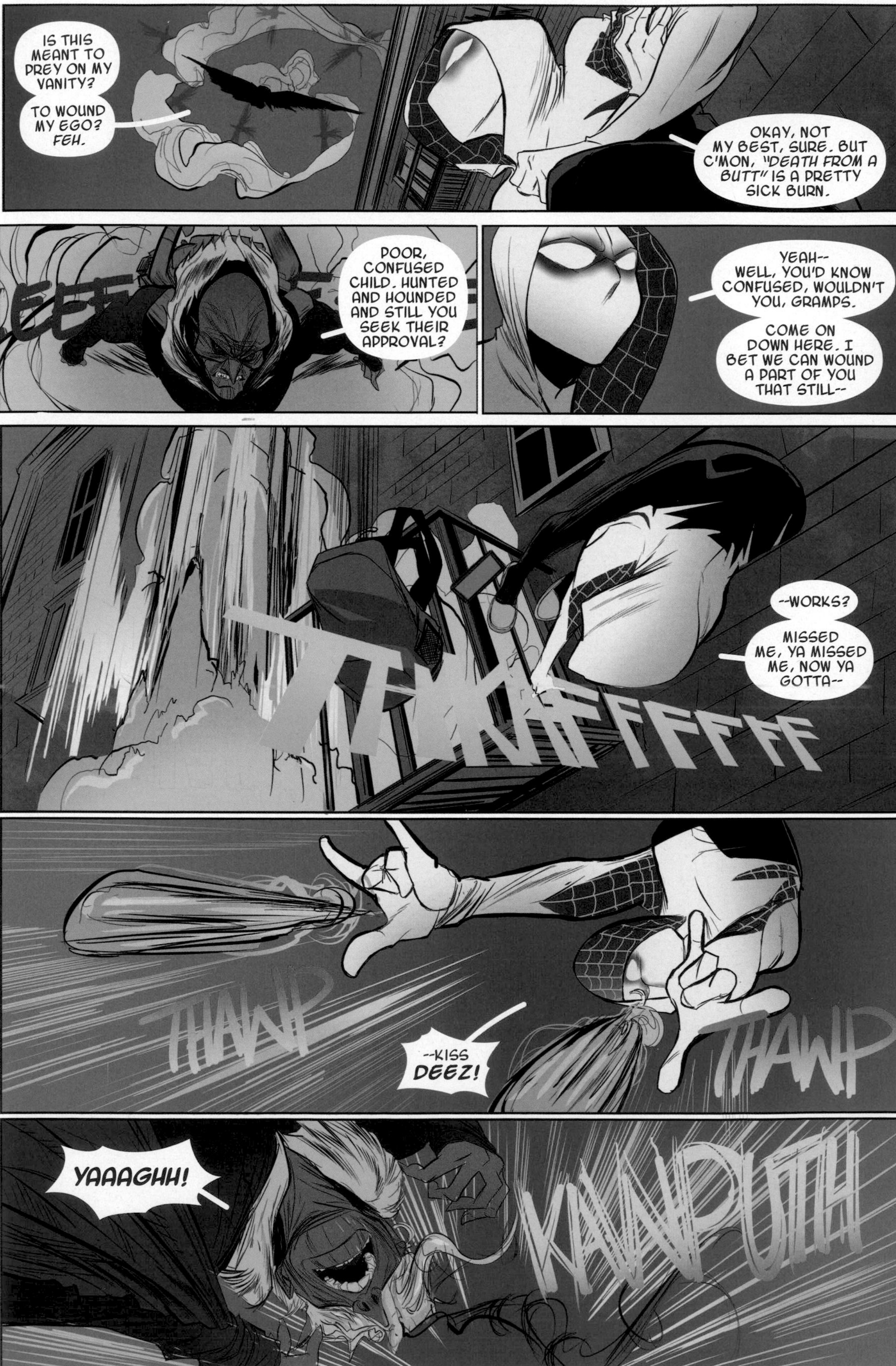

IS THIS MEANT TO PREY ON MY VANITY?
TO WOUND MY EGO? FEH.
OKAY, NOT MY BEST, SURE. BUT C'MON, "DEATH FROM A BUTT" IS A PRETTY SICK BURN.
POOR, CONFUSED CHILD. HUNTED AND HOUNDED AND STILL YOU SEEK THEIR APPROVAL?
YEAH-- WELL, YOU'D KNOW CONFUSED, WOULDN'T YOU, GRAMPS.
COME ON DOWN HERE. I BET WE CAN WOUND A PART OF YOU THAT STILL--
--WORKS?
MISSED ME, YA MISSED ME, NOW YA GOTTA--
THAWP
--KISS DEEZ!
THAWP
YAAAGHH!

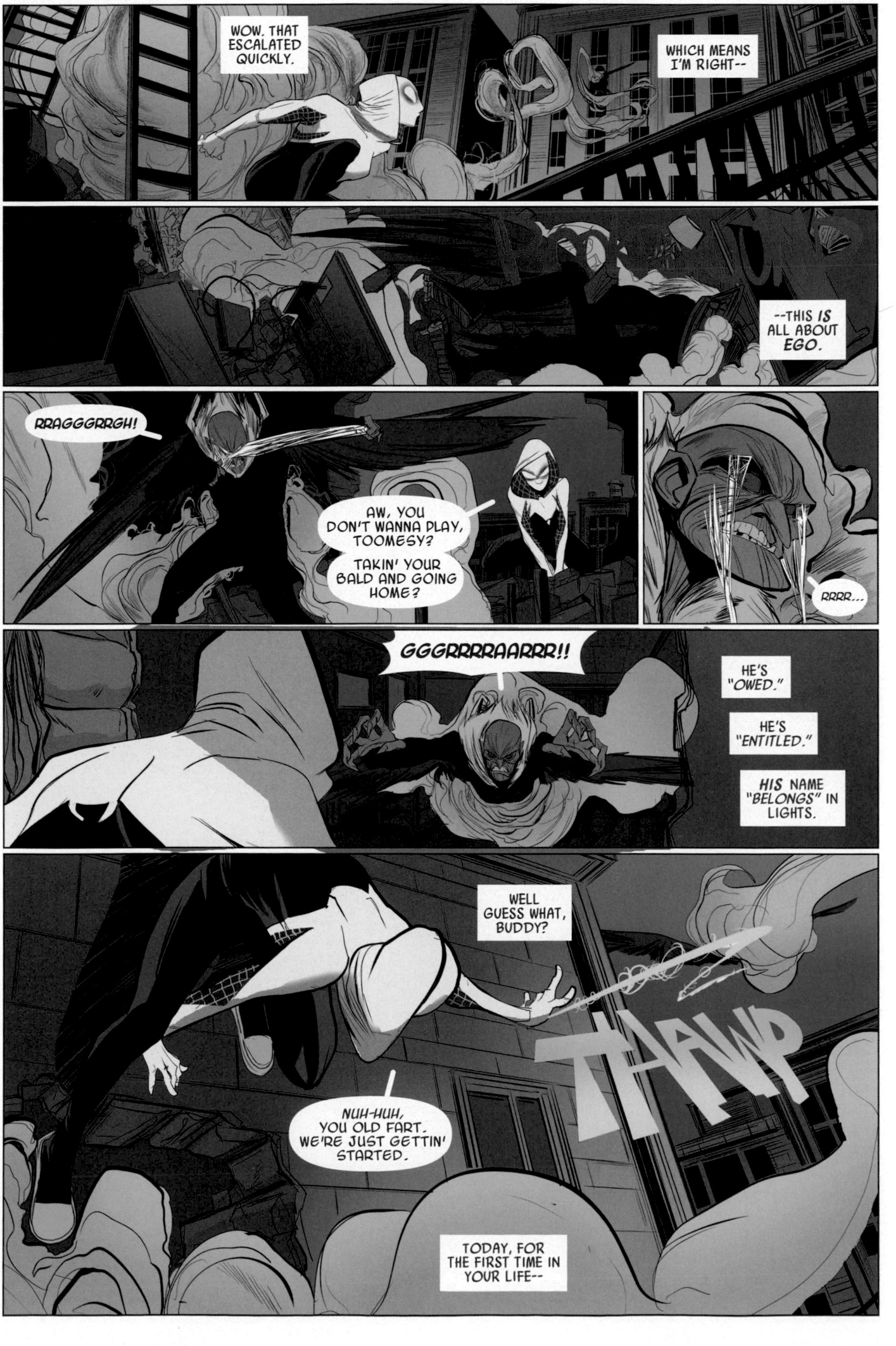
WOW. THAT ESCALATED QUICKLY.
WHICH MEANS I'M RIGHT--
--THIS IS ALL ABOUT EGO.
RRAGGGRRGH!
AW, YOU DON'T WANNA PLAY, TOOMESY?
TAKIN' YOUR BALD AND GOING HOME?
RRRR...
GGGRRRRAARRR!!
HE'S "OWED."
HE'S "ENTITLED."
HIS NAME "BELONGS" IN LIGHTS.
WELL GUESS WHAT, BUDDY?
THAWP
NUH-UH, YOU OLD FART. WE'RE JUST GETTIN' STARTED.
TODAY, FOR THE FIRST TIME IN YOUR LIFE--

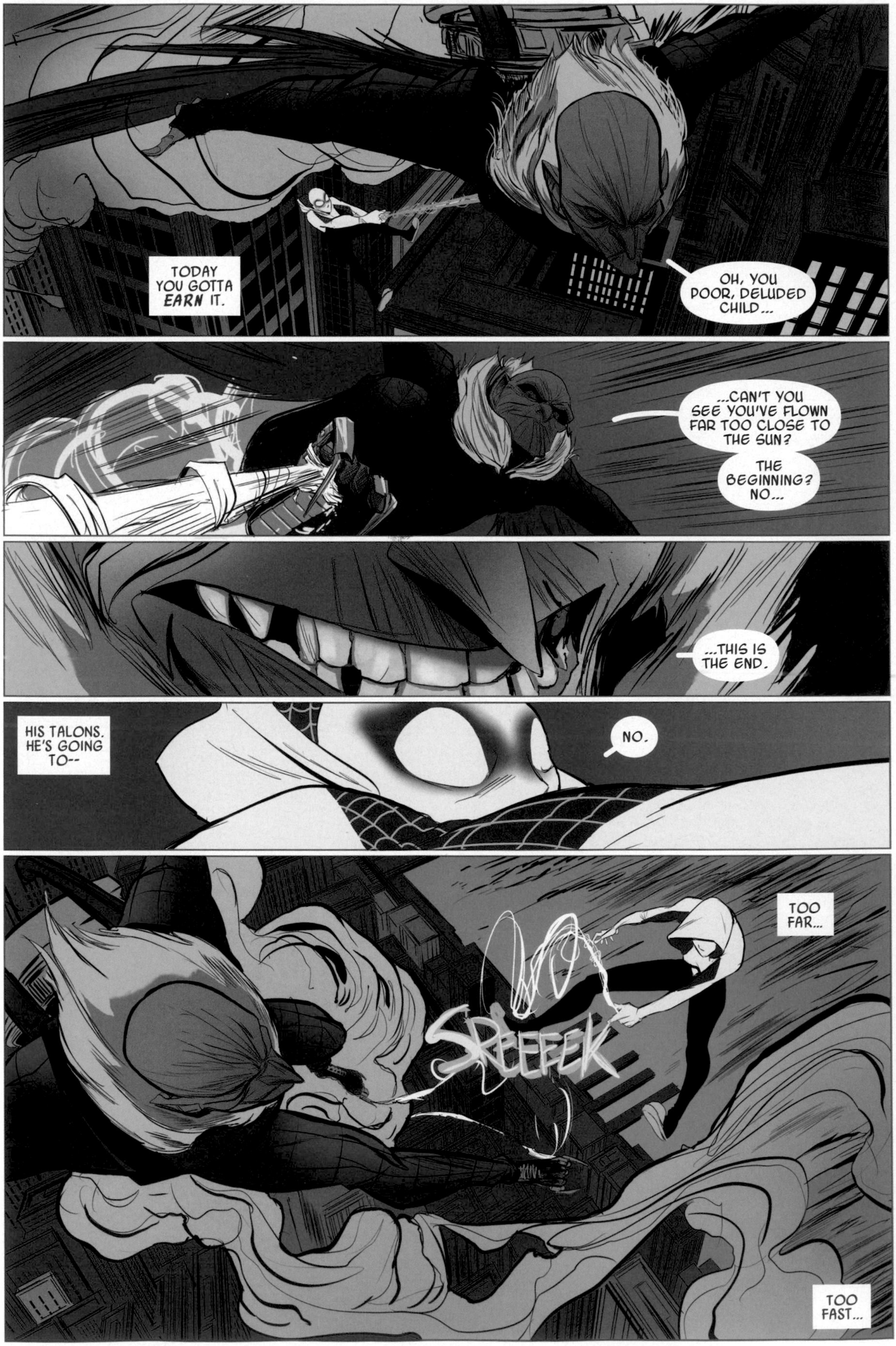
TODAY YOU GOTTA EARN IT.
OH, YOU POOR, DELUDED CHILD...
...CAN'T YOU SEE YOU'VE FLOWN FAR TOO CLOSE TO THE SUN?
THE BEGINNING? NO...
...THIS IS THE END.
HIS TALONS. HE'S GOING TO--
NO.
TOO FAR...
SREEEEK
TOO FAST...

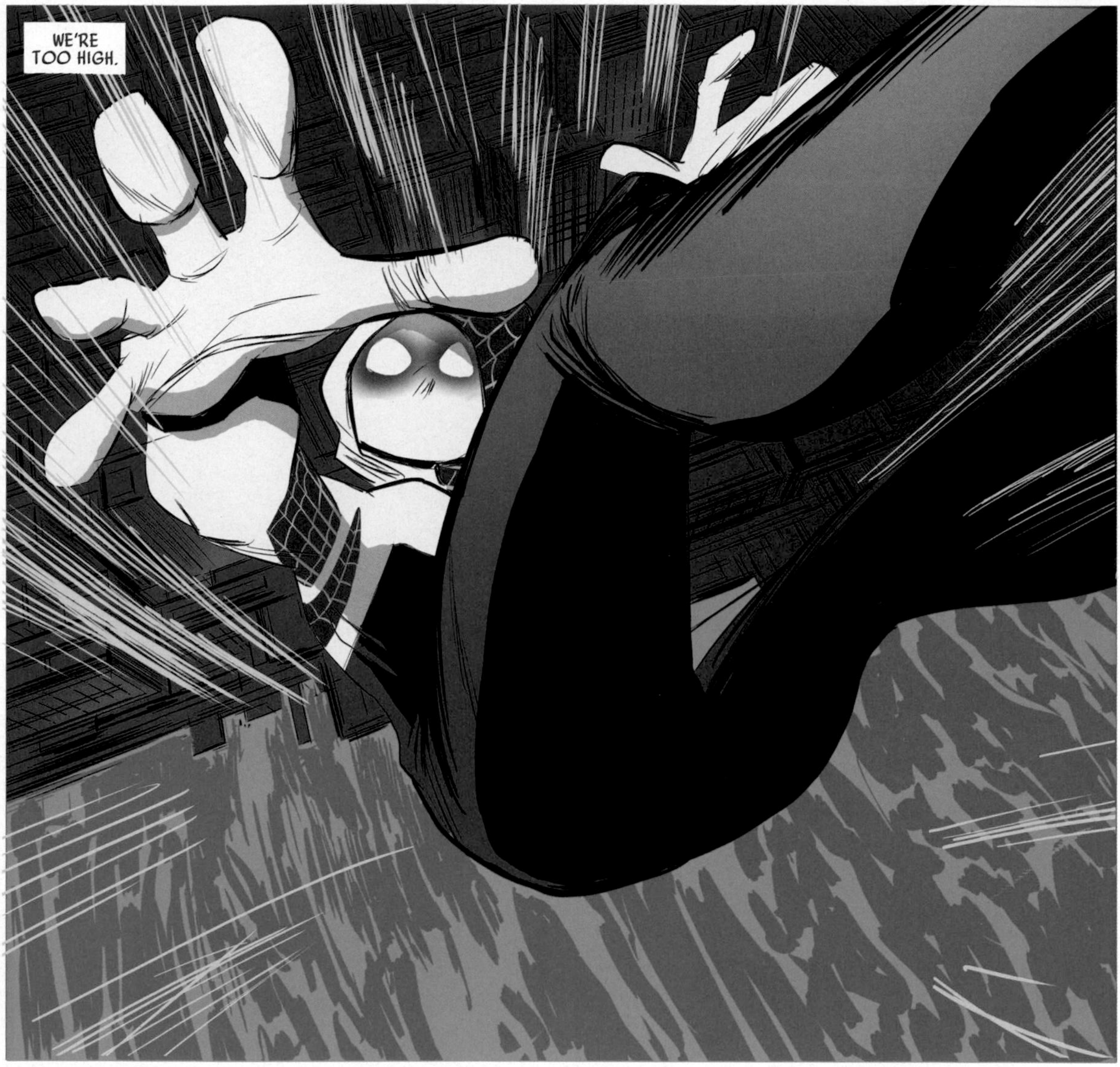
WE'RE TOO HIGH.

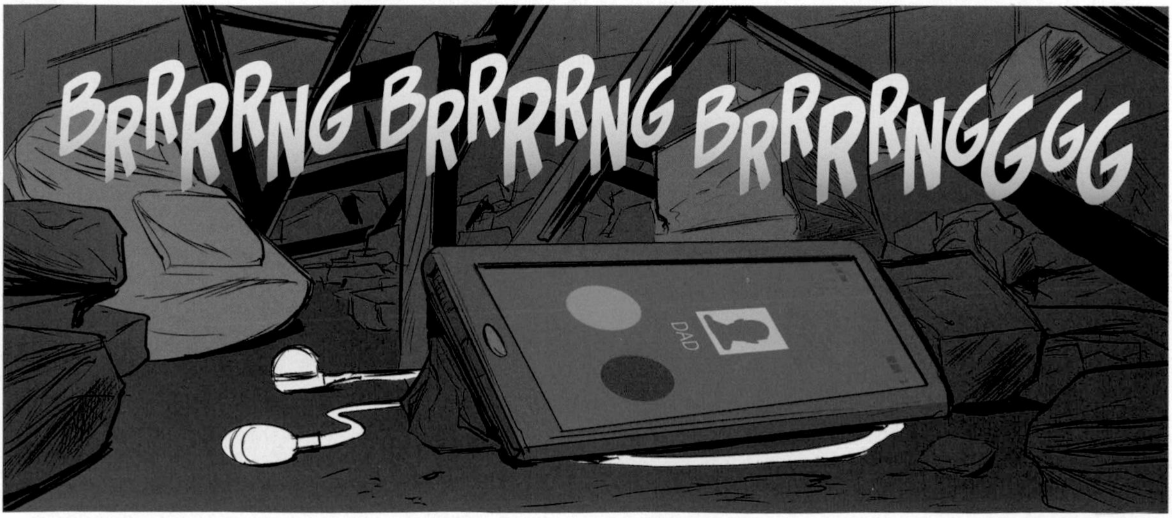
BRRRRNG BRRRRNG BRRRRNGGGG
DAD

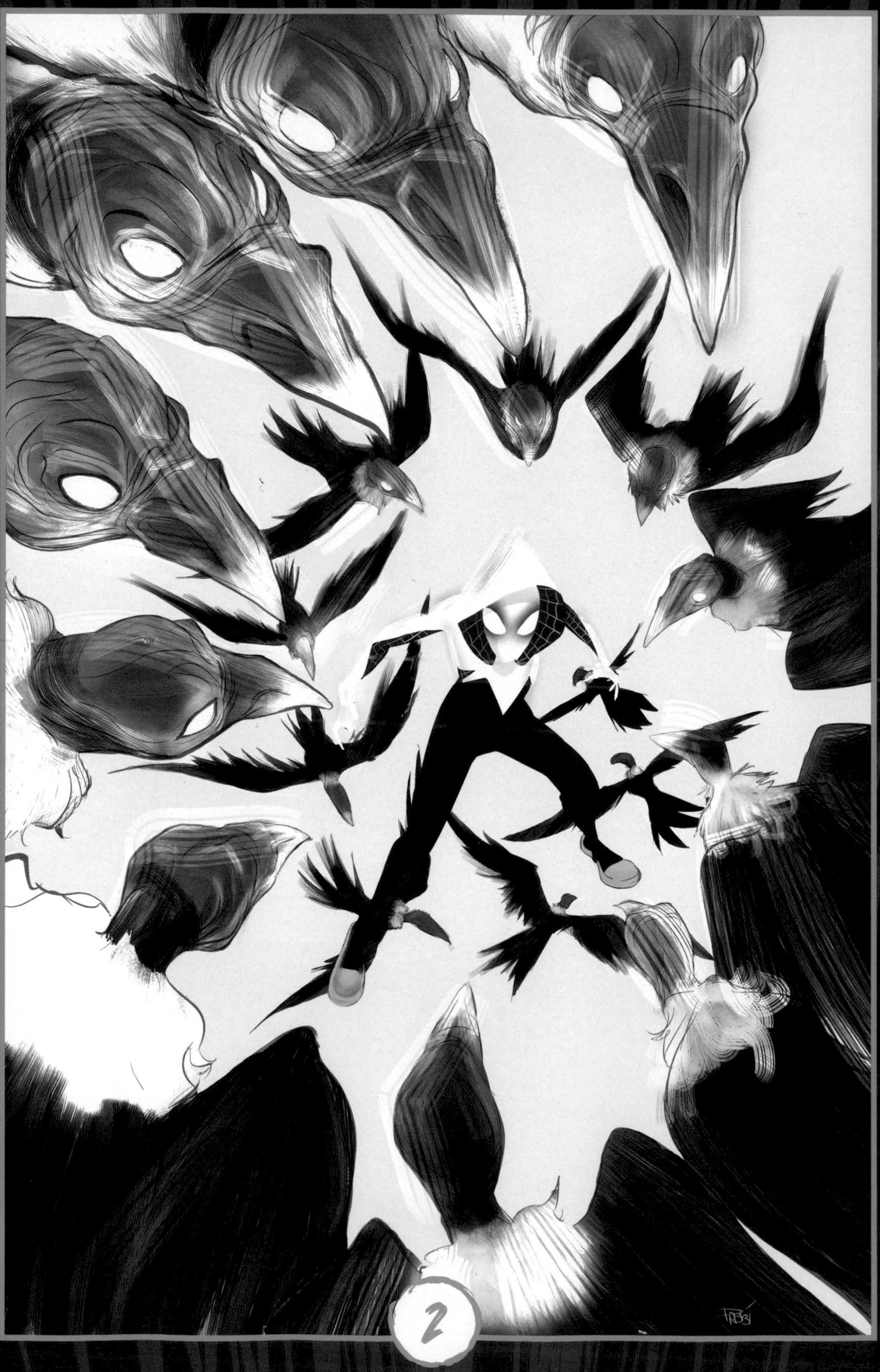
2

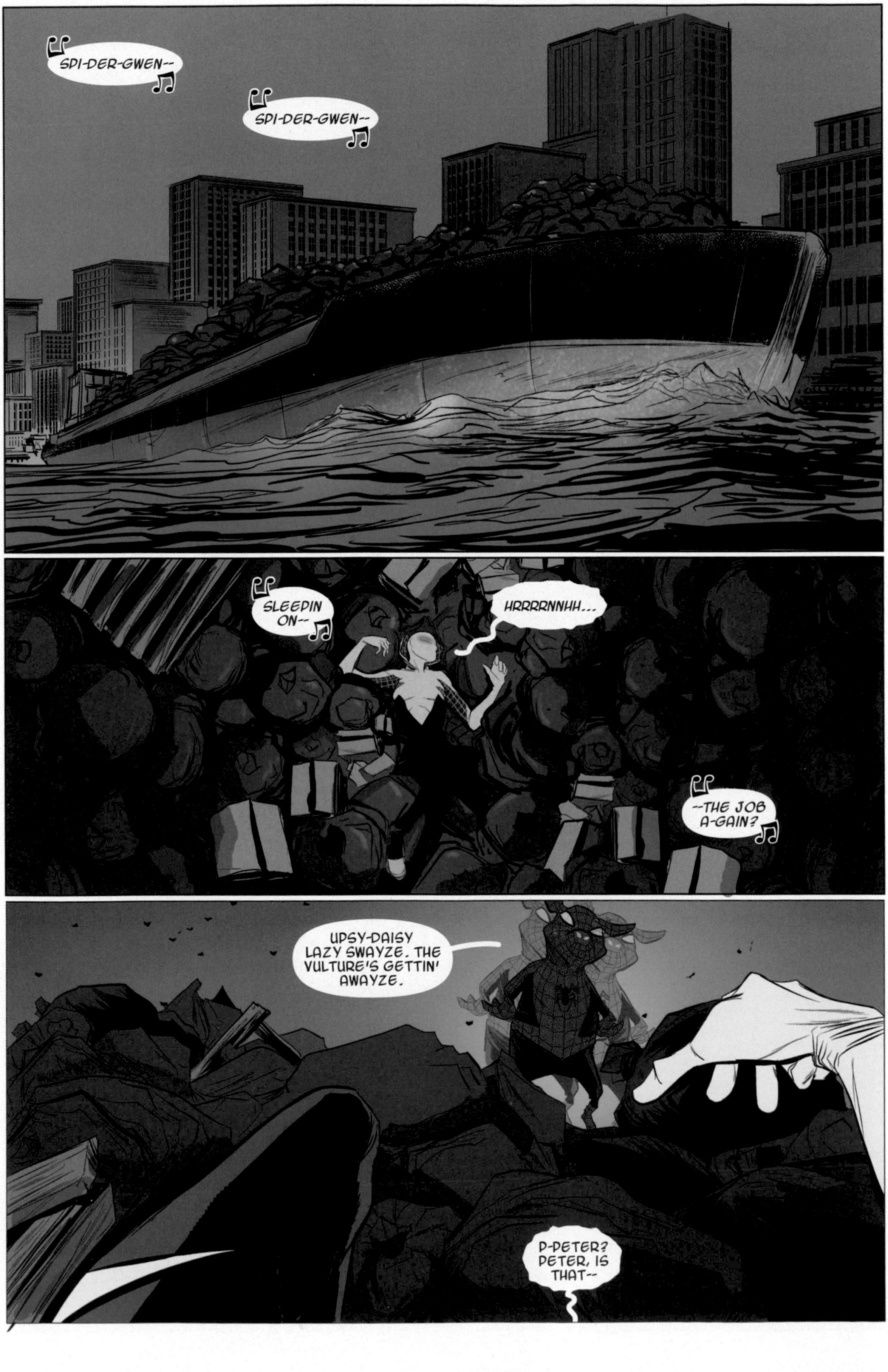
SPI-DER-GWEN--
SPI-DER-GWEN--
SLEEPIN ON--
HRRRRNNHH...
--THE JOB A-GAIN?
UPSY-DAISY LAZY SWAYZE. THE VULTURE'S GETTIN' AWAYZE.
P-PETER? PETER, IS THAT--

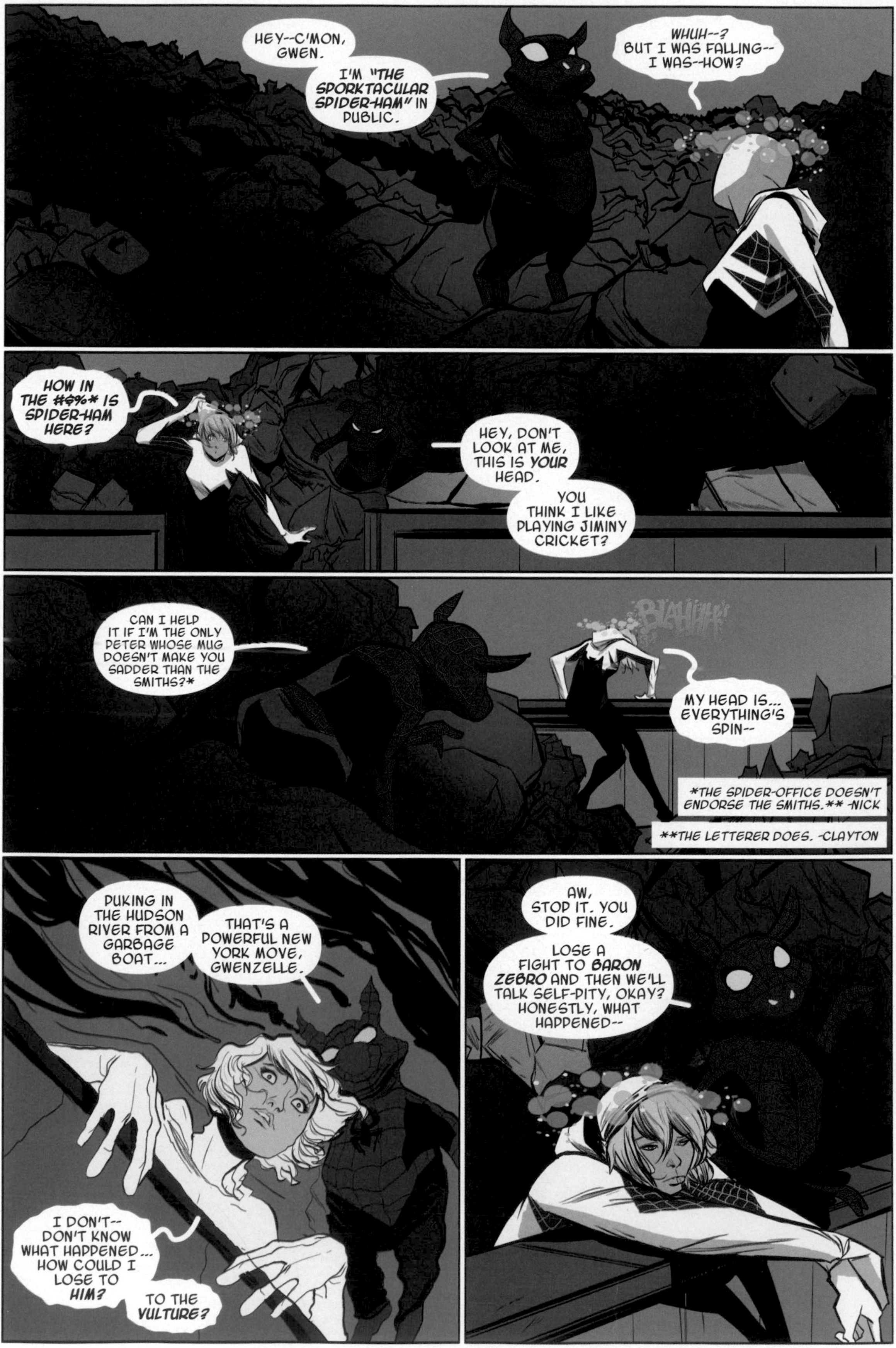
HEY--C'MON, GWEN.
I'M "THE SPORKTACULAR SPIDER-HAM" IN PUBLIC.
WHUH--? BUT I WAS FALLING-- I WAS--HOW?
HOW IN THE #$%* IS SPIDER-HAM HERE?
HEY, DON'T LOOK AT ME, THIS IS YOUR HEAD.
YOU THINK I LIKE PLAYING JIMINY CRICKET?
CAN I HELP IT IF I'M THE ONLY PETER WHOSE MUG DOESN'T MAKE YOU SADDER THAN THE SMITHS?*
MY HEAD IS... EVERYTHING'S SPIN--
*THE SPIDER-OFFICE DOESN'T ENDORSE THE SMITHS.** -NICK
**THE LETTERER DOES. -CLAYTON
PUKING IN THE HUDSON RIVER FROM A GARBAGE BOAT...
THAT'S A POWERFUL NEW YORK MOVE, GWENZELLE.
I DON'T-- DON'T KNOW WHAT HAPPENED... HOW COULD I LOSE TO HIM?
TO THE VULTURE?
AW, STOP IT. YOU DID FINE.
LOSE A FIGHT TO BARON ZEBRO AND THEN WE'LL TALK SELF-PITY, OKAY? HONESTLY, WHAT HAPPENED--

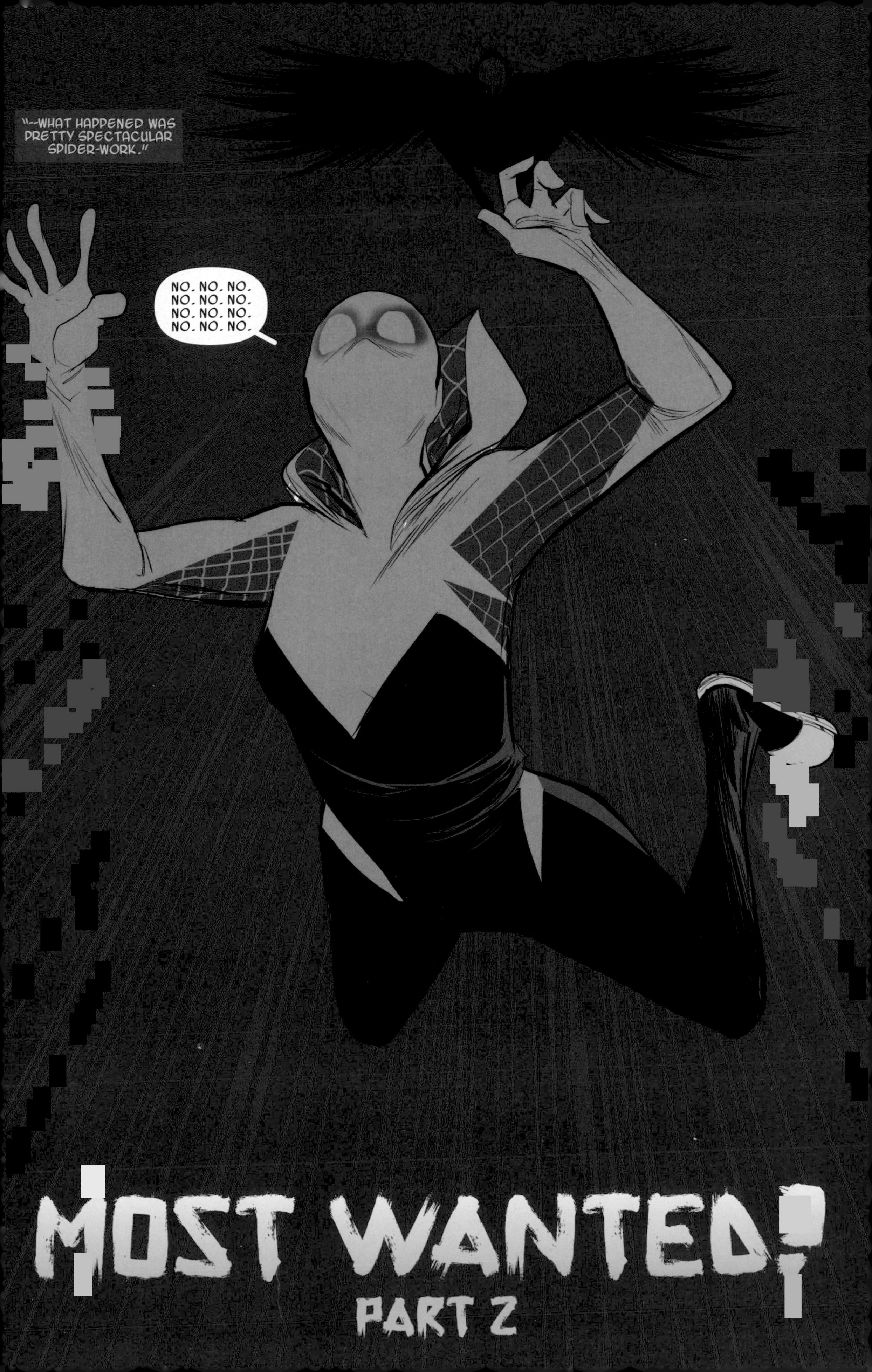
"--WHAT HAPPENED WAS PRETTY SPECTACULAR SPIDER-WORK."
NO. NO. NO. NO. NO. NO. NO. NO. NO. NO. NO. NO.
MOST WANTED?
PART 2

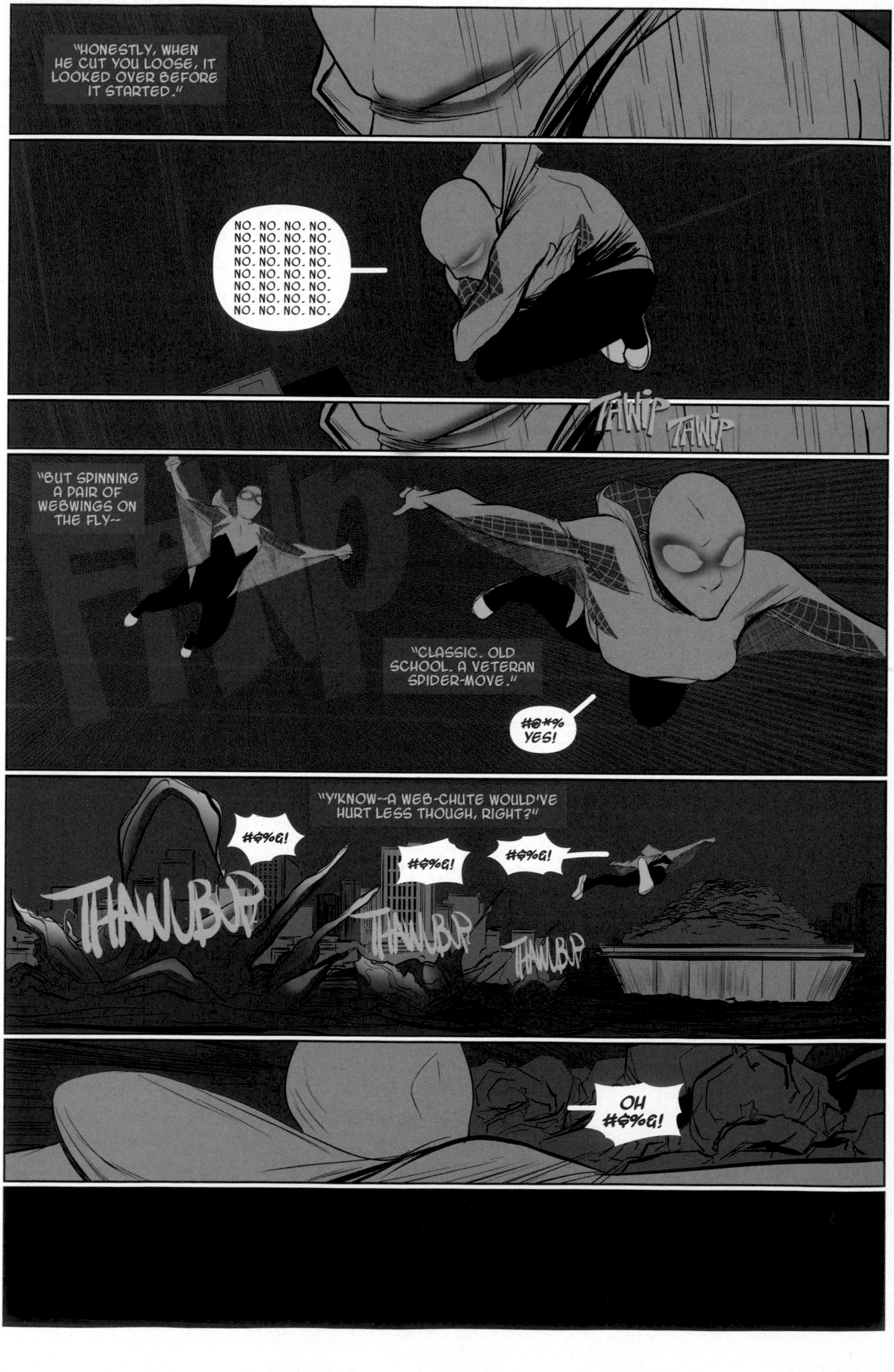
"HONESTLY, WHEN HE CUT YOU LOOSE, IT LOOKED OVER BEFORE IT STARTED."
NO. NO. NO. NO. NO. NO. NO. NO. NO. NO. NO. NO. NO. NO. NO. NO. NO. NO. NO. NO. NO. NO. NO. NO. NO. NO. NO. NO. NO. NO. NO. NO.
TAWIP TAWIP
"BUT SPINNING A PAIR OF WEBWINGS ON THE FLY--
"CLASSIC. OLD SCHOOL. A VETERAN SPIDER-MOVE."
#@*% YES!
"Y'KNOW--A WEB-CHUTE WOULD'VE HURT LESS THOUGH, RIGHT?"
#$%&!
#$%&!
#$%&!
THAWUBP
THAWUBP
THAWUBP
OH #$%&!

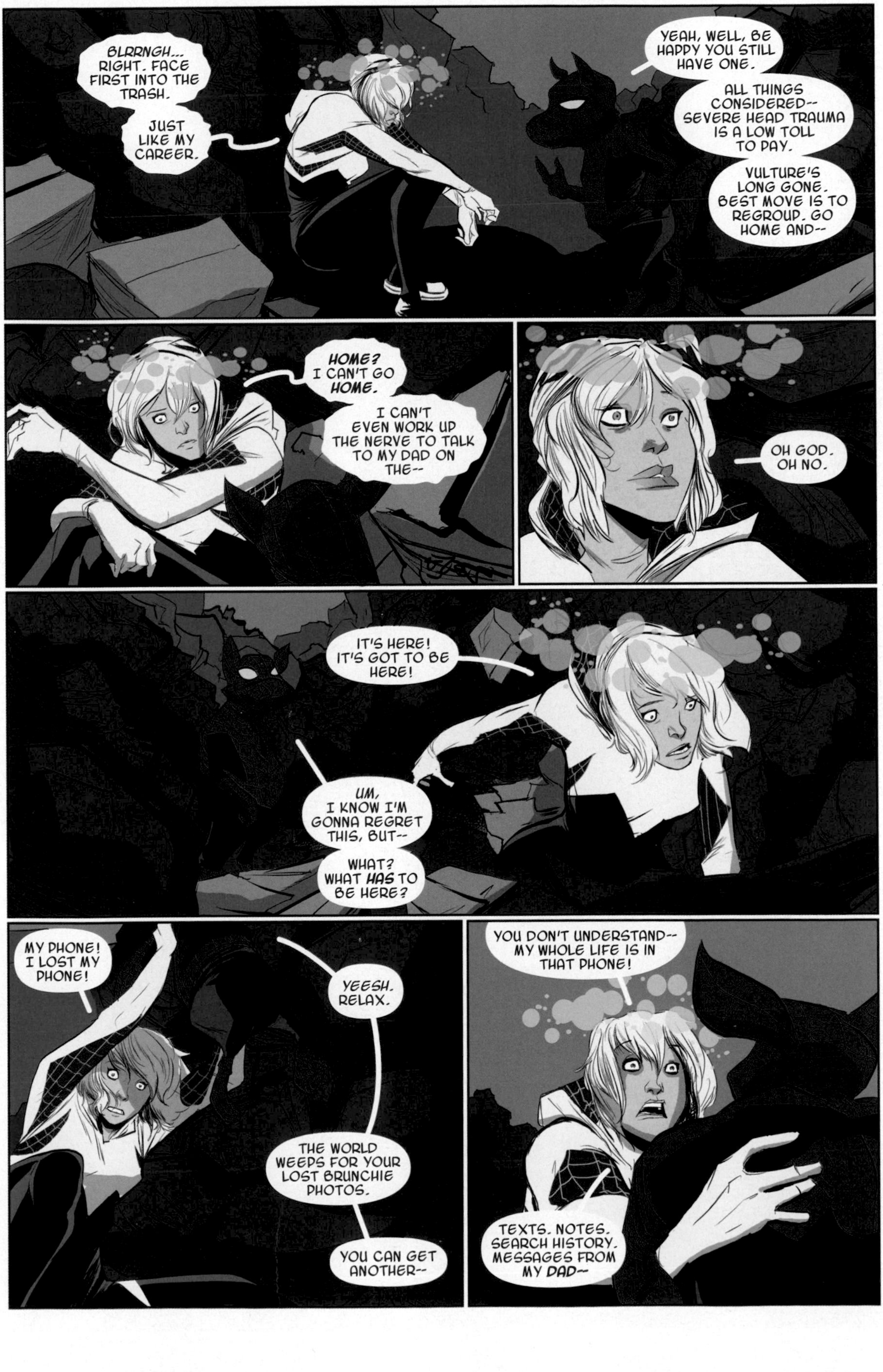
BLRRNGH... RIGHT. FACE FIRST INTO THE TRASH.
JUST LIKE MY CAREER.
YEAH, WELL, BE HAPPY YOU STILL HAVE ONE.
ALL THINGS CONSIDERED-- SEVERE HEAD TRAUMA IS A LOW TOLL TO PAY.
VULTURE'S LONG GONE. BEST MOVE IS TO REGROUP. GO HOME AND--
HOME? I CAN'T GO HOME.
I CAN'T EVEN WORK UP THE NERVE TO TALK TO MY DAD ON THE--
OH GOD. OH NO.
IT'S HERE! IT'S GOT TO BE HERE!
UM, I KNOW I'M GONNA REGRET THIS, BUT--
WHAT? WHAT HAS TO BE HERE?
MY PHONE! I LOST MY PHONE!
YEESH. RELAX.
THE WORLD WEEPS FOR YOUR LOST BRUNCHIE PHOTOS.
YOU CAN GET ANOTHER--
YOU DON'T UNDERSTAND-- MY WHOLE LIFE IS IN THAT PHONE!
TEXTS. NOTES. SEARCH HISTORY. MESSAGES FROM MY DAD--

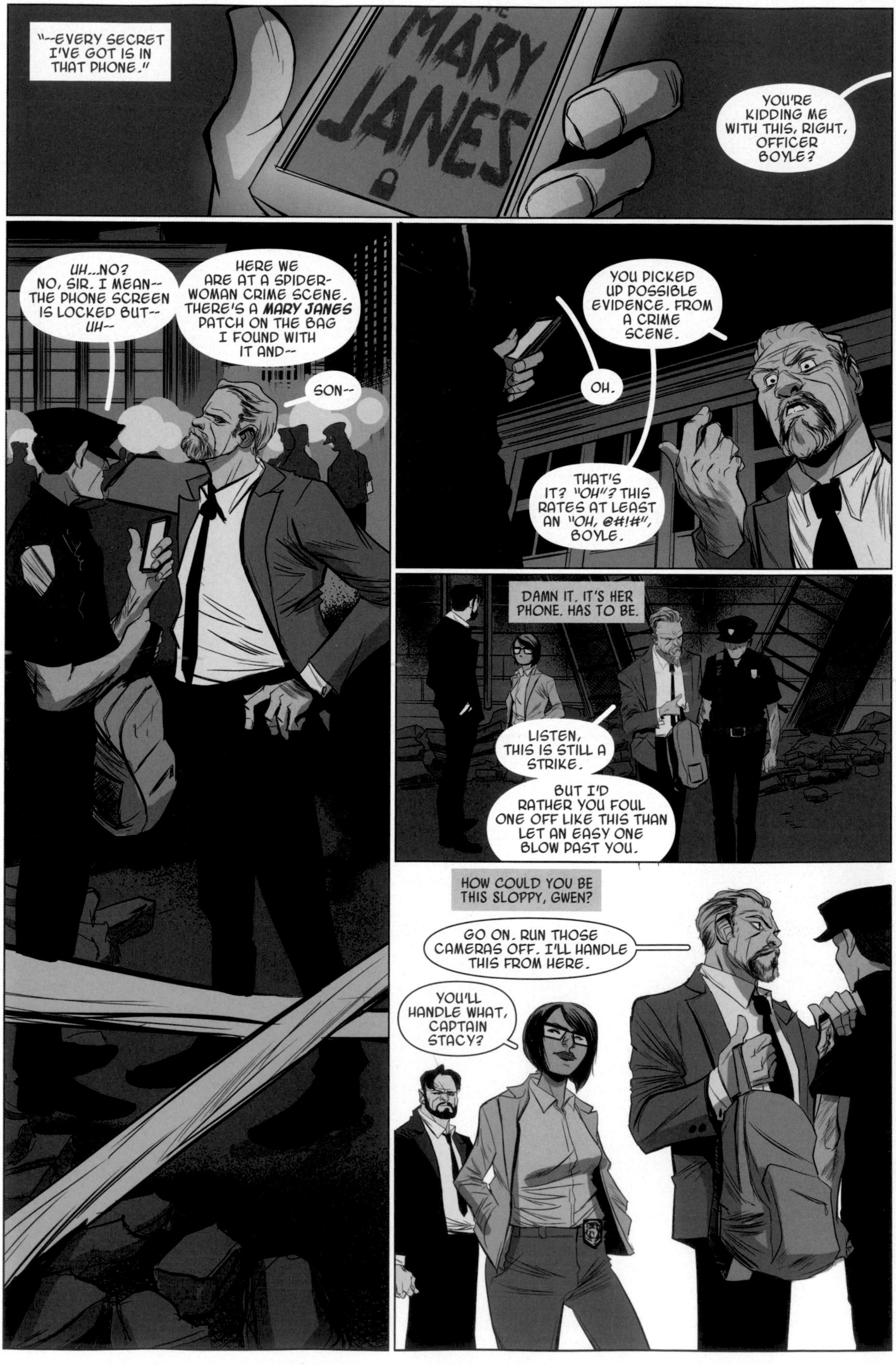
"--EVERY SECRET I'VE GOT IS IN THAT PHONE."
MARY JANES
YOU'RE KIDDING ME WITH THIS, RIGHT, OFFICER BOYLE?
UH...NO? NO, SIR. I MEAN-- THE PHONE SCREEN IS LOCKED BUT-- UH--
HERE WE ARE AT A SPIDER-WOMAN CRIME SCENE. THERE'S A MARY JANES PATCH ON THE BAG I FOUND WITH IT AND--
SON--
YOU PICKED UP POSSIBLE EVIDENCE. FROM A CRIME SCENE.
OH.
THAT'S IT? "OH"? THIS RATES AT LEAST AN "OH, @#!#", BOYLE.
DAMN IT. IT'S HER PHONE. HAS TO BE.
LISTEN, THIS IS STILL A STRIKE.
BUT I'D RATHER YOU FOUL ONE OFF LIKE THIS THAN LET AN EASY ONE BLOW PAST YOU.
HOW COULD YOU BE THIS SLOPPY, GWEN?
GO ON. RUN THOSE CAMERAS OFF. I'LL HANDLE THIS FROM HERE.
YOU'LL HANDLE WHAT, CAPTAIN STACY?

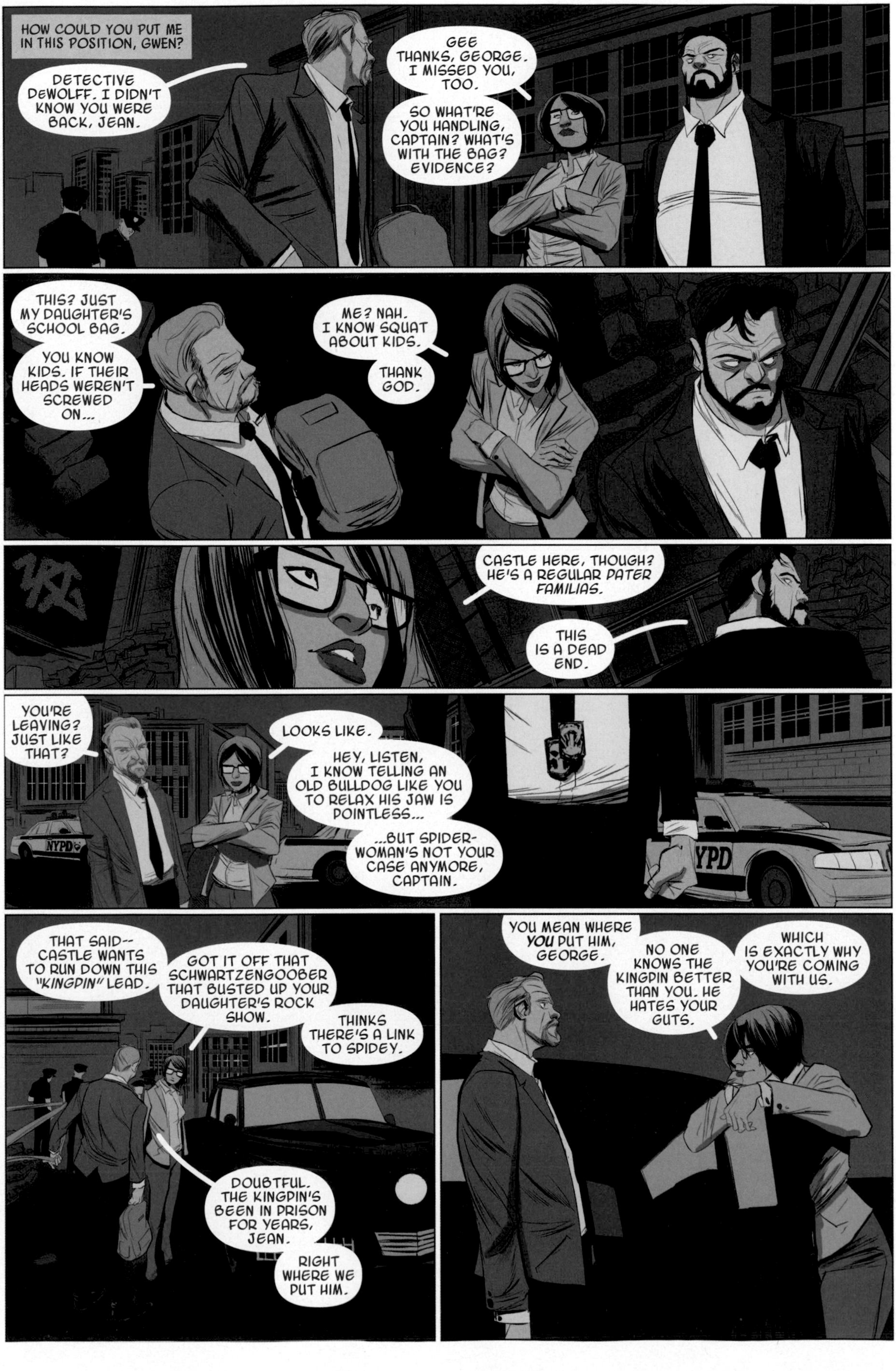
HOW COULD YOU PUT ME IN THIS POSITION, GWEN?
DETECTIVE DeWOLFF. I DIDN'T KNOW YOU WERE BACK, JEAN.
GEE THANKS, GEORGE. I MISSED YOU, TOO.
SO WHAT'RE YOU HANDLING, CAPTAIN? WHAT'S WITH THE BAG? EVIDENCE?
THIS? JUST MY DAUGHTER'S SCHOOL BAG.
YOU KNOW KIDS. IF THEIR HEADS WEREN'T SCREWED ON...
ME? NAH. I KNOW SQUAT ABOUT KIDS.
THANK GOD.
CASTLE HERE, THOUGH? HE'S A REGULAR PATER FAMILIAS.
THIS IS A DEAD END.
YOU'RE LEAVING? JUST LIKE THAT?
LOOKS LIKE.
HEY, LISTEN, I KNOW TELLING AN OLD BULLDOG LIKE YOU TO RELAX HIS JAW IS POINTLESS...
...BUT SPIDER-WOMAN'S NOT YOUR CASE ANYMORE, CAPTAIN.
NYPD
NYPD
THAT SAID-- CASTLE WANTS TO RUN DOWN THIS "KINGPIN" LEAD.
GOT IT OFF THAT SCHWARTZENGOOBER THAT BUSTED UP YOUR DAUGHTER'S ROCK SHOW.
THINKS THERE'S A LINK TO SPIDEY.
DOUBTFUL. THE KINGPIN'S BEEN IN PRISON FOR YEARS, JEAN.
RIGHT WHERE WE PUT HIM.
YOU MEAN WHERE YOU PUT HIM, GEORGE.
NO ONE KNOWS THE KINGPIN BETTER THAN YOU. HE HATES YOUR GUTS.
WHICH IS EXACTLY WHY YOU'RE COMING WITH US.

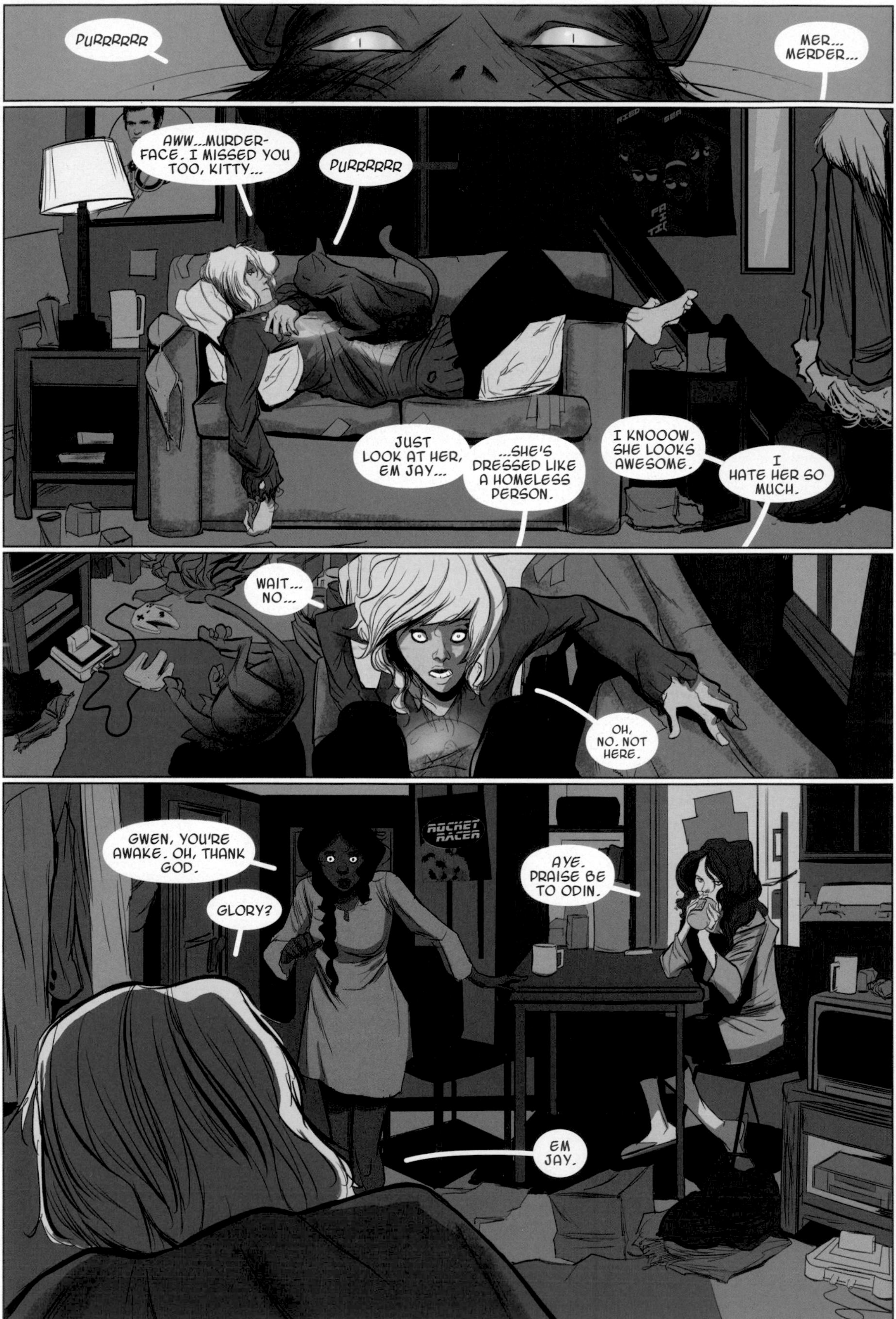
PURRRRRR
MER... MERDER...
AWW...MURDER-FACE. I MISSED YOU TOO, KITTY...
PURRRRRR
JUST LOOK AT HER, EM JAY...
...SHE'S DRESSED LIKE A HOMELESS PERSON.
I KNOOOW. SHE LOOKS AWESOME.
I HATE HER SO MUCH.
WAIT... NO...
OH, NO. NOT HERE.
ROCKET RACER
GWEN, YOU'RE AWAKE. OH, THANK GOD.
GLORY?
AYE. PRAISE BE TO ODIN.
EM JAY.

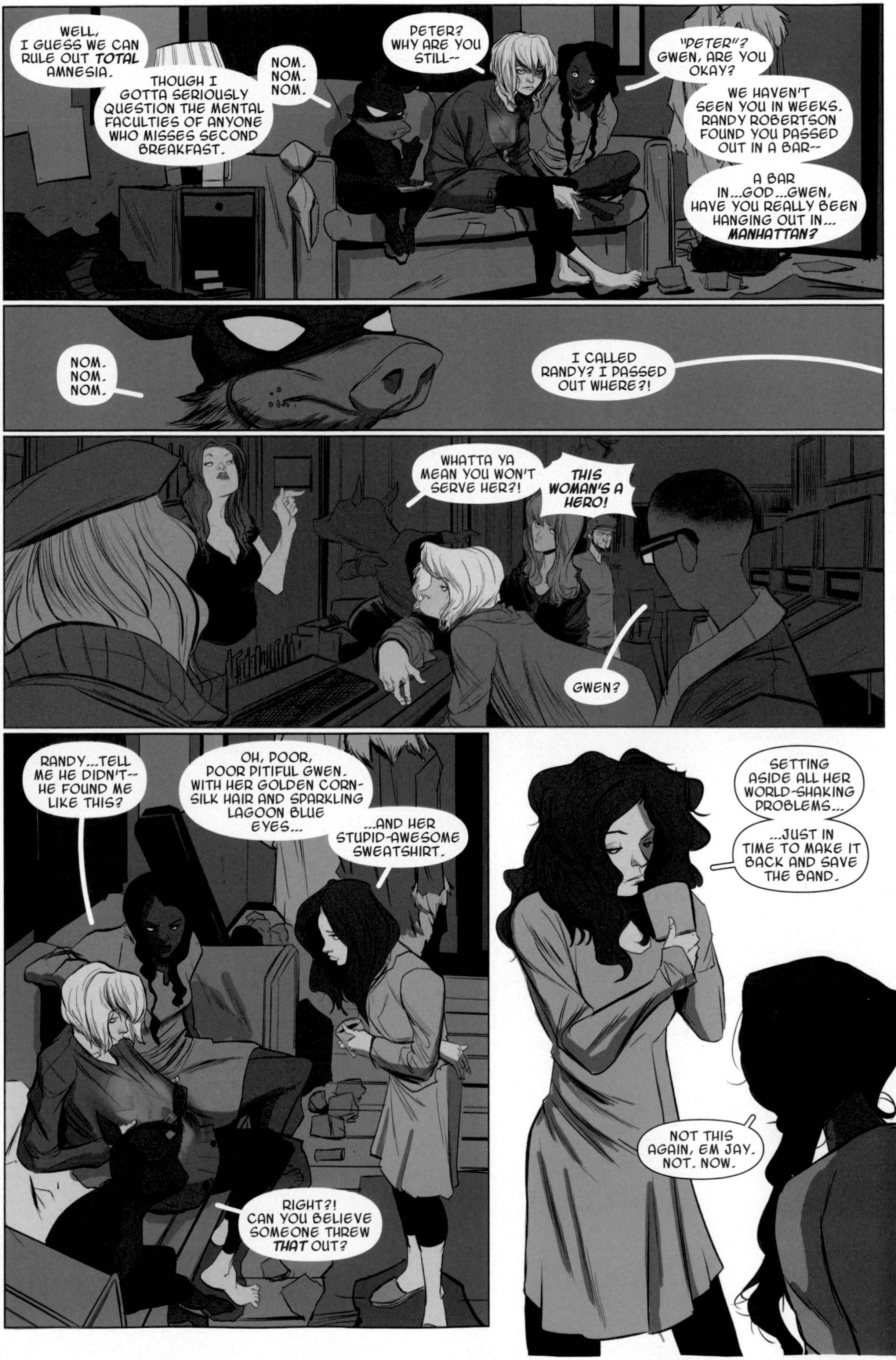
WELL, I GUESS WE CAN RULE OUT TOTAL AMNESIA.
THOUGH I GOTTA SERIOUSLY QUESTION THE MENTAL FACULTIES OF ANYONE WHO MISSES SECOND BREAKFAST.
NOM. NOM. NOM.
PETER? WHY ARE YOU STILL--
"PETER"? GWEN, ARE YOU OKAY?
WE HAVEN'T SEEN YOU IN WEEKS. RANDY ROBERTSON FOUND YOU PASSED OUT IN A BAR--
A BAR IN...GOD...GWEN, HAVE YOU REALLY BEEN HANGING OUT IN... MANHATTAN?
NOM. NOM. NOM.
I CALLED RANDY? I PASSED OUT WHERE?!
WHATTA YA MEAN YOU WON'T SERVE HER?!
THIS WOMAN'S A HERO!
GWEN?
RANDY...TELL ME HE DIDN'T-- HE FOUND ME LIKE THIS?
OH, POOR, POOR PITIFUL GWEN. WITH HER GOLDEN CORN-SILK HAIR AND SPARKLING LAGOON BLUE EYES...
...AND HER STUPID-AWESOME SWEATSHIRT.
RIGHT?! CAN YOU BELIEVE SOMEONE THREW THAT OUT?
SETTING ASIDE ALL HER WORLD-SHAKING PROBLEMS...
...JUST IN TIME TO MAKE IT BACK AND SAVE THE BAND.
NOT THIS AGAIN, EM JAY. NOT. NOW.

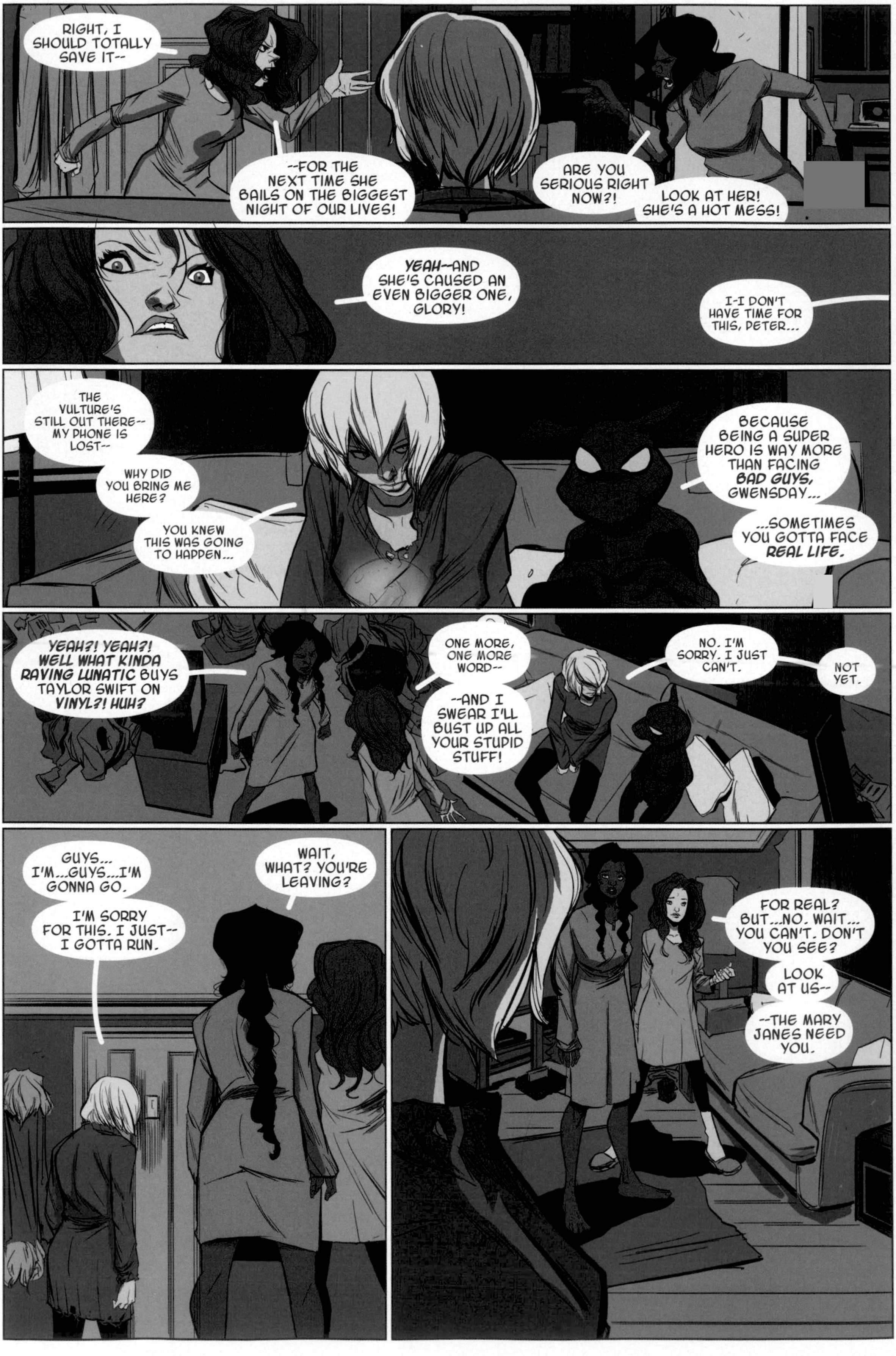
RIGHT, I SHOULD TOTALLY SAVE IT--
--FOR THE NEXT TIME SHE BAILS ON THE BIGGEST NIGHT OF OUR LIVES!
ARE YOU SERIOUS RIGHT NOW?!
LOOK AT HER! SHE'S A HOT MESS!
YEAH--AND SHE'S CAUSED AN EVEN BIGGER ONE, GLORY!
I-I DON'T HAVE TIME FOR THIS, PETER...
THE VULTURE'S STILL OUT THERE-- MY PHONE IS LOST--
WHY DID YOU BRING ME HERE?
YOU KNEW THIS WAS GOING TO HAPPEN...
BECAUSE BEING A SUPER HERO IS WAY MORE THAN FACING BAD GUYS, GWENSDAY...
...SOMETIMES YOU GOTTA FACE REAL LIFE.
YEAH?! YEAH?! WELL WHAT KINDA RAVING LUNATIC BUYS TAYLOR SWIFT ON VINYL?! HUH?
ONE MORE, ONE MORE WORD--
--AND I SWEAR I'LL BUST UP ALL YOUR STUPID STUFF!
NO. I'M SORRY. I JUST CAN'T.
NOT YET.
GUYS... I'M...GUYS...I'M GONNA GO.
I'M SORRY FOR THIS. I JUST-- I GOTTA RUN.
WAIT, WHAT? YOU'RE LEAVING?
FOR REAL? BUT...NO. WAIT... YOU CAN'T. DON'T YOU SEE?
LOOK AT US--
--THE MARY JANES NEED YOU.

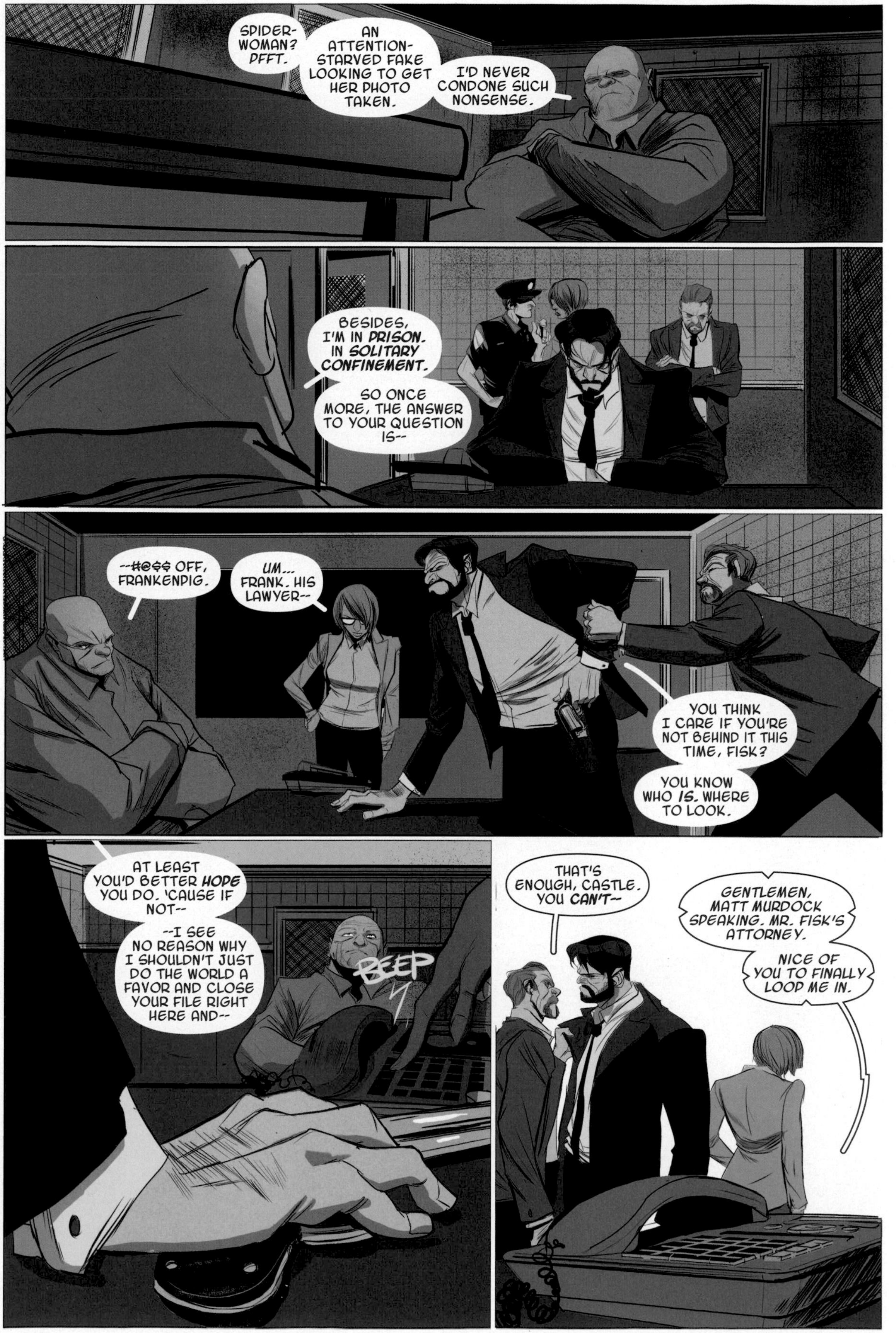

SPIDER-WOMAN? PFFT.
AN ATTENTION-STARVED FAKE LOOKING TO GET HER PHOTO TAKEN.
I'D NEVER CONDONE SUCH NONSENSE.
BESIDES, I'M IN PRISON. IN SOLITARY CONFINEMENT.
SO ONCE MORE, THE ANSWER TO YOUR QUESTION IS--
--#@$$ OFF, FRANKENPIG.
UM... FRANK. HIS LAWYER--
YOU THINK I CARE IF YOU'RE NOT BEHIND IT THIS TIME, FISK?
YOU KNOW WHO IS. WHERE TO LOOK.
AT LEAST YOU'D BETTER HOPE YOU DO. 'CAUSE IF NOT--
--I SEE NO REASON WHY I SHOULDN'T JUST DO THE WORLD A FAVOR AND CLOSE YOUR FILE RIGHT HERE AND--
BEEP
THAT'S ENOUGH, CASTLE. YOU CAN'T--
GENTLEMEN, MATT MURDOCK SPEAKING. MR. FISK'S ATTORNEY.
NICE OF YOU TO FINALLY LOOP ME IN.

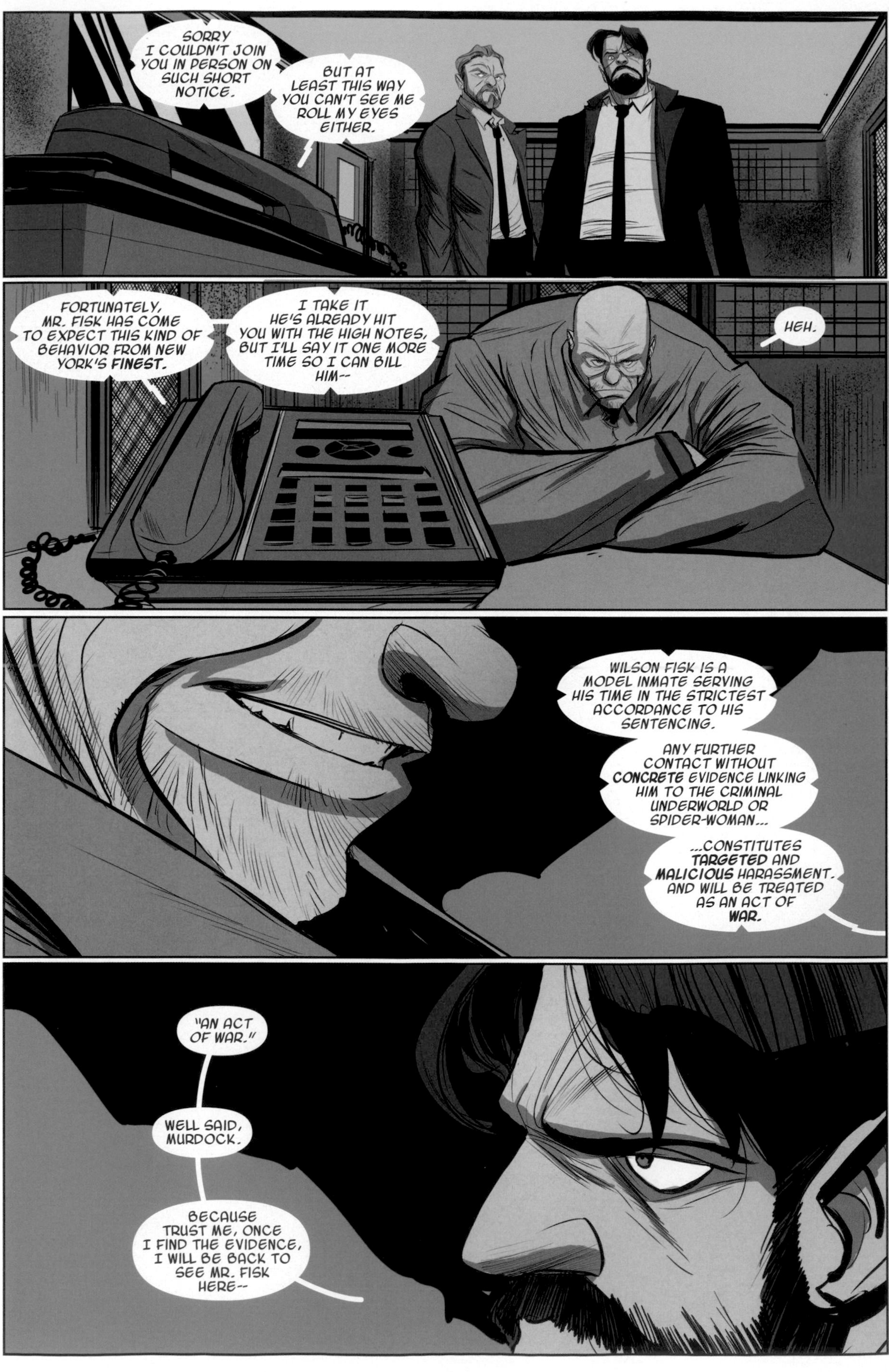
SORRY I COULDN'T JOIN YOU IN PERSON ON SUCH SHORT NOTICE.
BUT AT LEAST THIS WAY YOU CAN'T SEE ME ROLL MY EYES EITHER.
FORTUNATELY, MR. FISK HAS COME TO EXPECT THIS KIND OF BEHAVIOR FROM NEW YORK'S FINEST.
I TAKE IT HE'S ALREADY HIT YOU WITH THE HIGH NOTES, BUT I'LL SAY IT ONE MORE TIME SO I CAN BILL HIM--
HEH.
WILSON FISK IS A MODEL INMATE SERVING HIS TIME IN THE STRICTEST ACCORDANCE TO HIS SENTENCING.
ANY FURTHER CONTACT WITHOUT CONCRETE EVIDENCE LINKING HIM TO THE CRIMINAL UNDERWORLD OR SPIDER-WOMAN...
...CONSTITUTES TARGETED AND MALICIOUS HARASSMENT. AND WILL BE TREATED AS AN ACT OF WAR.
"AN ACT OF WAR."
WELL SAID, MURDOCK.
BECAUSE TRUST ME, ONCE I FIND THE EVIDENCE, I WILL BE BACK TO SEE MR. FISK HERE--

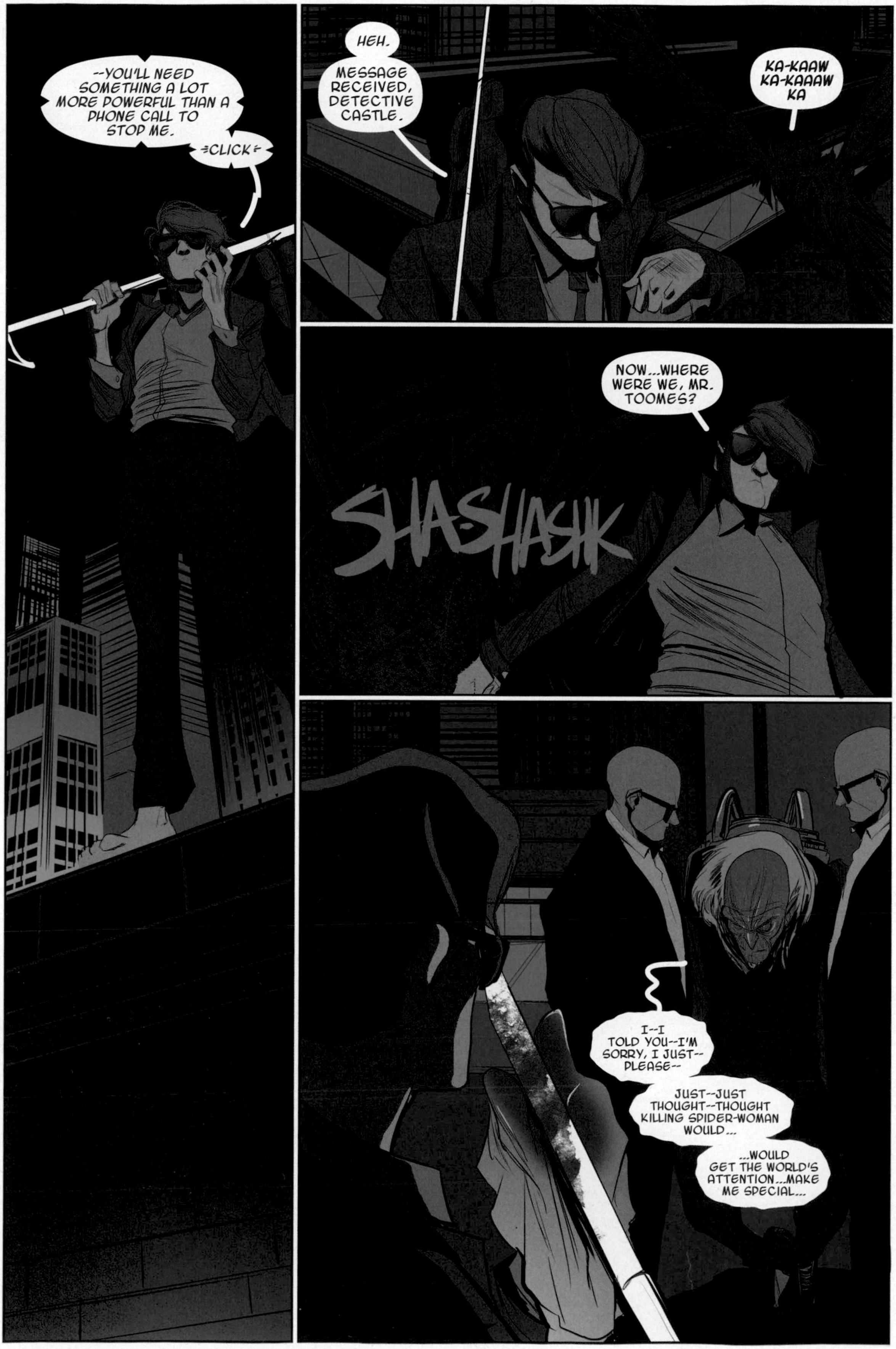
--YOU'LL NEED SOMETHING A LOT MORE POWERFUL THAN A PHONE CALL TO STOP ME.
=CLICK=
HEH.
MESSAGE RECEIVED, DETECTIVE CASTLE.
KA-KAAW KA-KAAAW KA
NOW...WHERE WERE WE, MR. TOOMES?
SHASHASHK
I--I TOLD YOU--I'M SORRY, I JUST-- PLEASE--
JUST--JUST THOUGHT--THOUGHT KILLING SPIDER-WOMAN WOULD...
...WOULD GET THE WORLD'S ATTENTION...MAKE ME SPECIAL...

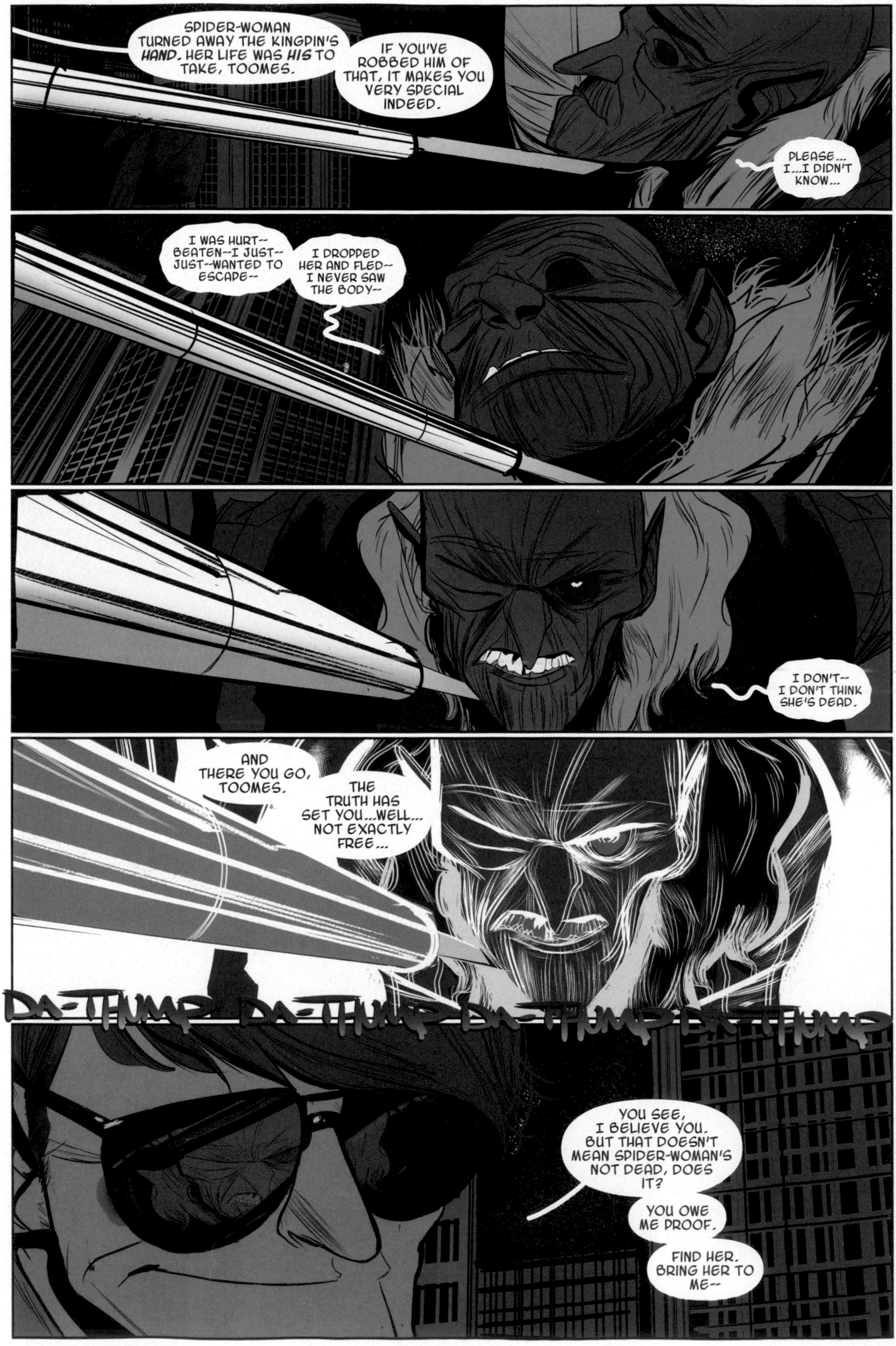
SPIDER-WOMAN TURNED AWAY THE KINGPIN'S HAND. HER LIFE WAS HIS TO TAKE, TOOMES.
IF YOU'VE ROBBED HIM OF THAT, IT MAKES YOU VERY SPECIAL INDEED.
PLEASE... I...I DIDN'T KNOW...
I WAS HURT-- BEATEN--I JUST-- JUST--WANTED TO ESCAPE--
I DROPPED HER AND FLED-- I NEVER SAW THE BODY--
I DON'T-- I DON'T THINK SHE'S DEAD.
AND THERE YOU GO, TOOMES.
THE TRUTH HAS SET YOU...WELL... NOT EXACTLY FREE...
DA-THUMP DA-THUMP DA-THUMP DA-THUMP
YOU SEE, I BELIEVE YOU. BUT THAT DOESN'T MEAN SPIDER-WOMAN'S NOT DEAD, DOES IT?
YOU OWE ME PROOF.
FIND HER. BRING HER TO ME--

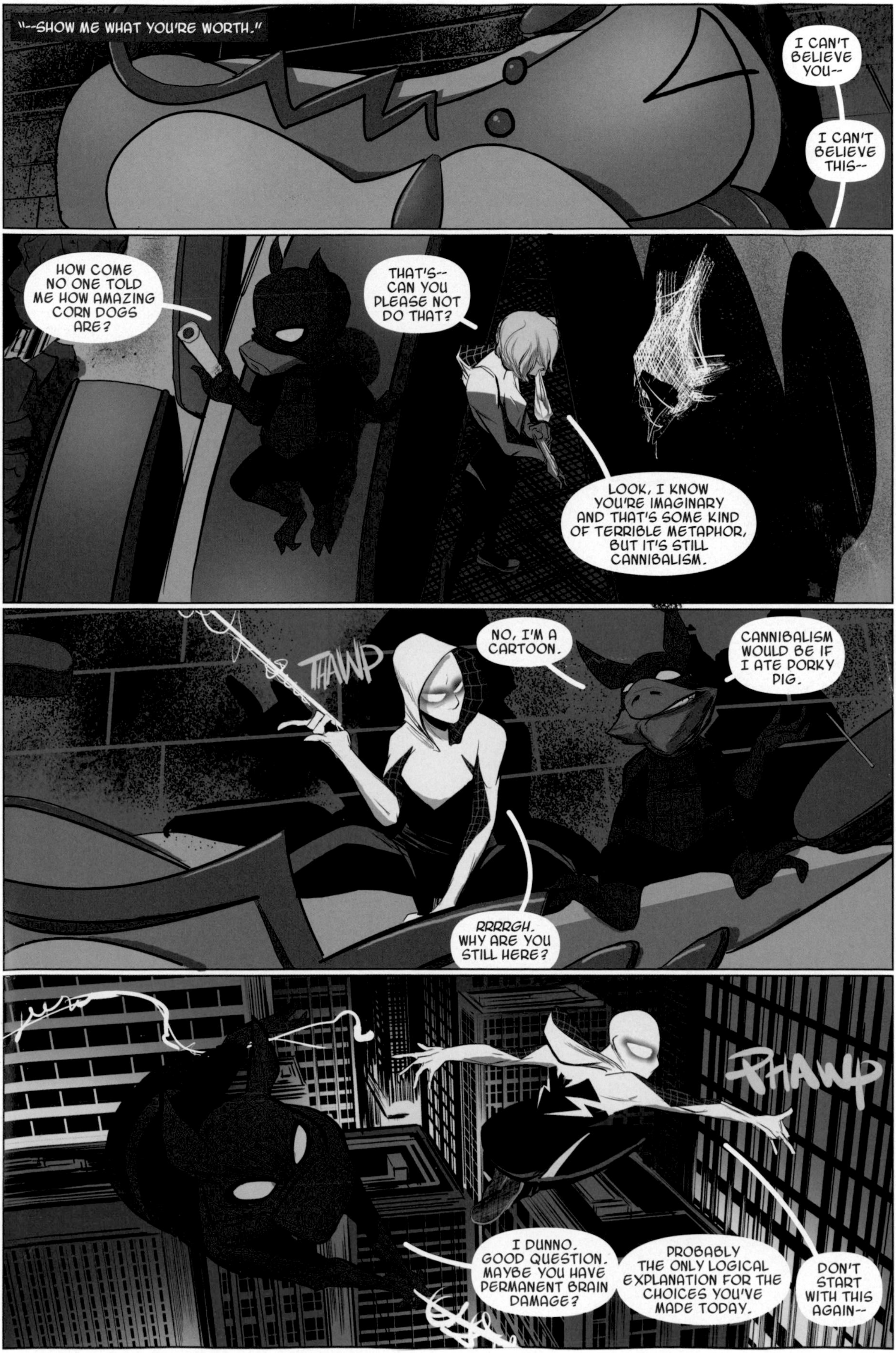
"--SHOW ME WHAT YOU'RE WORTH."
I CAN'T BELIEVE YOU--
I CAN'T BELIEVE THIS--
HOW COME NO ONE TOLD ME HOW AMAZING CORN DOGS ARE?
THAT'S-- CAN YOU PLEASE NOT DO THAT?
LOOK, I KNOW YOU'RE IMAGINARY AND THAT'S SOME KIND OF TERRIBLE METAPHOR, BUT IT'S STILL CANNIBALISM.
THAWP
NO, I'M A CARTOON.
CANNIBALISM WOULD BE IF I ATE PORKY PIG.
RRRRGH. WHY ARE YOU STILL HERE?
THAWP
I DUNNO. GOOD QUESTION. MAYBE YOU HAVE PERMANENT BRAIN DAMAGE?
PROBABLY THE ONLY LOGICAL EXPLANATION FOR THE CHOICES YOU'VE MADE TODAY.
DON'T START WITH THIS AGAIN--

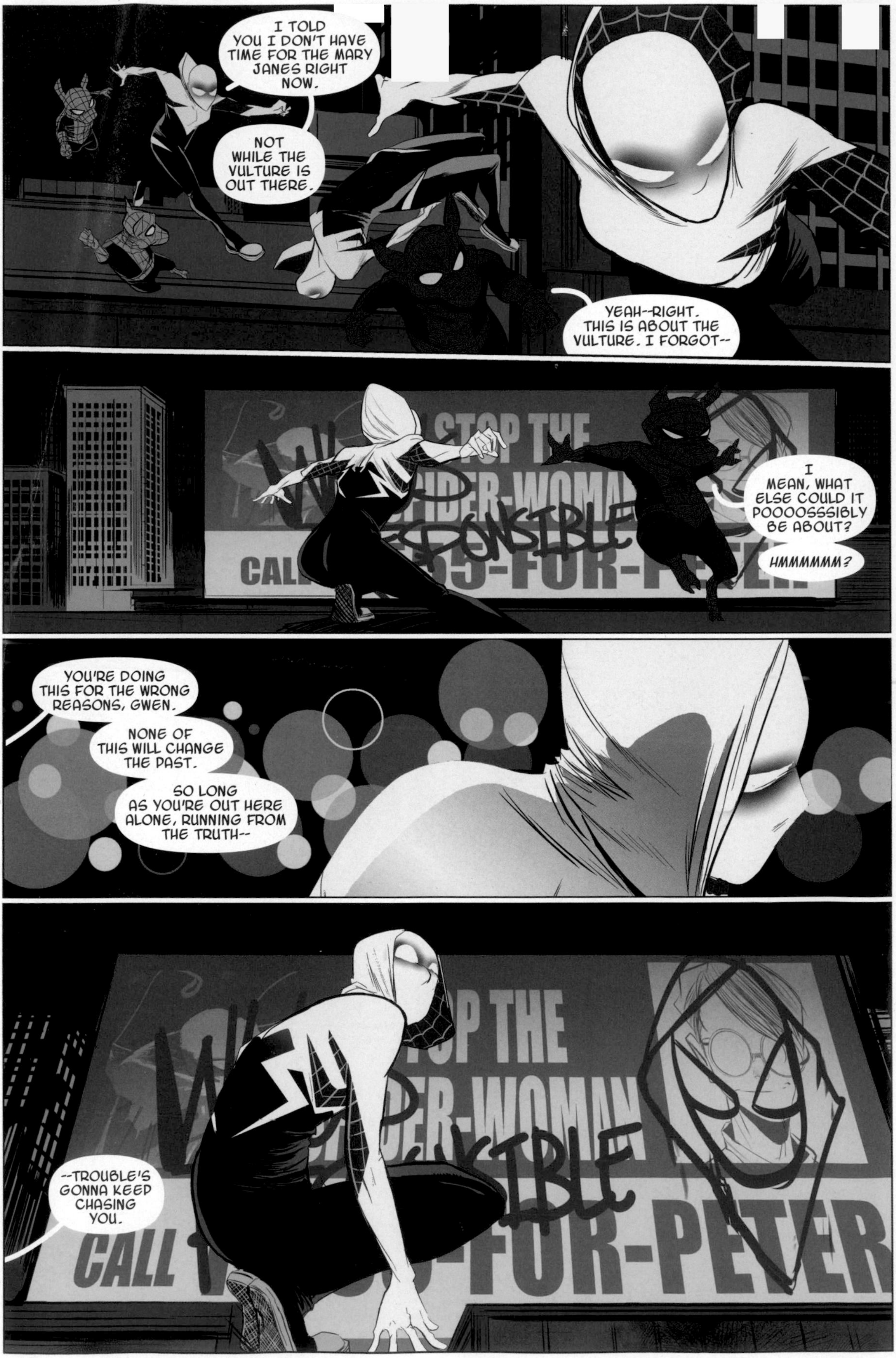
I TOLD YOU I DON'T HAVE TIME FOR THE MARY JANES RIGHT NOW.
NOT WHILE THE VULTURE IS OUT THERE.
YEAH--RIGHT. THIS IS ABOUT THE VULTURE. I FORGOT--
STOP THE SPIDER-WOMAN
SPONSIBLE
CALL 5-FOR-PETER
I MEAN, WHAT ELSE COULD IT POOOOSSSIBLY BE ABOUT?
HMMMMMM?
YOU'RE DOING THIS FOR THE WRONG REASONS, GWEN.
NONE OF THIS WILL CHANGE THE PAST.
SO LONG AS YOU'RE OUT HERE ALONE, RUNNING FROM THE TRUTH--
--TROUBLE'S GONNA KEEP CHASING YOU.
OP THE
ER-WOMAN
IBLE
CALL
-FOR-PETER

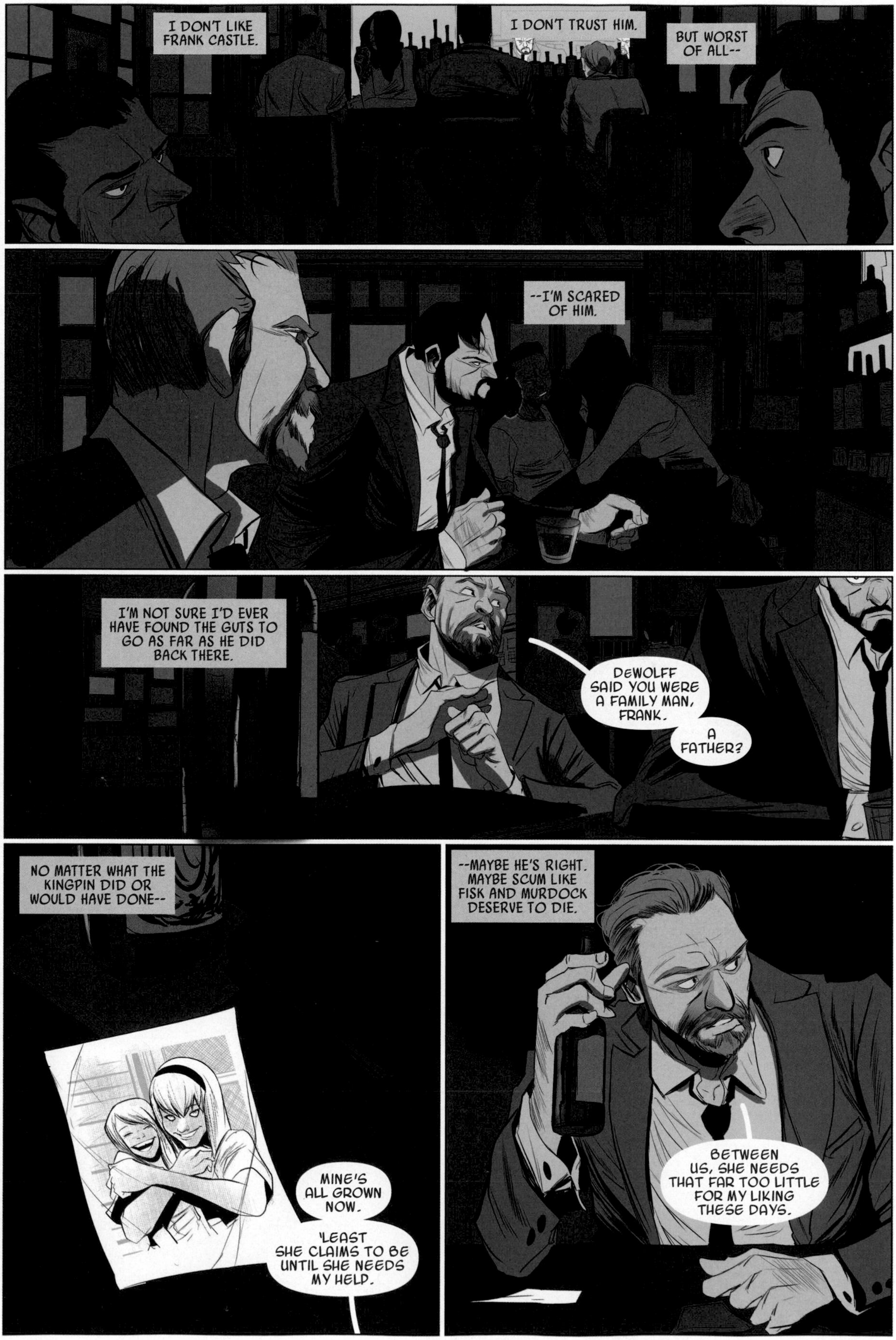
I DON'T LIKE FRANK CASTLE.
I DON'T TRUST HIM.
BUT WORST OF ALL--
--I'M SCARED OF HIM.
I'M NOT SURE I'D EVER HAVE FOUND THE GUTS TO GO AS FAR AS HE DID BACK THERE.
DEWOLFF SAID YOU WERE A FAMILY MAN, FRANK.
A FATHER?
NO MATTER WHAT THE KINGPIN DID OR WOULD HAVE DONE--
--MAYBE HE'S RIGHT. MAYBE SCUM LIKE FISK AND MURDOCK DESERVE TO DIE.
MINE'S ALL GROWN NOW.
'LEAST SHE CLAIMS TO BE UNTIL SHE NEEDS MY HELP.
BETWEEN US, SHE NEEDS THAT FAR TOO LITTLE FOR MY LIKING THESE DAYS.

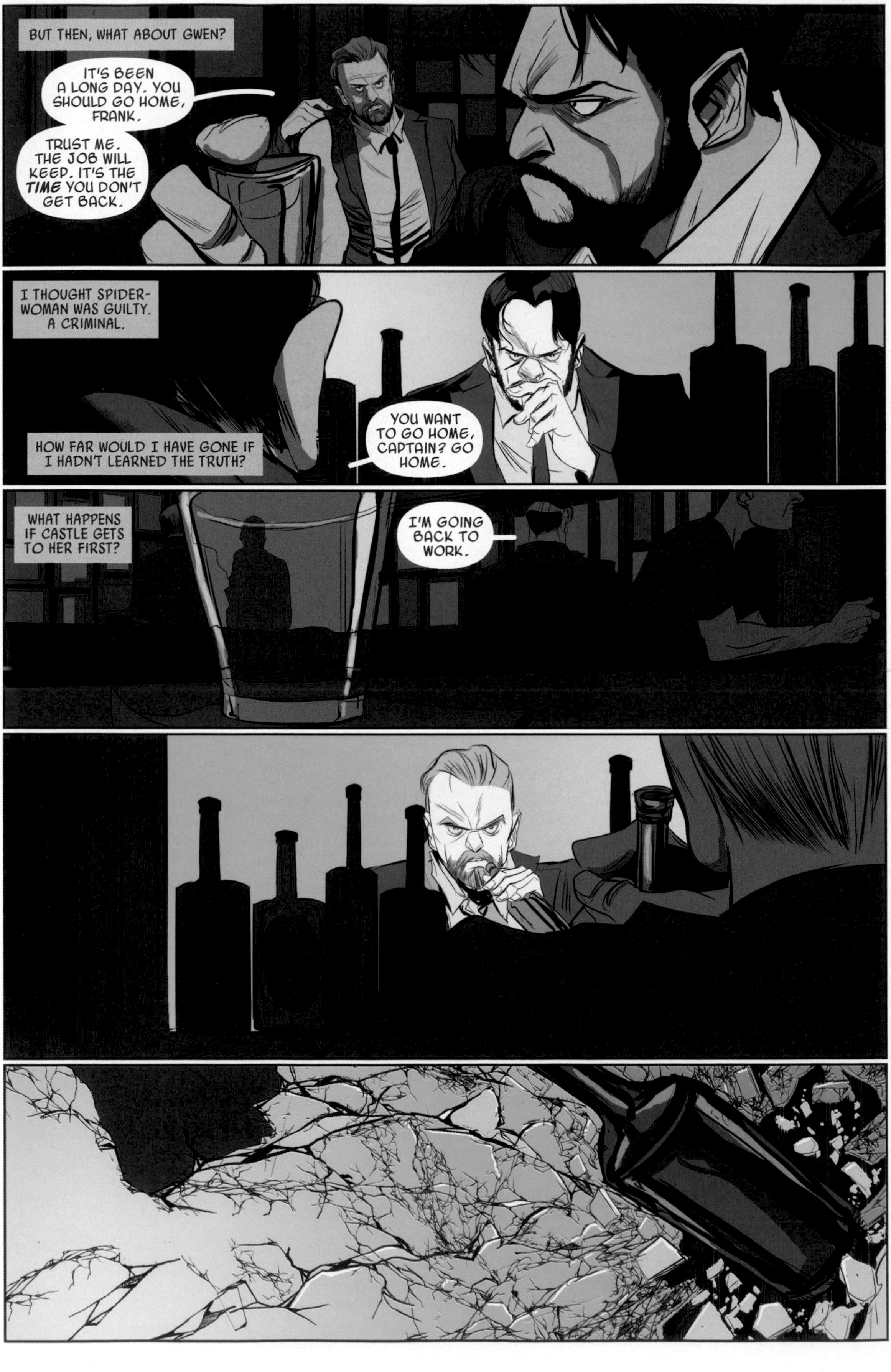

BUT THEN, WHAT ABOUT GWEN?
IT'S BEEN A LONG DAY. YOU SHOULD GO HOME, FRANK.
TRUST ME. THE JOB WILL KEEP. IT'S THE *TIME* YOU DON'T GET BACK.
I THOUGHT SPIDER-WOMAN WAS GUILTY. A CRIMINAL.
HOW FAR WOULD I HAVE GONE IF I HADN'T LEARNED THE TRUTH?
YOU WANT TO GO HOME, CAPTAIN? GO HOME.
WHAT HAPPENS IF CASTLE GETS TO HER FIRST?
I'M GOING BACK TO WORK.

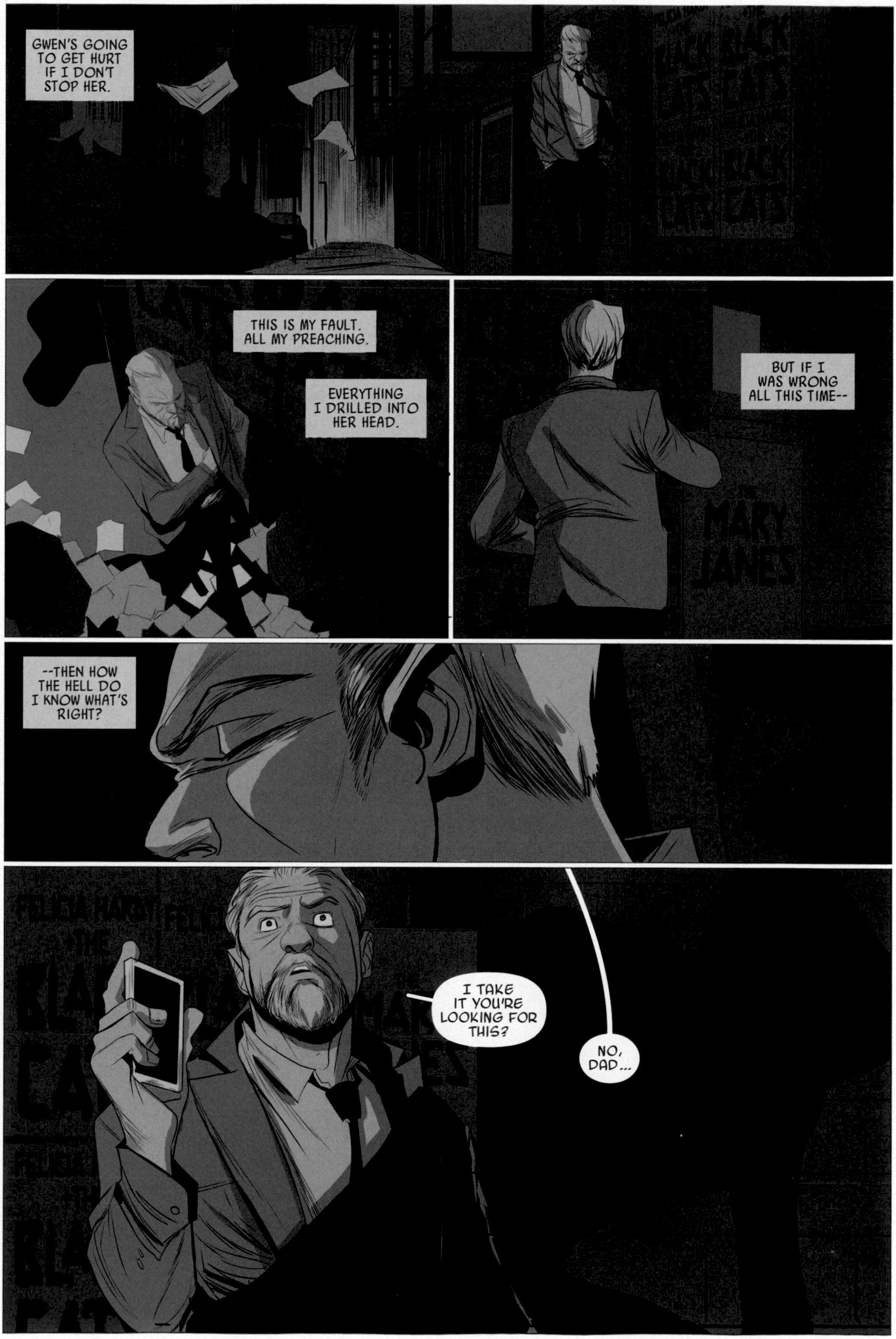
GWEN'S GOING TO GET HURT IF I DON'T STOP HER.
THIS IS MY FAULT. ALL MY PREACHING.
EVERYTHING I DRILLED INTO HER HEAD.
BUT IF I WAS WRONG ALL THIS TIME--
MARY JANES
--THEN HOW THE HELL DO I KNOW WHAT'S RIGHT?
I TAKE IT YOU'RE LOOKING FOR THIS?
NO, DAD...

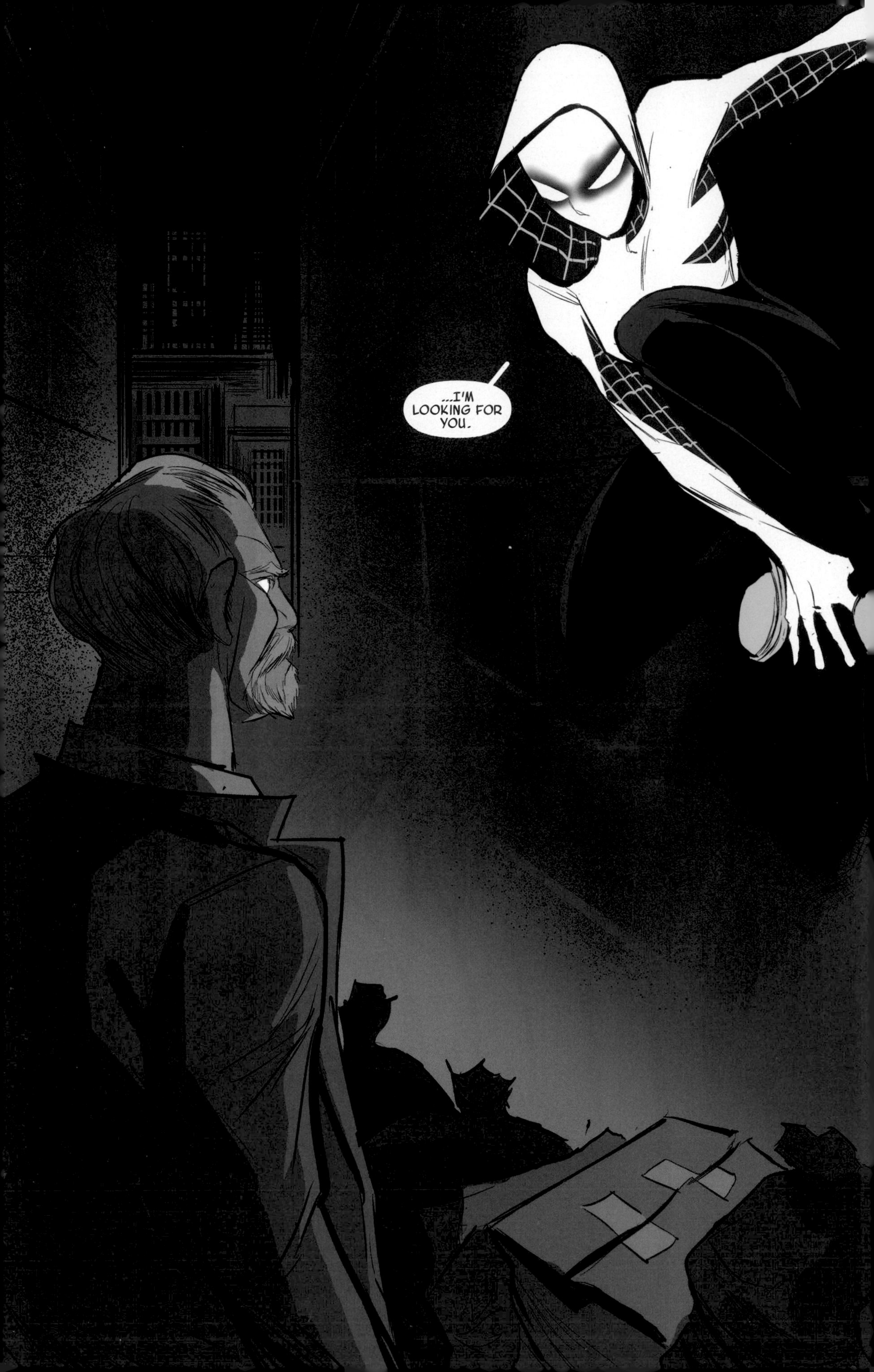
...I'M LOOKING FOR YOU.

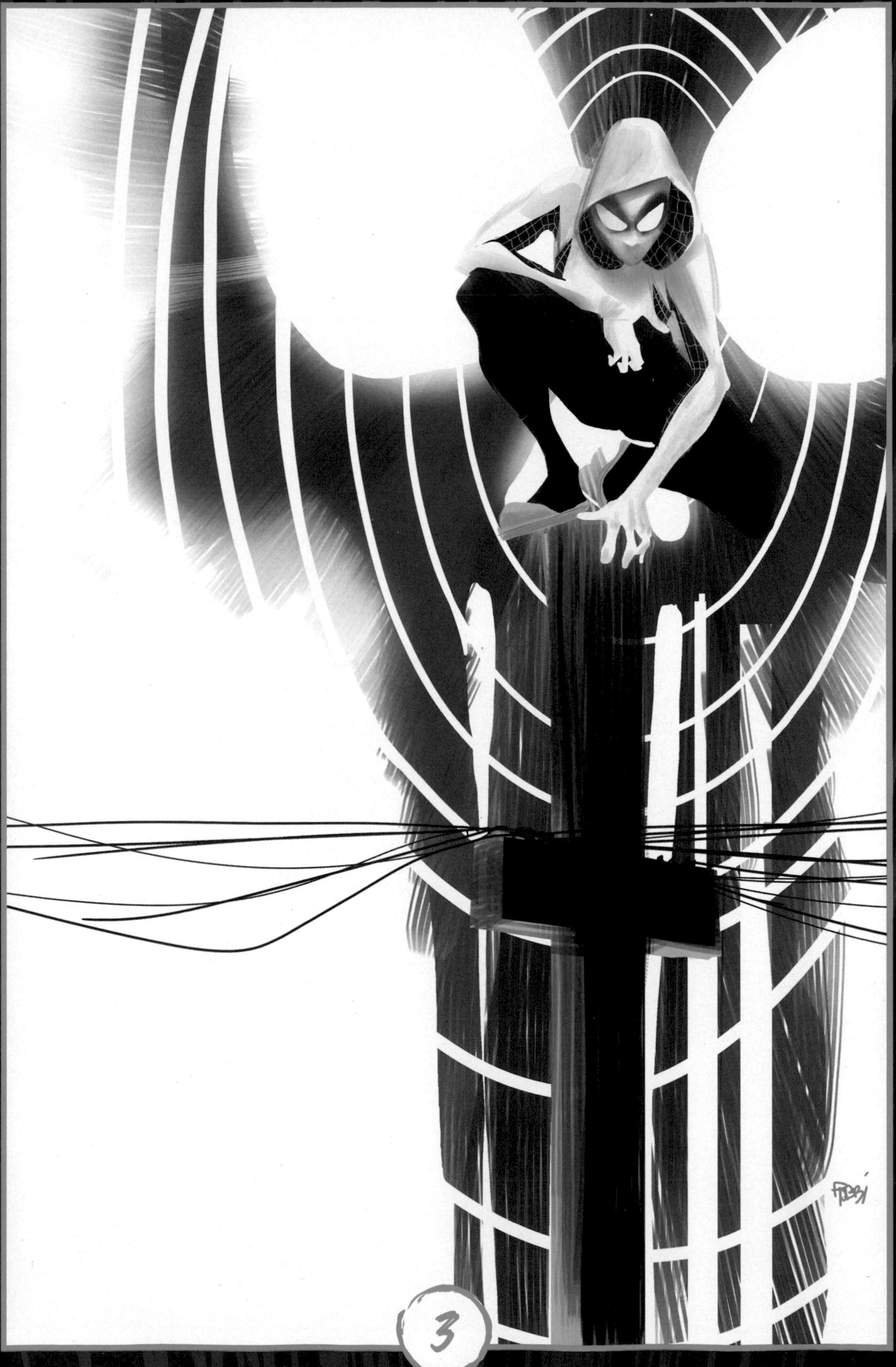
3

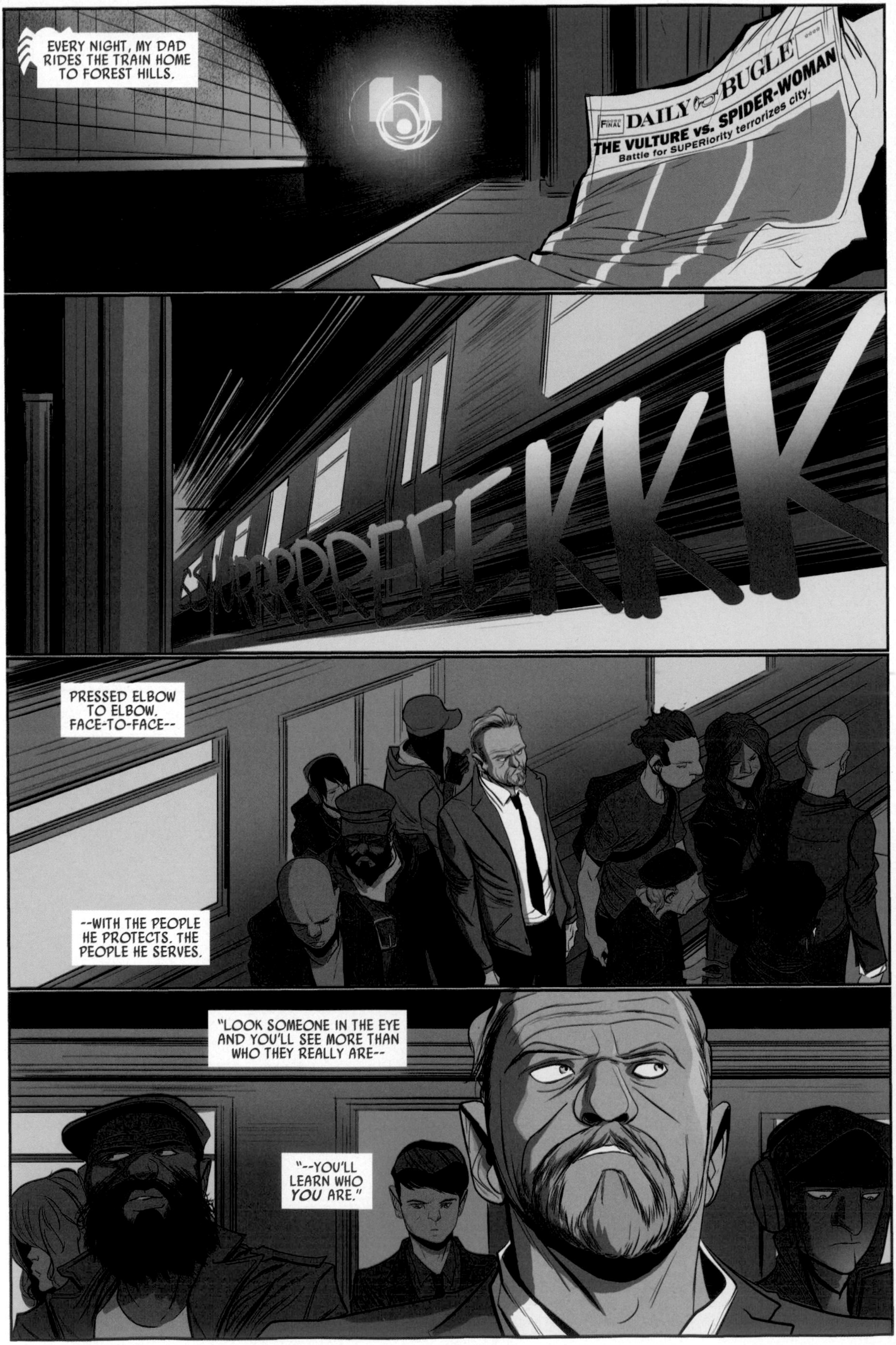
EVERY NIGHT, MY DAD RIDES THE TRAIN HOME TO FOREST HILLS.
DAILY BUGLE
FINAL
THE VULTURE vs. SPIDER-WOMAN
Battle for SUPERiority terrorizes city.
SHRRRRREEEEKKK
PRESSED ELBOW TO ELBOW. FACE-TO-FACE--
--WITH THE PEOPLE HE PROTECTS. THE PEOPLE HE SERVES.
"LOOK SOMEONE IN THE EYE AND YOU'LL SEE MORE THAN WHO THEY REALLY ARE--
"--YOU'LL LEARN WHO YOU ARE."

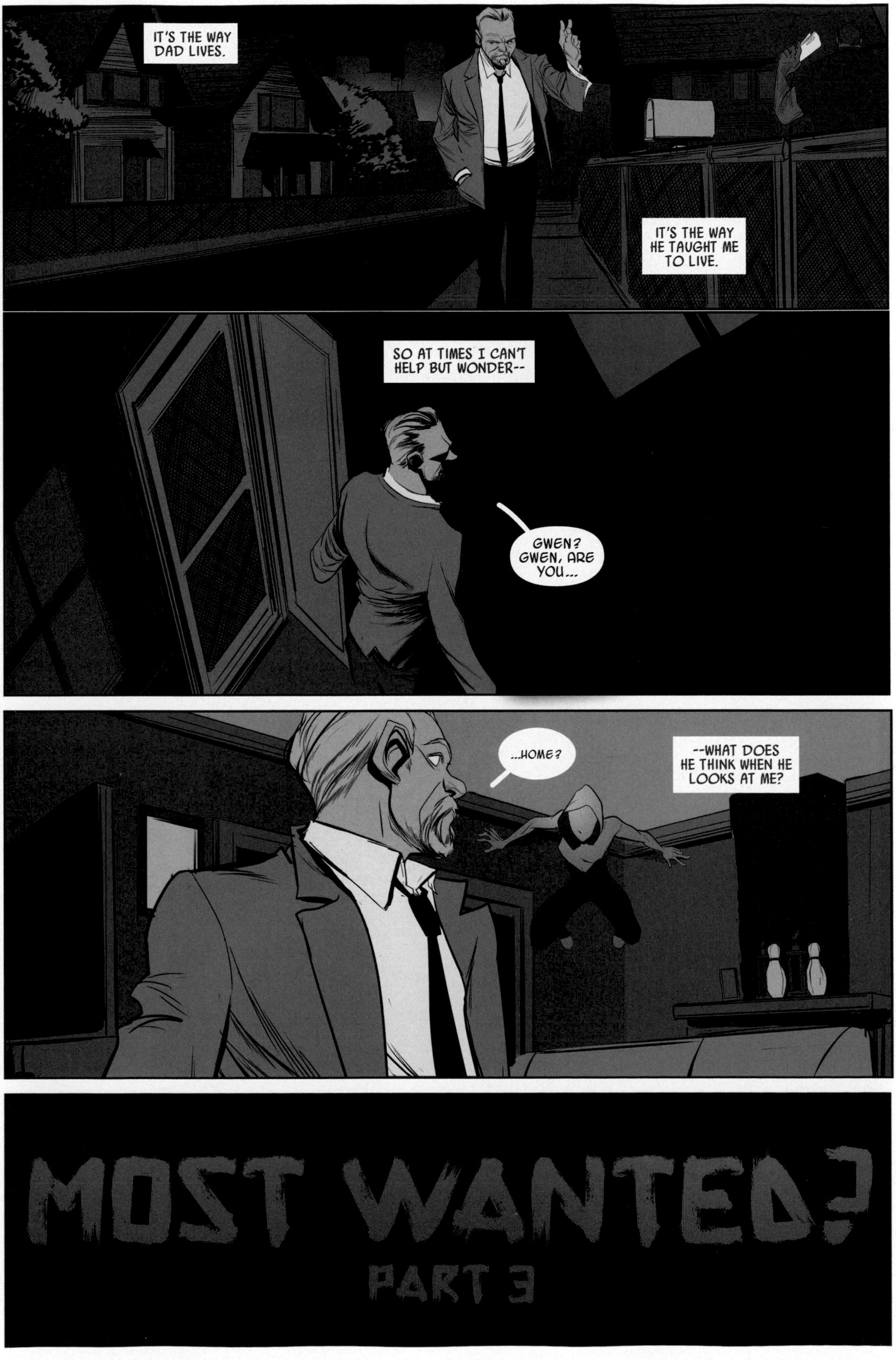
IT'S THE WAY DAD LIVES.
IT'S THE WAY HE TAUGHT ME TO LIVE.
SO AT TIMES I CAN'T HELP BUT WONDER--
GWEN? GWEN, ARE YOU...
...HOME?
--WHAT DOES HE THINK WHEN HE LOOKS AT ME?
MOST WANTED?
PART 3

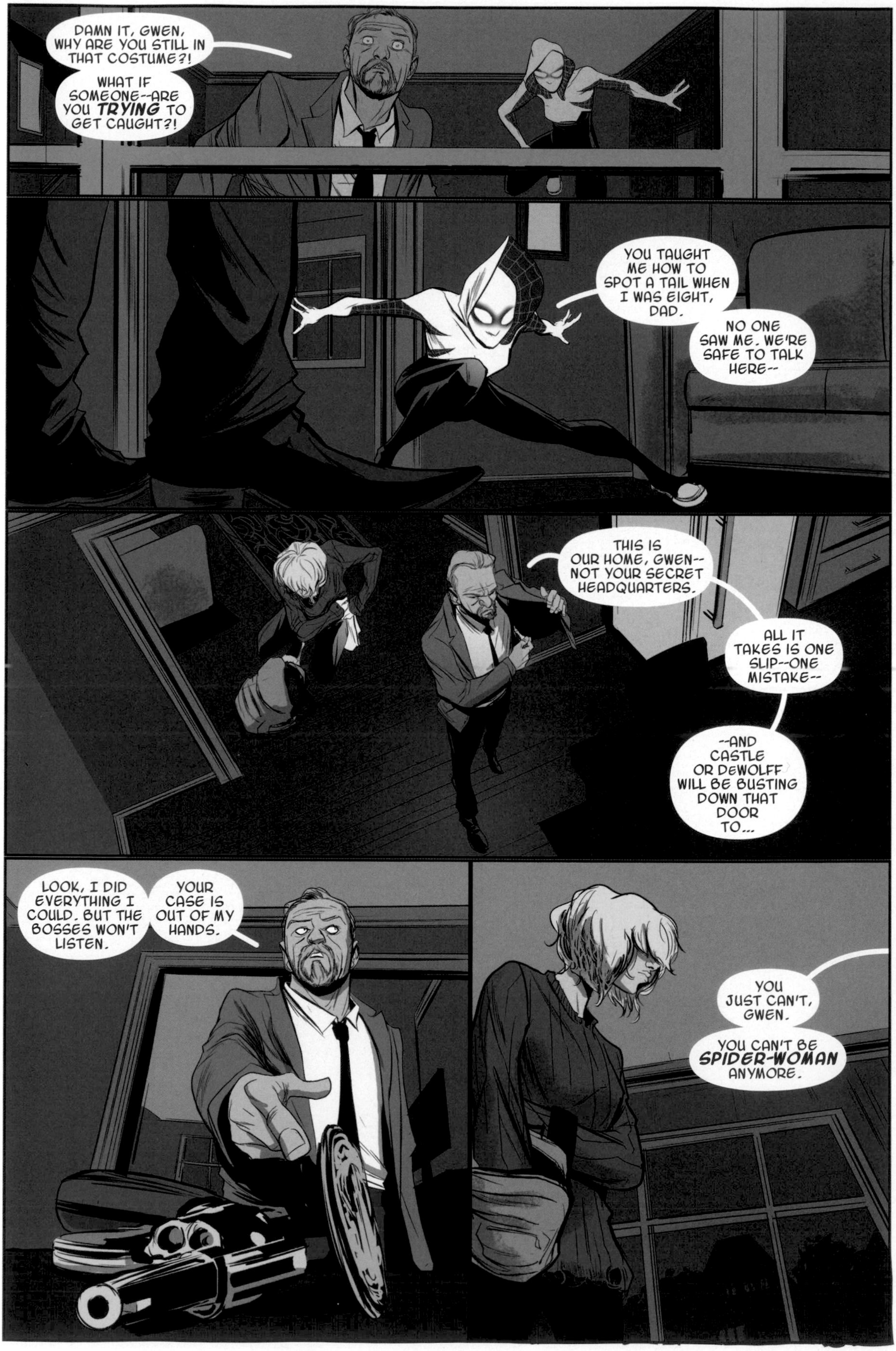
DAMN IT, GWEN, WHY ARE YOU STILL IN THAT COSTUME?!
WHAT IF SOMEONE--ARE YOU *TRYING* TO GET CAUGHT?!
YOU TAUGHT ME HOW TO SPOT A TAIL WHEN I WAS EIGHT, DAD.
NO ONE SAW ME. WE'RE SAFE TO TALK HERE--
THIS IS OUR HOME, GWEN--NOT YOUR SECRET HEADQUARTERS.
ALL IT TAKES IS ONE SLIP--ONE MISTAKE--
--AND CASTLE OR DEWOLFF WILL BE BUSTING DOWN THAT DOOR TO...
LOOK, I DID EVERYTHING I COULD. BUT THE BOSSES WON'T LISTEN.
YOUR CASE IS OUT OF MY HANDS.
YOU JUST CAN'T, GWEN.
YOU CAN'T BE **SPIDER-WOMAN** ANYMORE.

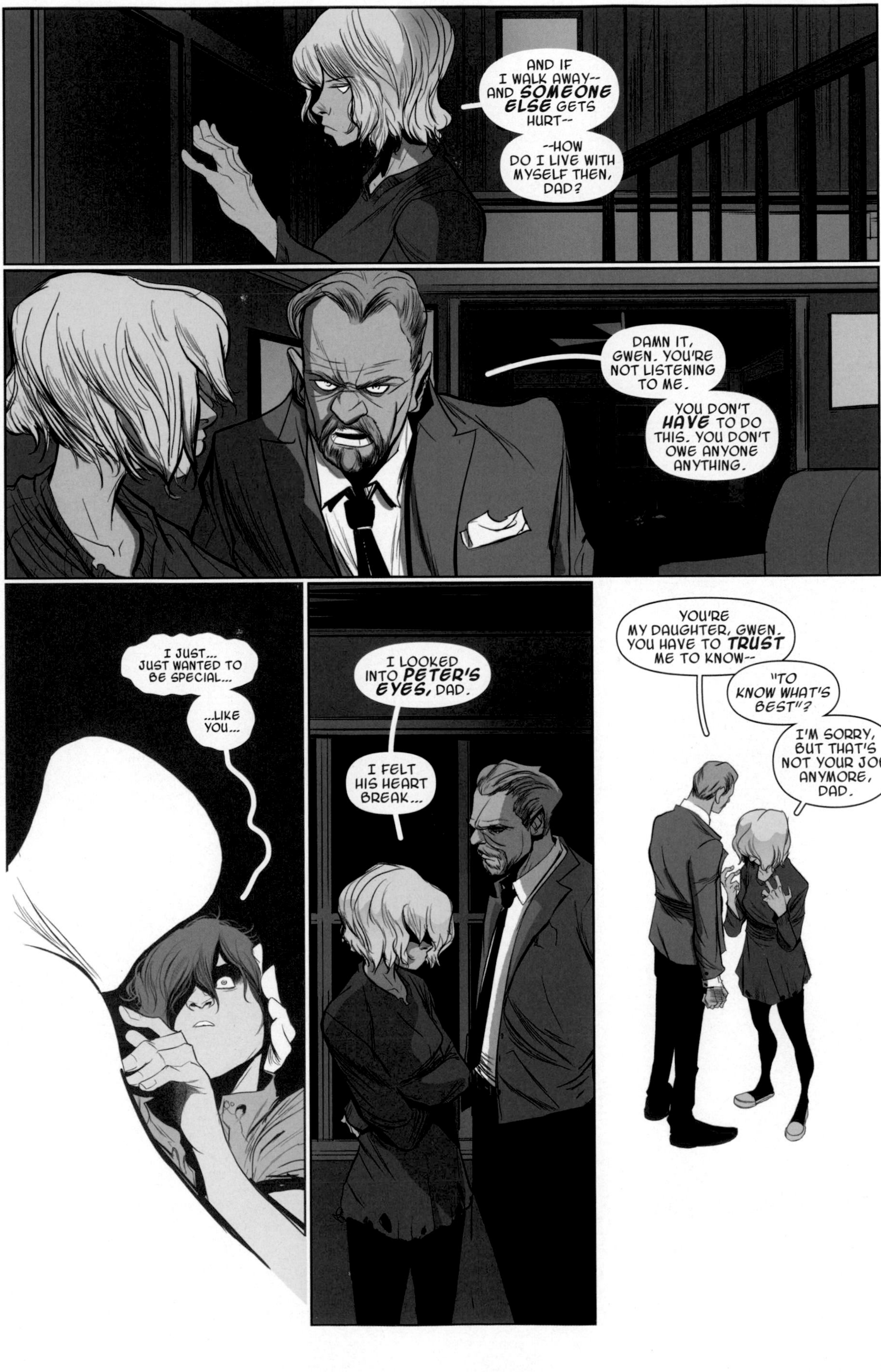

AND IF I WALK AWAY-- AND SOMEONE ELSE GETS HURT--
--HOW DO I LIVE WITH MYSELF THEN, DAD?
DAMN IT, GWEN. YOU'RE NOT LISTENING TO ME.
YOU DON'T HAVE TO DO THIS. YOU DON'T OWE ANYONE ANYTHING.
I JUST... JUST WANTED TO BE SPECIAL...
...LIKE YOU...
I LOOKED INTO PETER'S EYES, DAD.
I FELT HIS HEART BREAK...
YOU'RE MY DAUGHTER, GWEN. YOU HAVE TO TRUST ME TO KNOW--
"TO KNOW WHAT'S BEST"?
I'M SORRY, BUT THAT'S NOT YOUR JOB ANYMORE, DAD.

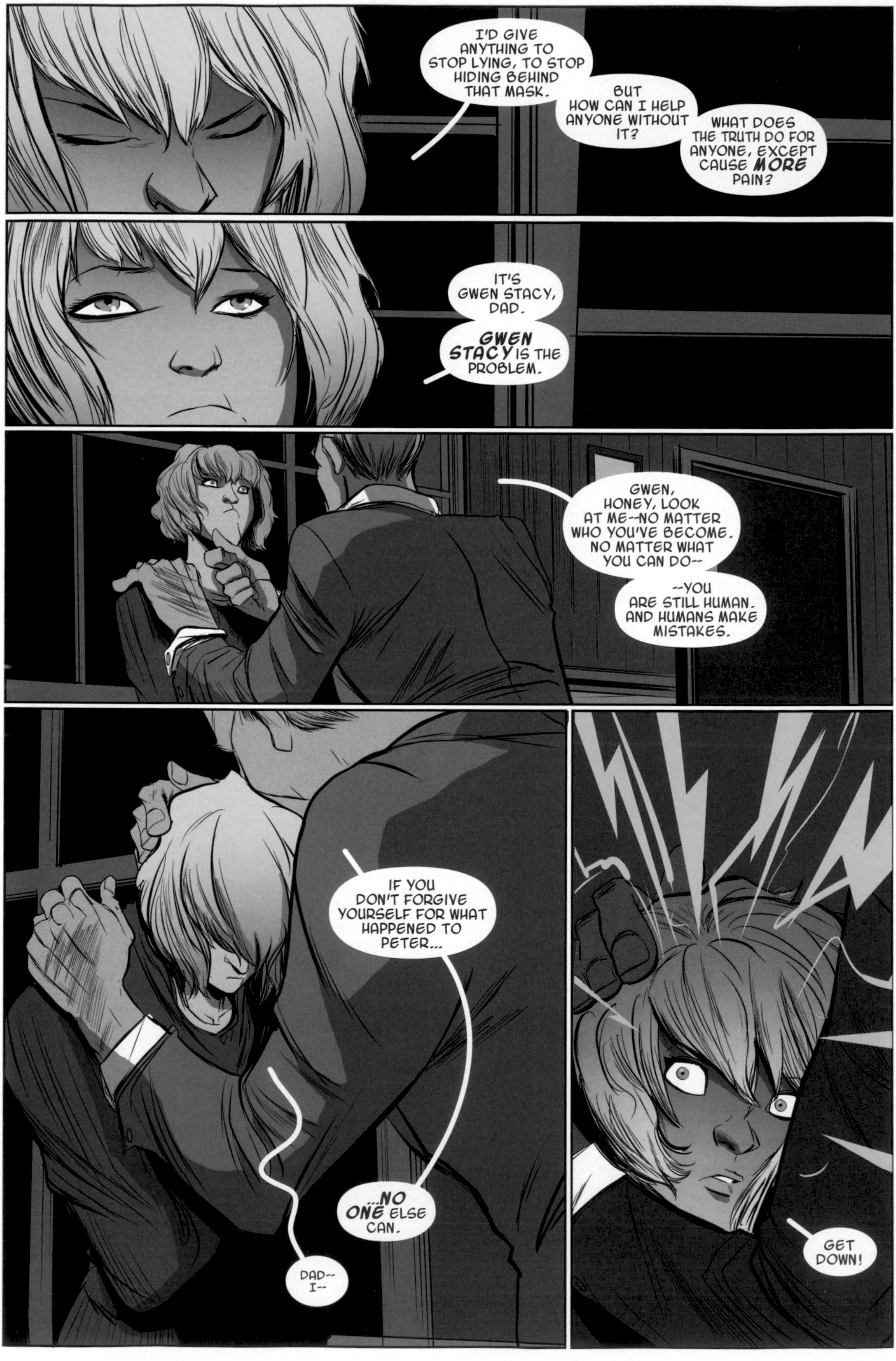
I'D GIVE ANYTHING TO STOP LYING, TO STOP HIDING BEHIND THAT MASK.
BUT HOW CAN I HELP ANYONE WITHOUT IT?
WHAT DOES THE TRUTH DO FOR ANYONE, EXCEPT CAUSE MORE PAIN?
IT'S GWEN STACY, DAD.
GWEN STACY IS THE PROBLEM.
GWEN, HONEY, LOOK AT ME--NO MATTER WHO YOU'VE BECOME. NO MATTER WHAT YOU CAN DO--
--YOU ARE STILL HUMAN. AND HUMANS MAKE MISTAKES.
IF YOU DON'T FORGIVE YOURSELF FOR WHAT HAPPENED TO PETER...
...NO ONE ELSE CAN.
DAD-- I--
GET DOWN!

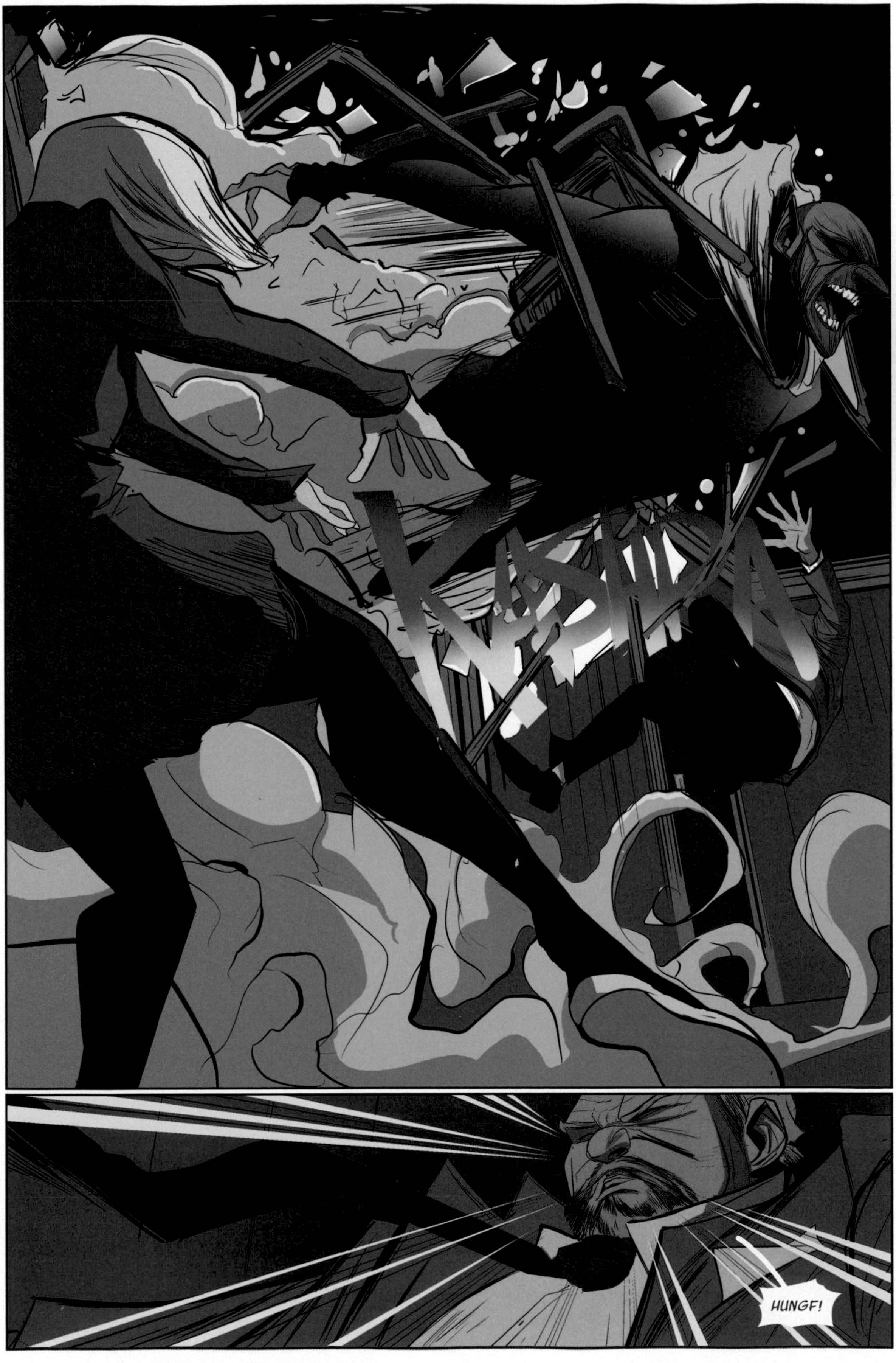
HUNGF!

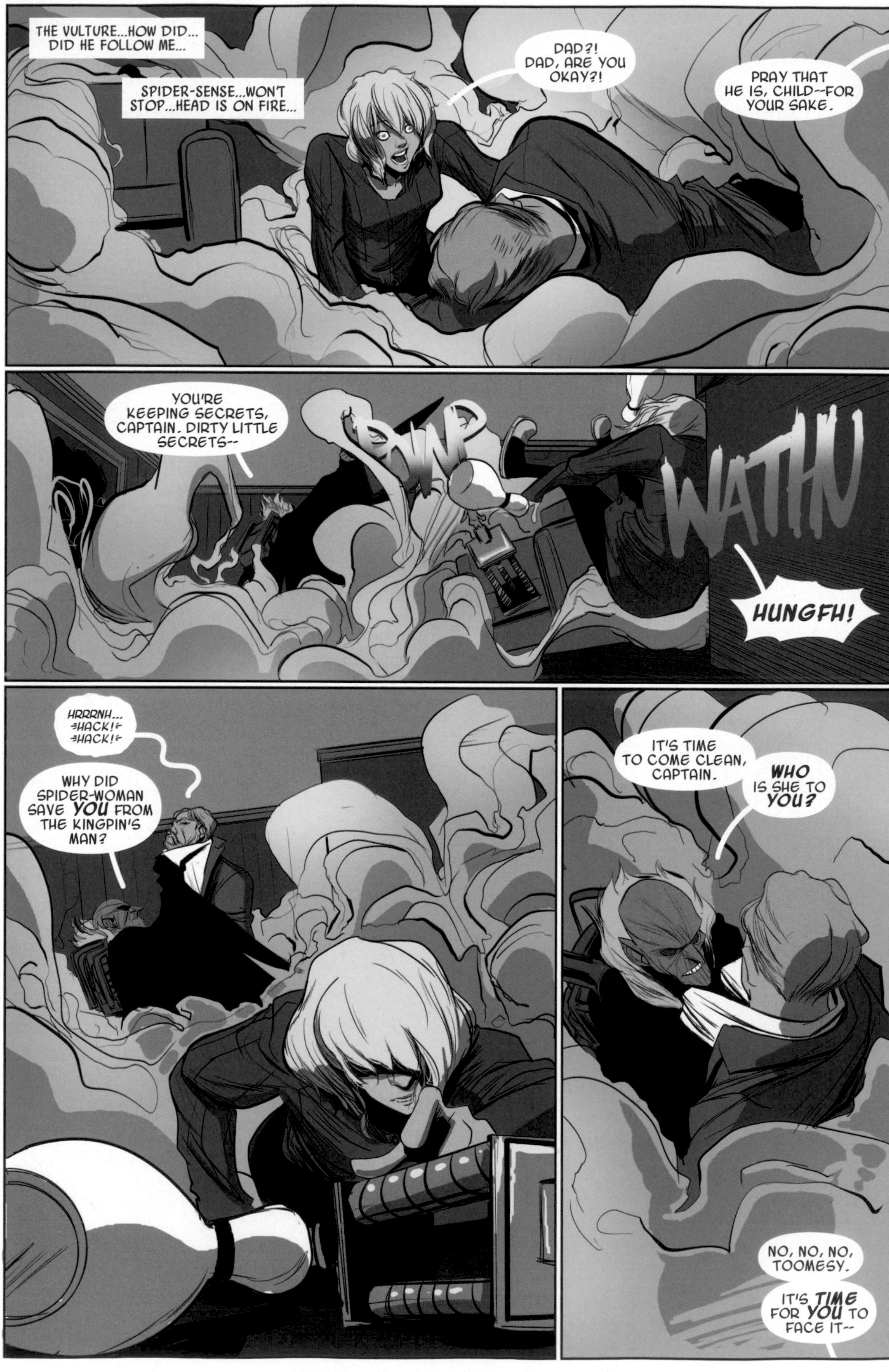

THE VULTURE...HOW DID... DID HE FOLLOW ME...
SPIDER-SENSE...WON'T STOP...HEAD IS ON FIRE...
DAD?! DAD, ARE YOU OKAY?!
PRAY THAT HE IS, CHILD--FOR YOUR SAKE.
YOU'RE KEEPING SECRETS, CAPTAIN. DIRTY LITTLE SECRETS--
WATHU
HUNGFH!
HRRRNH... HACK! HACK!
WHY DID SPIDER-WOMAN SAVE YOU FROM THE KINGPIN'S MAN?
IT'S TIME TO COME CLEAN, CAPTAIN.
WHO IS SHE TO YOU?
NO, NO, NO, TOOMESY.
IT'S TIME FOR YOU TO FACE IT--

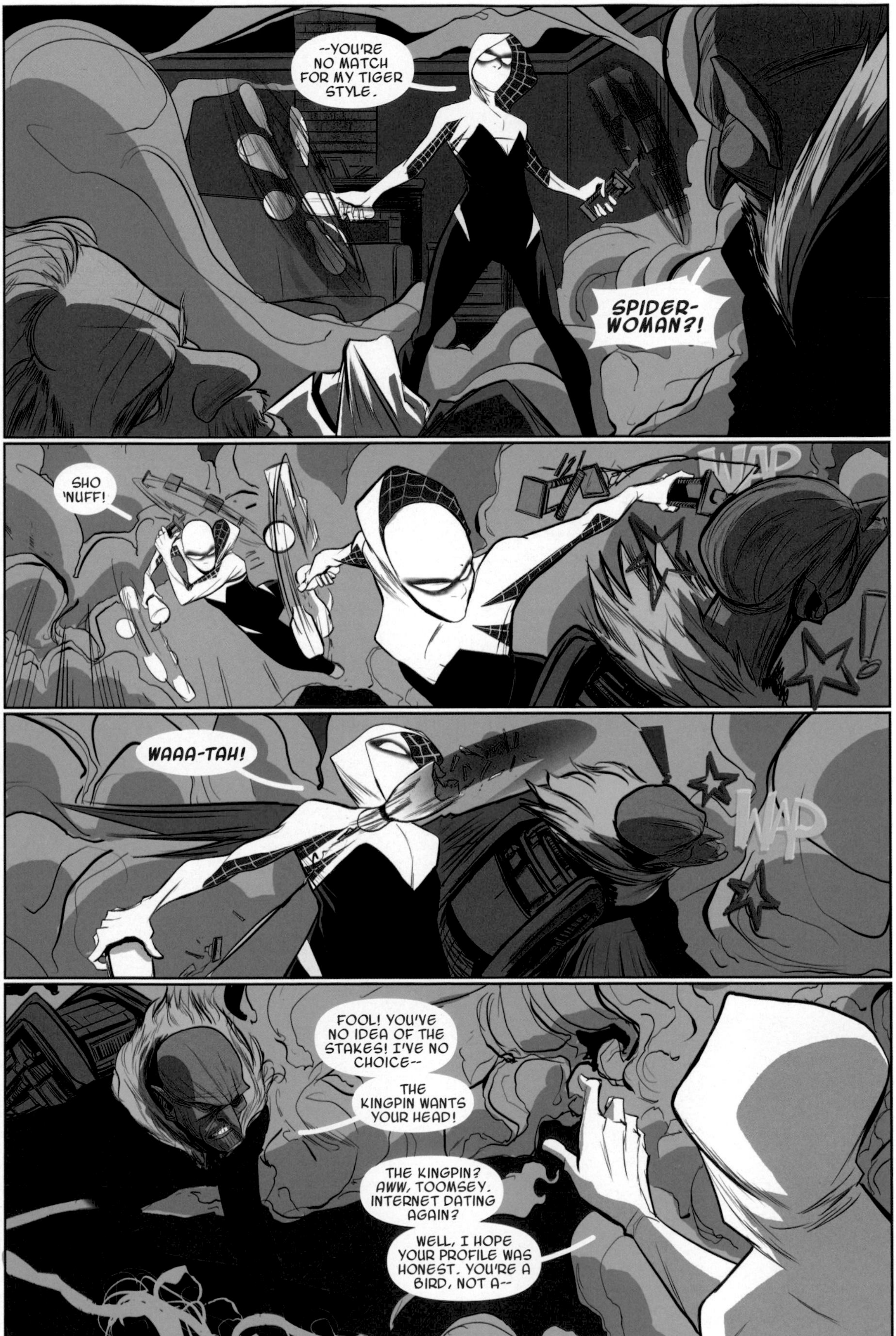
--YOU'RE NO MATCH FOR MY TIGER STYLE.
SPIDER-WOMAN?!
SHO 'NUFF!
WAP
WAAA-TAH!
WAP
FOOL! YOU'VE NO IDEA OF THE STAKES! I'VE NO CHOICE--
THE KINGPIN WANTS YOUR HEAD!
THE KINGPIN? AWW, TOOMSEY. INTERNET DATING AGAIN?
WELL, I HOPE YOUR PROFILE WAS HONEST. YOU'RE A BIRD, NOT A--

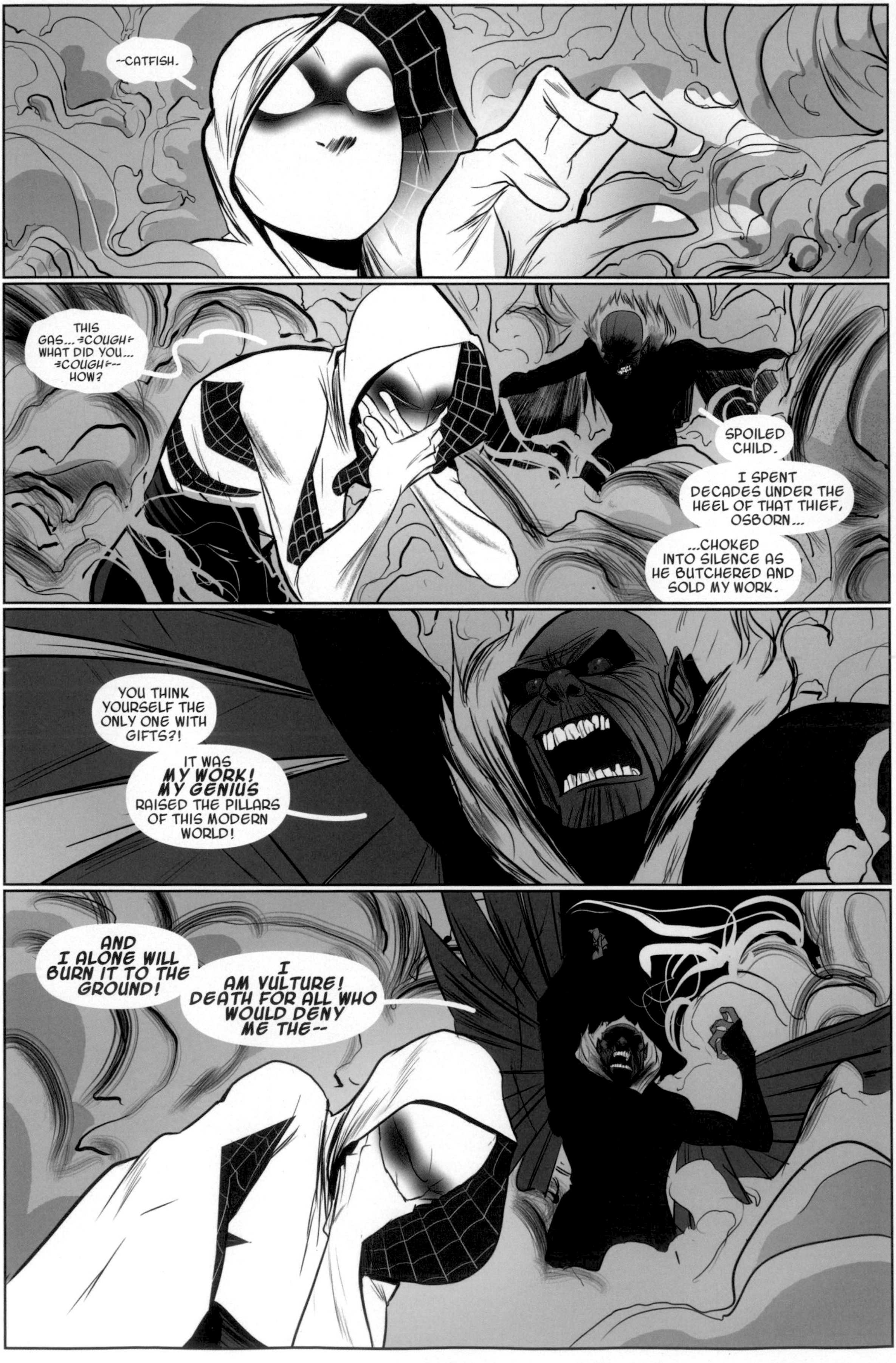
--CATFISH.
THIS GAS... ⇉COUGH⇇ WHAT DID YOU... ⇉COUGH⇇-- HOW?
SPOILED CHILD.
I SPENT DECADES UNDER THE HEEL OF THAT THIEF, OSBORN...
...CHOKED INTO SILENCE AS HE BUTCHERED AND SOLD MY WORK.
YOU THINK YOURSELF THE ONLY ONE WITH GIFTS?!
IT WAS MY WORK! MY GENIUS RAISED THE PILLARS OF THIS MODERN WORLD!
AND I ALONE WILL BURN IT TO THE GROUND!
I AM VULTURE! DEATH FOR ALL WHO WOULD DENY ME THE--

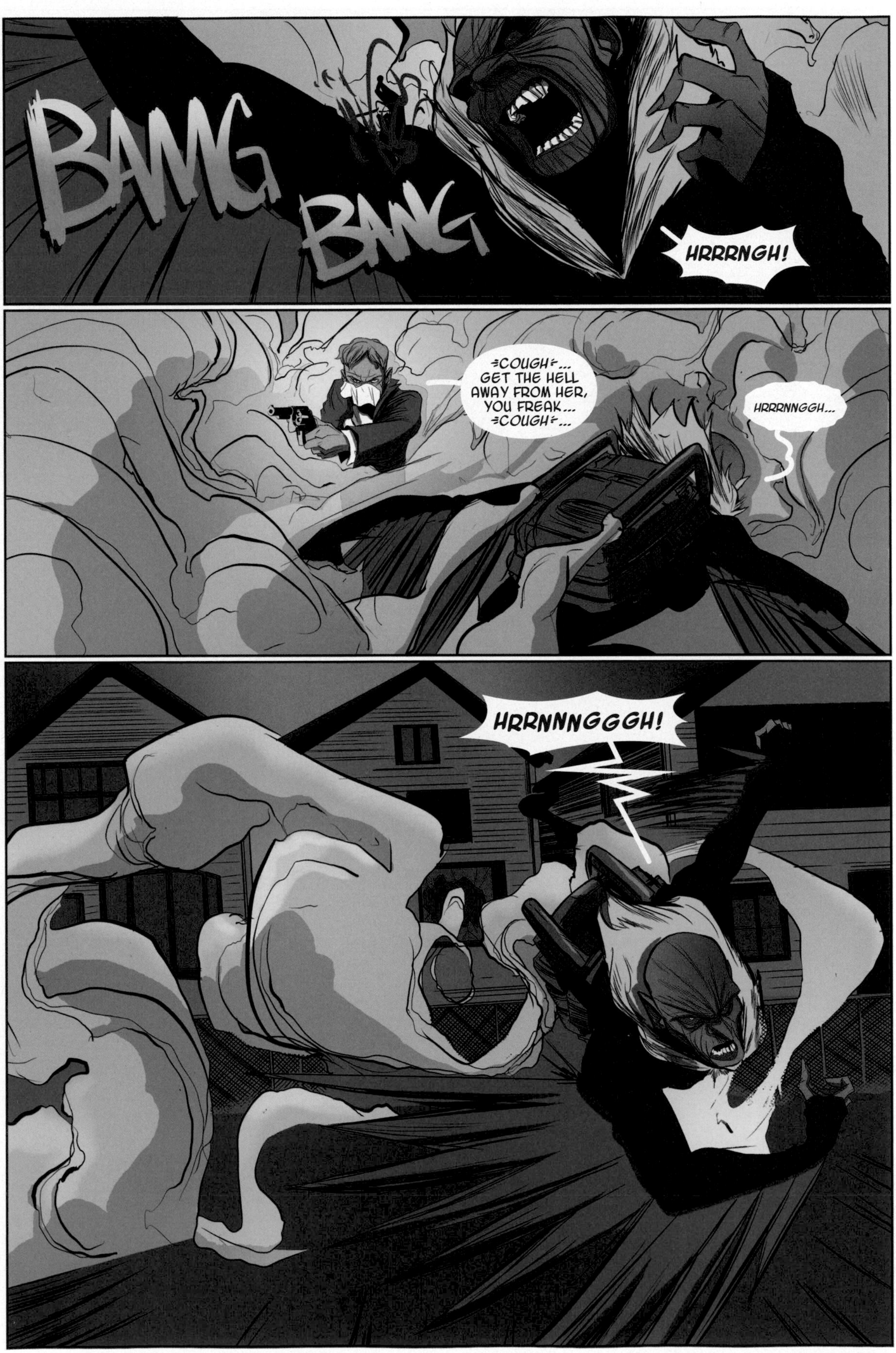
BAMG
BANG
HRRRNGH!
=COUGH=... GET THE HELL AWAY FROM HER, YOU FREAK... =COUGH=...
HRRRNNGGH...
HRRNNNGGGH!

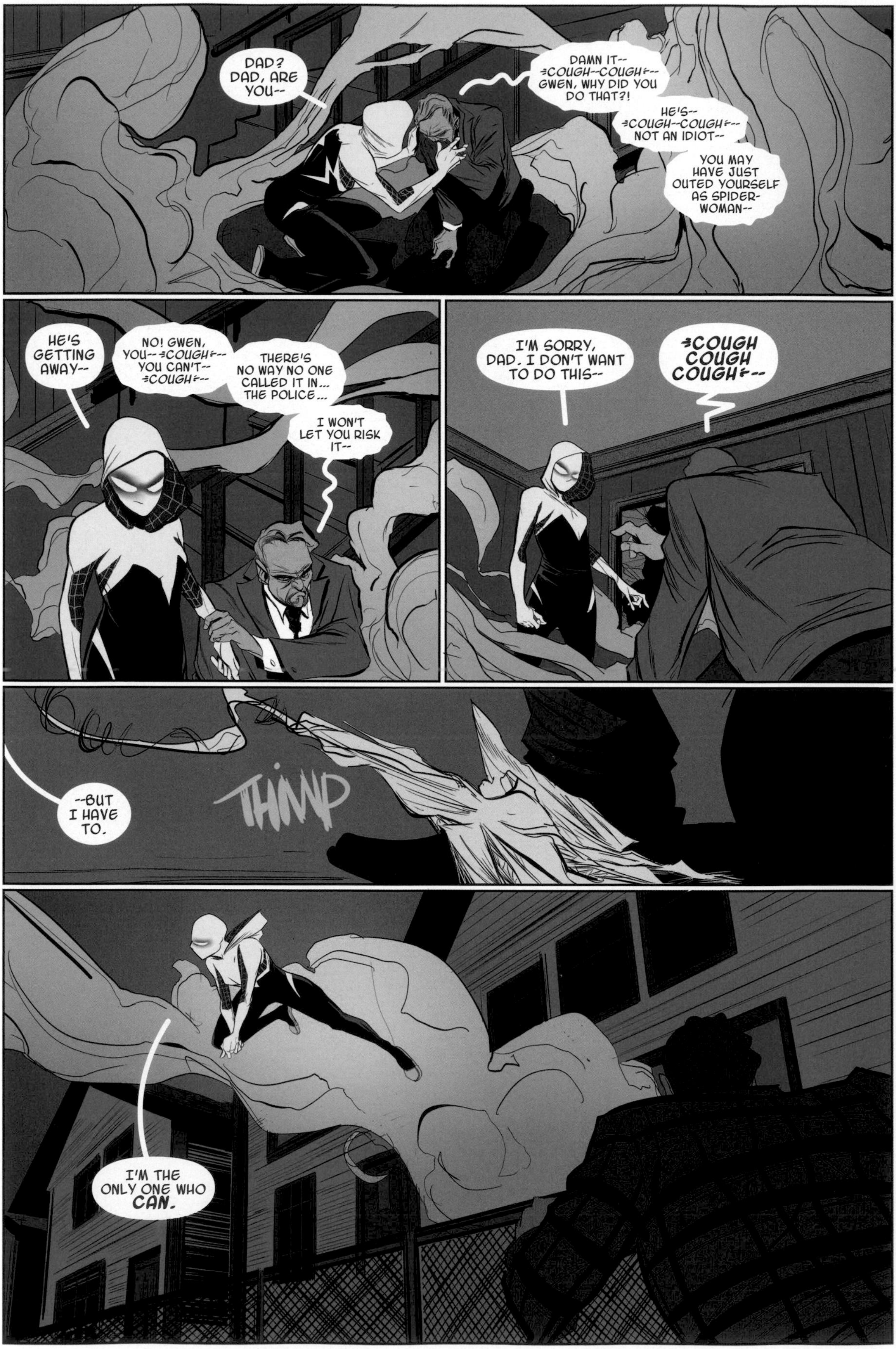
DAD? DAD, ARE YOU--
DAMN IT-- =COUGH--COUGH=-- GWEN, WHY DID YOU DO THAT?!
HE'S-- =COUGH--COUGH=-- NOT AN IDIOT--
YOU MAY HAVE JUST OUTED YOURSELF AS SPIDER-WOMAN--
HE'S GETTING AWAY--
NO! GWEN, YOU-- =COUGH=-- YOU CAN'T-- =COUGH=--
THERE'S NO WAY NO ONE CALLED IT IN... THE POLICE...
I WON'T LET YOU RISK IT--
I'M SORRY, DAD. I DON'T WANT TO DO THIS--
=COUGH COUGH COUGH=--
THWP
--BUT I HAVE TO.
I'M THE ONLY ONE WHO CAN.

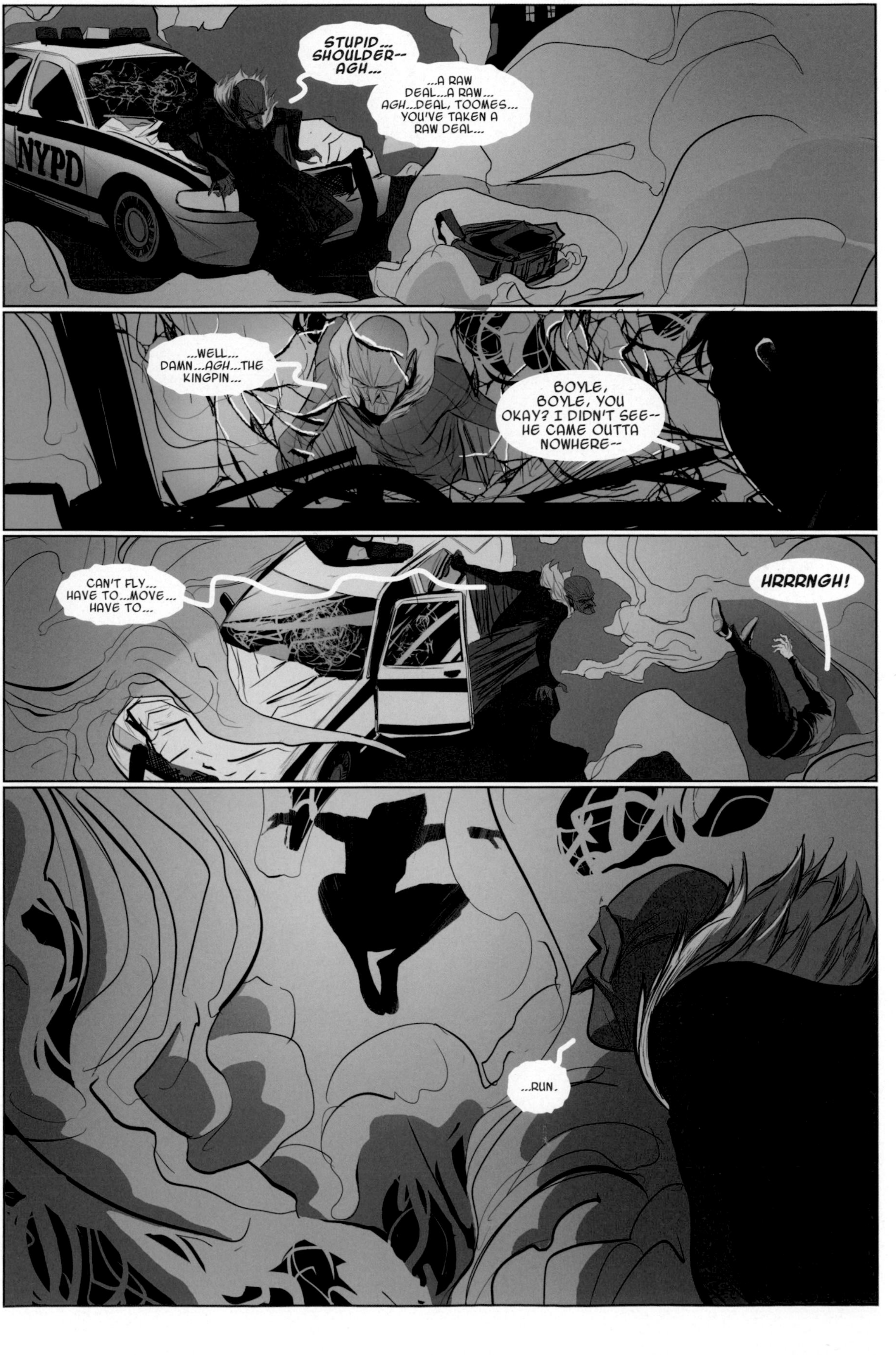
STUPID... SHOULDER-- AGH...
...A RAW DEAL...A RAW... AGH...DEAL, TOOMES... YOU'VE TAKEN A RAW DEAL...
...WELL... DAMN...AGH...THE KINGPIN...
BOYLE, BOYLE, YOU OKAY? I DIDN'T SEE-- HE CAME OUTTA NOWHERE--
CAN'T FLY... HAVE TO...MOVE... HAVE TO...
HRRRNGH!
...RUN.

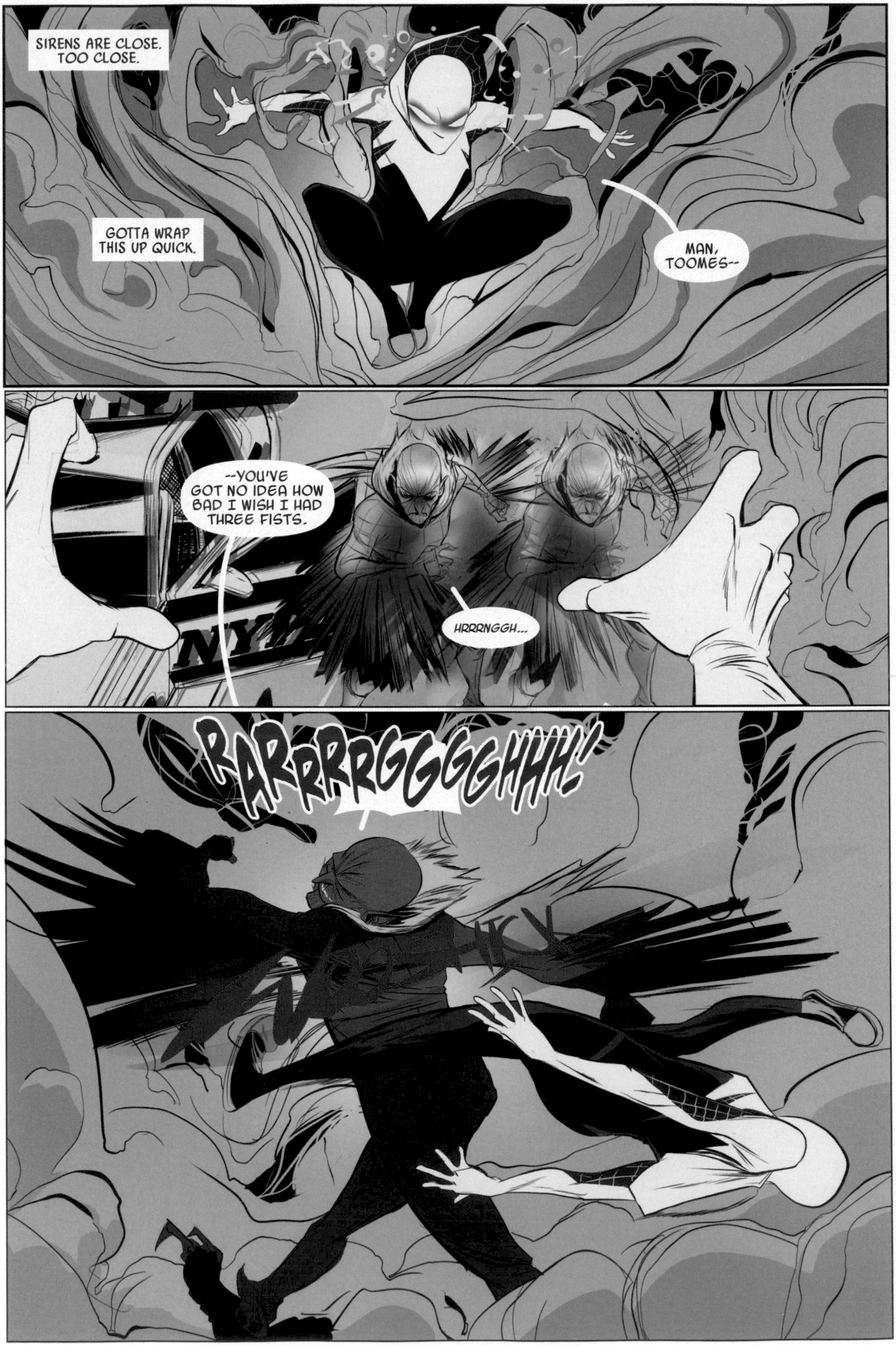
SIRENS ARE CLOSE. TOO CLOSE.
GOTTA WRAP THIS UP QUICK.
MAN, TOOMES--
--YOU'VE GOT NO IDEA HOW BAD I WISH I HAD THREE FISTS.
HRRRNGGH...
RARRRRGGGGHHH!

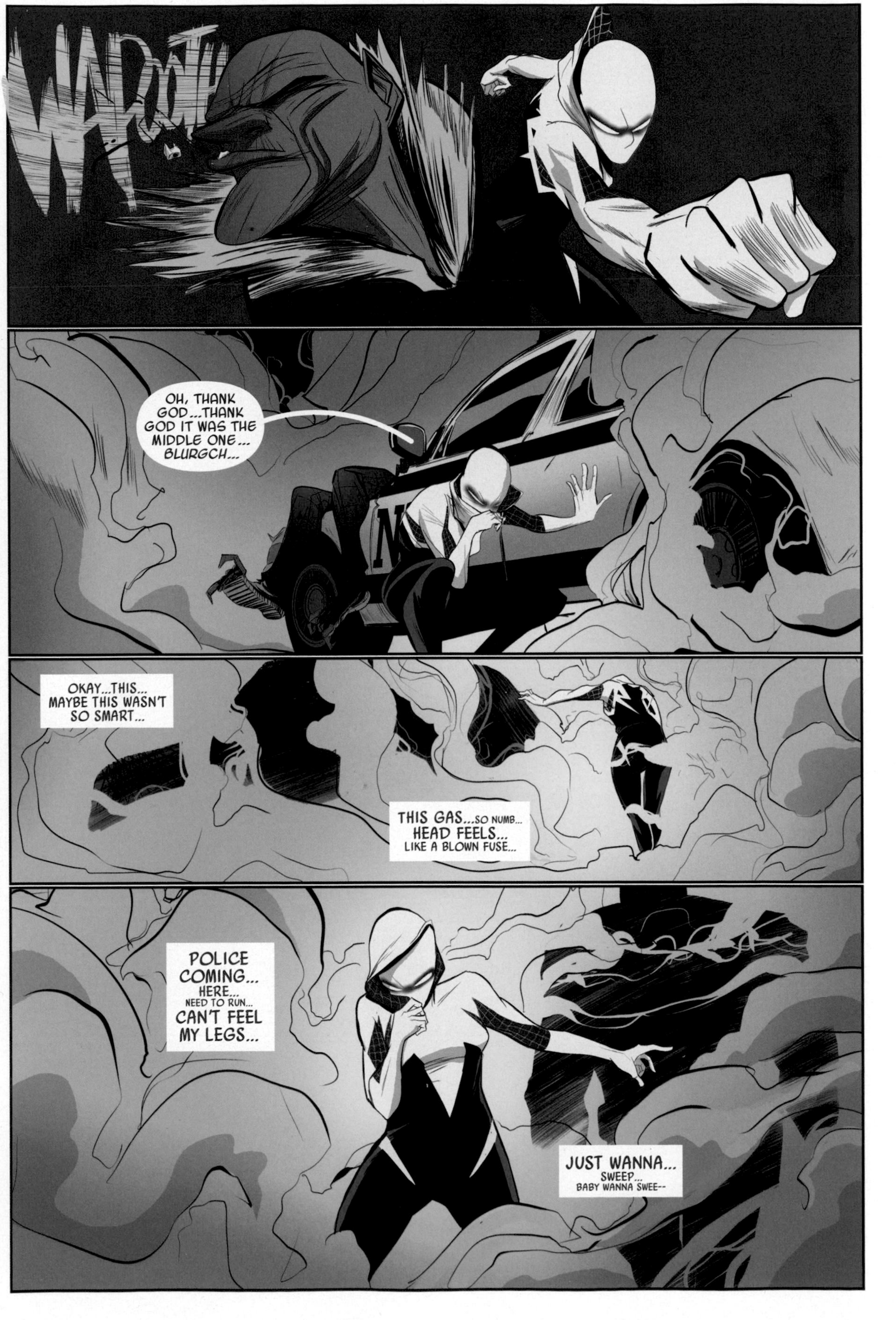
WHOOMP
OH, THANK GOD...THANK GOD IT WAS THE MIDDLE ONE... BLURGCH...
OKAY...THIS... MAYBE THIS WASN'T SO SMART...
THIS GAS...SO NUMB... HEAD FEELS... LIKE A BLOWN FUSE...
POLICE COMING... HERE... NEED TO RUN... CAN'T FEEL MY LEGS...
JUST WANNA... SWEEP... BABY WANNA SWEE--

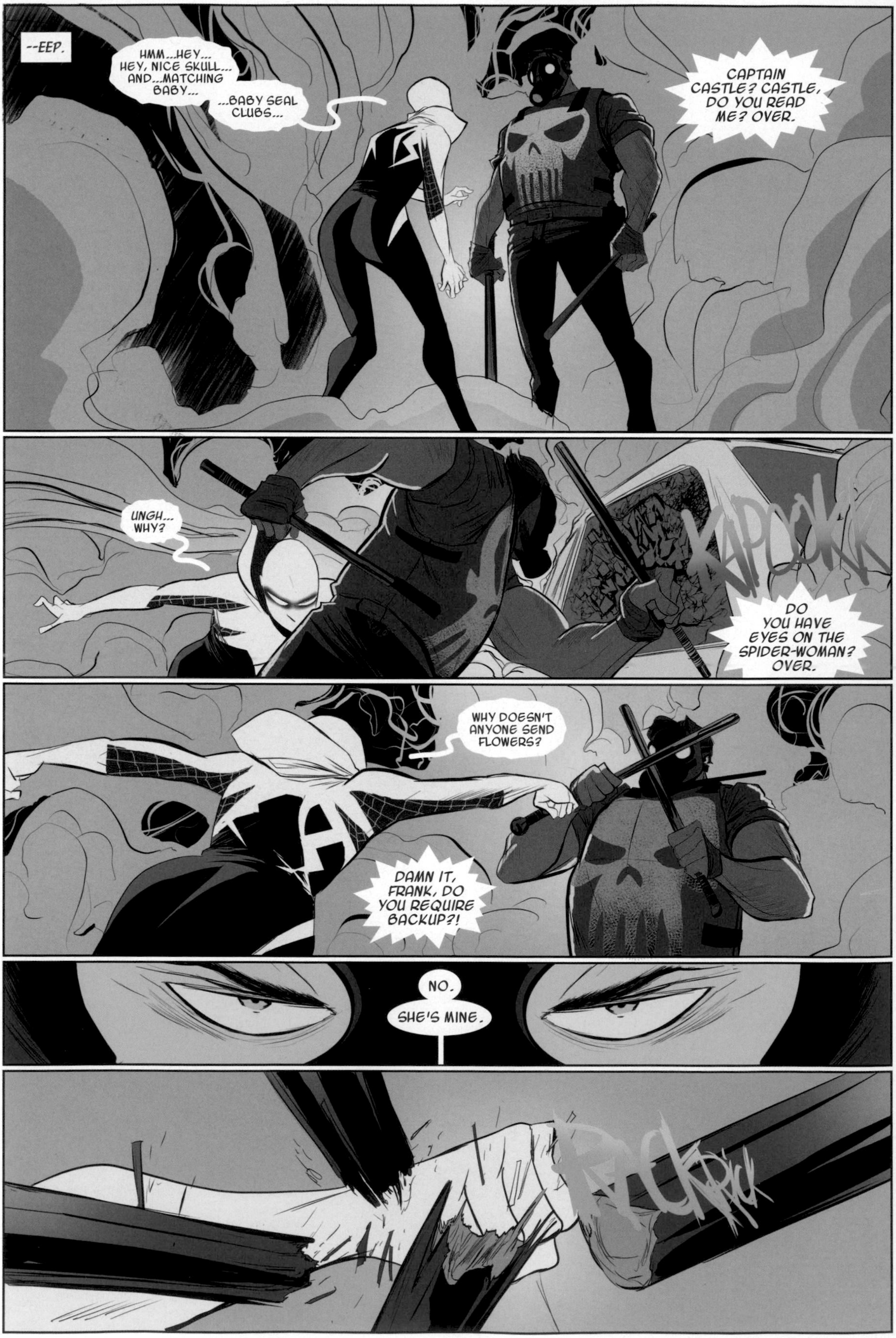
--EEP.
HMM...HEY... HEY, NICE SKULL... AND...MATCHING BABY...
...BABY SEAL CLUBS...
CAPTAIN CASTLE? CASTLE, DO YOU READ ME? OVER.
UNGH... WHY?
KAPOOKK
DO YOU HAVE EYES ON THE SPIDER-WOMAN? OVER.
WHY DOESN'T ANYONE SEND FLOWERS?
DAMN IT, FRANK, DO YOU REQUIRE BACKUP?!
NO.
SHE'S MINE.

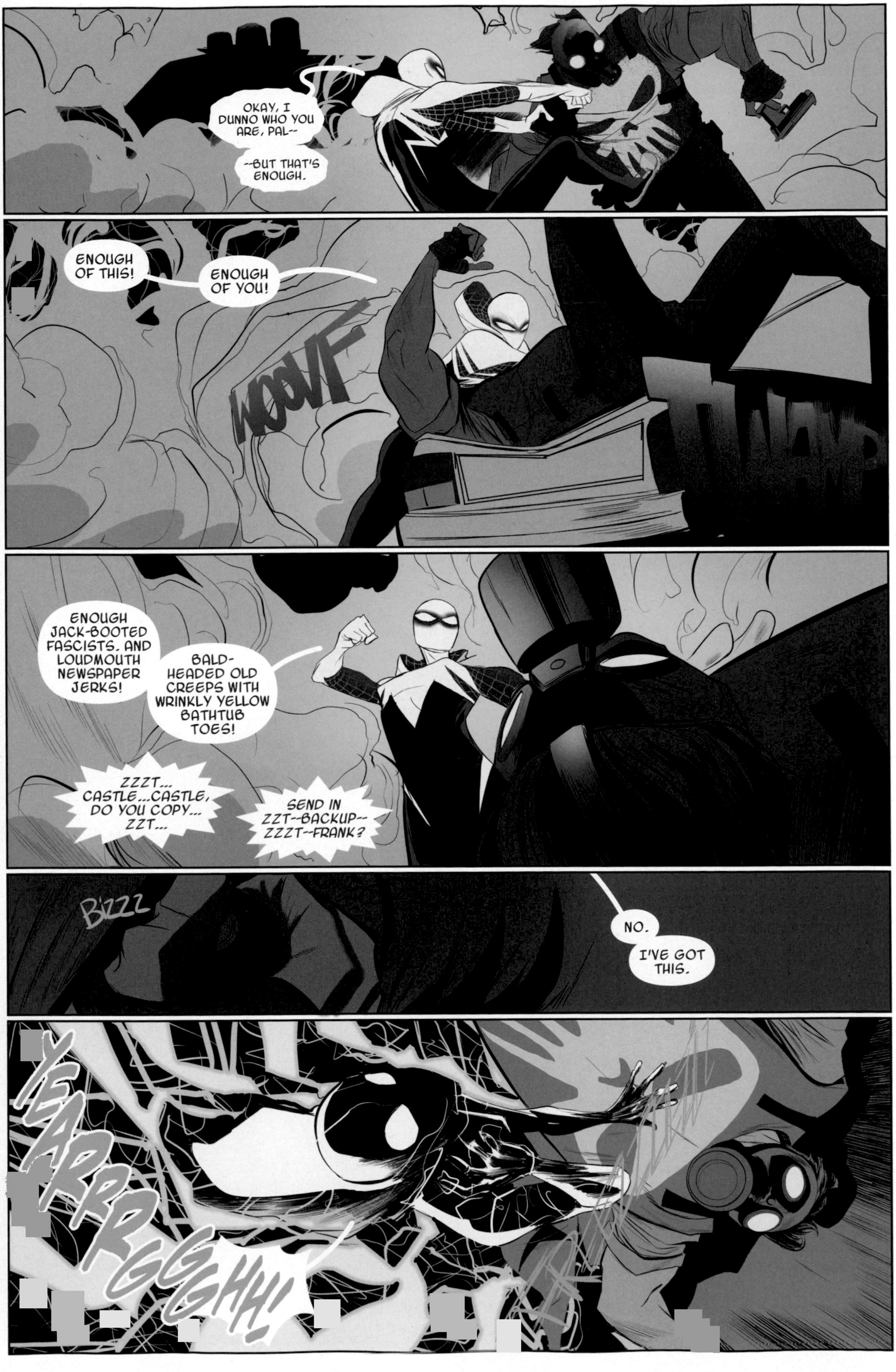

OKAY, I DUNNO WHO YOU ARE, PAL--
--BUT THAT'S ENOUGH.
ENOUGH OF THIS!
ENOUGH OF YOU!
WOOVF
THWAMP
ENOUGH JACK-BOOTED FASCISTS. AND LOUDMOUTH NEWSPAPER JERKS!
BALD-HEADED OLD CREEPS WITH WRINKLY YELLOW BATHTUB TOES!
ZZZT... CASTLE...CASTLE, DO YOU COPY... ZZT...
SEND IN ZZT--BACKUP-- ZZZT--FRANK?
BZZZ
NO.
I'VE GOT THIS.
YEARRRGGGHH!

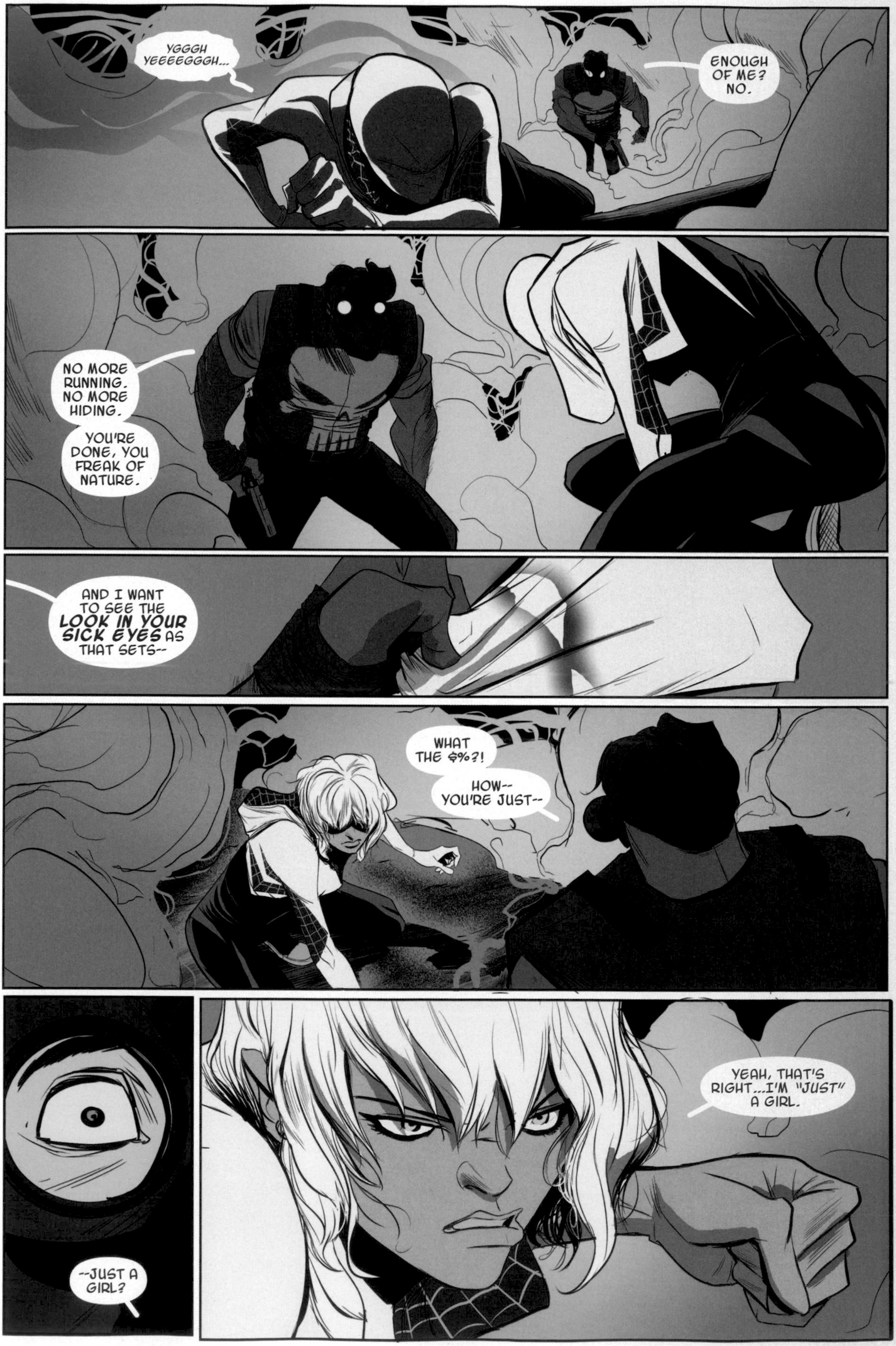
YGGGH YEEEEGGGH...
ENOUGH OF ME? NO.
NO MORE RUNNING. NO MORE HIDING.
YOU'RE DONE, YOU FREAK OF NATURE.
AND I WANT TO SEE THE ***LOOK IN YOUR SICK EYES*** AS THAT SETS--
WHAT THE $%?!
HOW-- YOU'RE JUST--
--JUST A GIRL?
YEAH, THAT'S RIGHT...I'M "JUST" A GIRL.

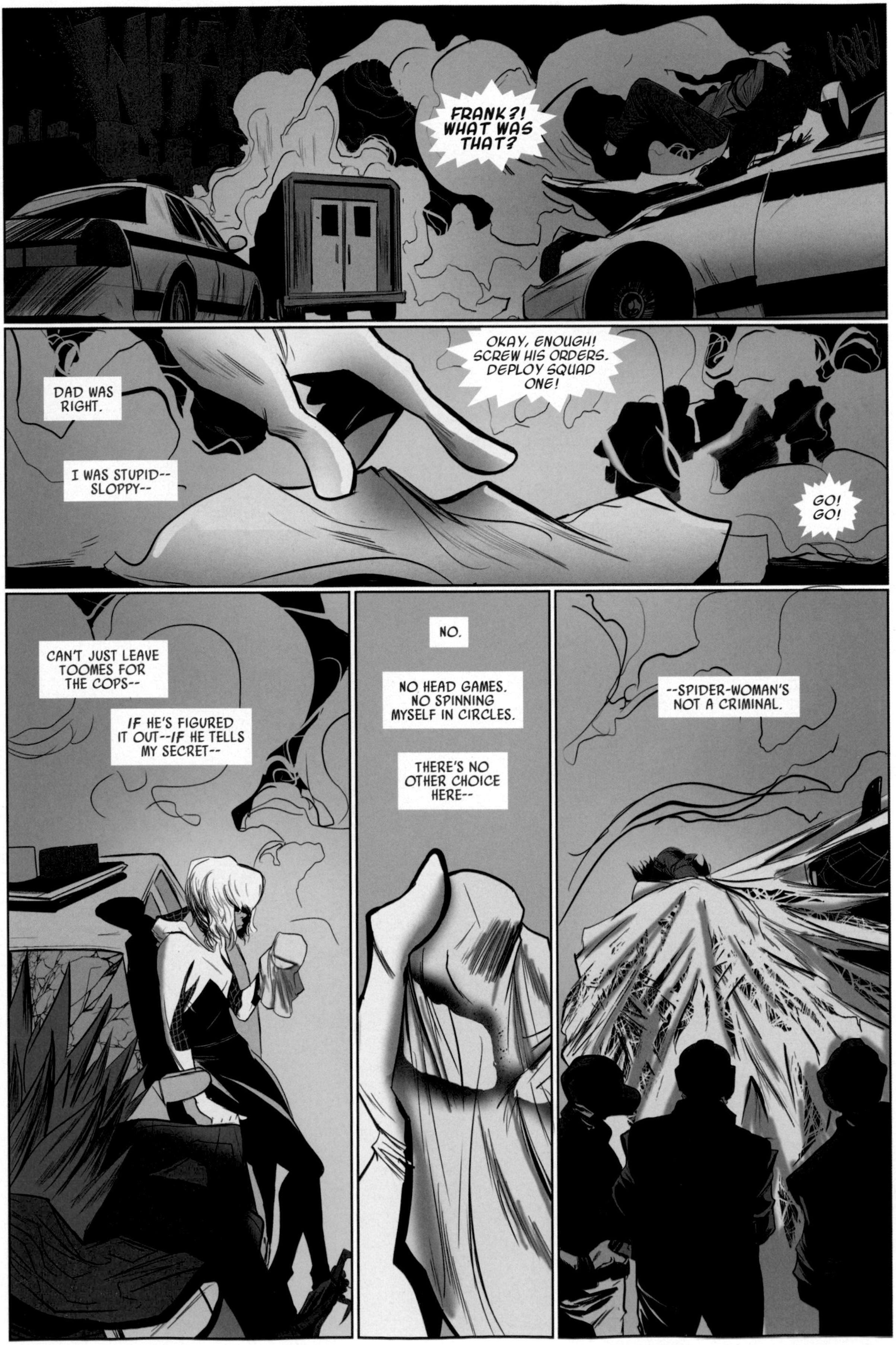
FRANK?! WHAT WAS THAT?
DAD WAS RIGHT.
I WAS STUPID--SLOPPY--
OKAY, ENOUGH! SCREW HIS ORDERS. DEPLOY SQUAD ONE!
GO! GO!
CAN'T JUST LEAVE TOOMES FOR THE COPS--
*IF* HE'S FIGURED IT OUT--*IF* HE TELLS MY SECRET--
NO.
NO HEAD GAMES. NO SPINNING MYSELF IN CIRCLES.
THERE'S NO OTHER CHOICE HERE--
--SPIDER-WOMAN'S NOT A CRIMINAL.

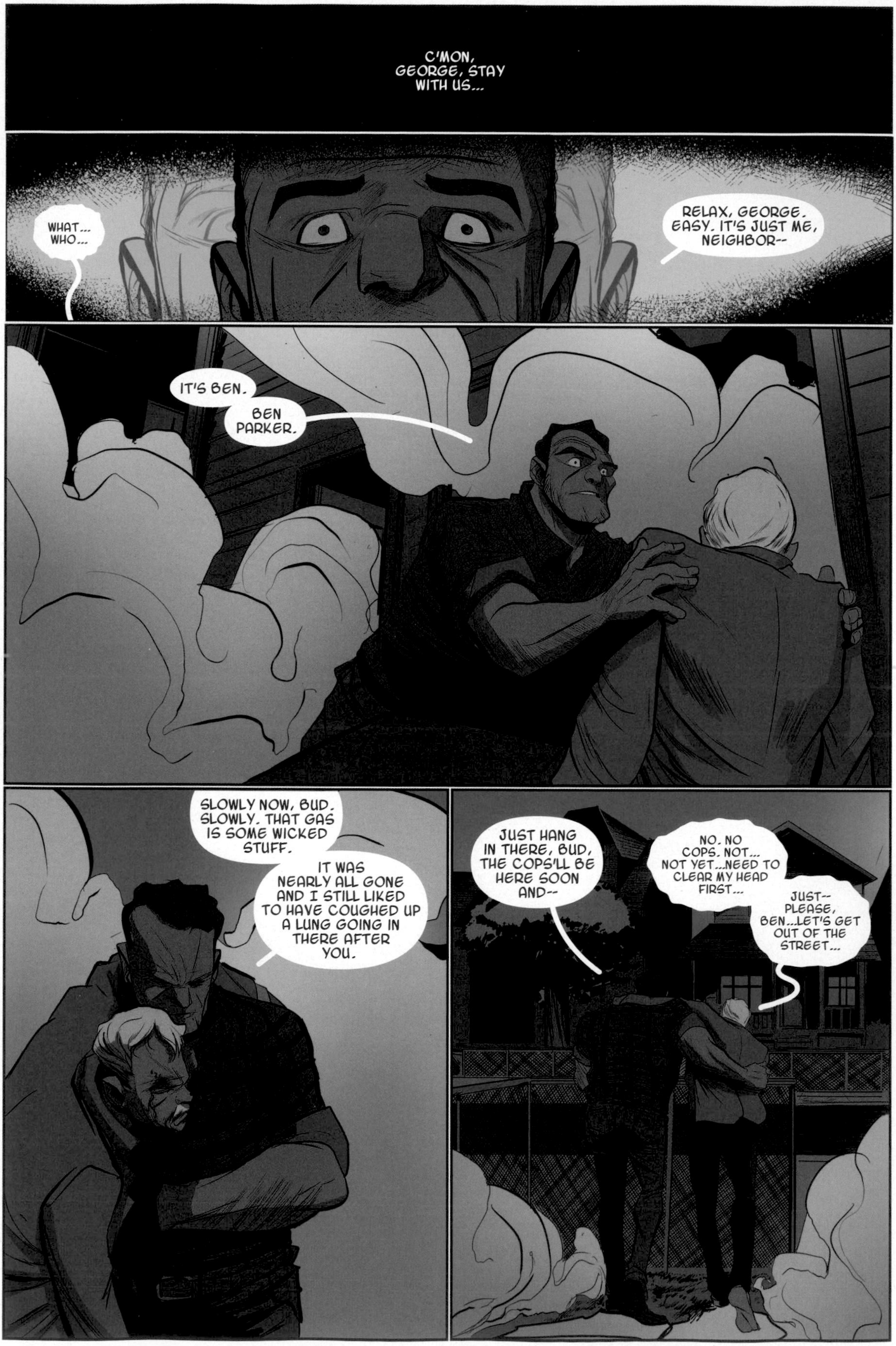

C'MON, GEORGE, STAY WITH US...
WHAT... WHO...
RELAX, GEORGE. EASY. IT'S JUST ME, NEIGHBOR--
IT'S BEN.
BEN PARKER.
SLOWLY NOW, BUD. SLOWLY. THAT GAS IS SOME WICKED STUFF.
IT WAS NEARLY ALL GONE AND I STILL LIKED TO HAVE COUGHED UP A LUNG GOING IN THERE AFTER YOU.
JUST HANG IN THERE, BUD, THE COPS'LL BE HERE SOON AND--
NO. NO COPS. NOT... NOT YET...NEED TO CLEAR MY HEAD FIRST...
JUST-- PLEASE, BEN...LET'S GET OUT OF THE STREET...

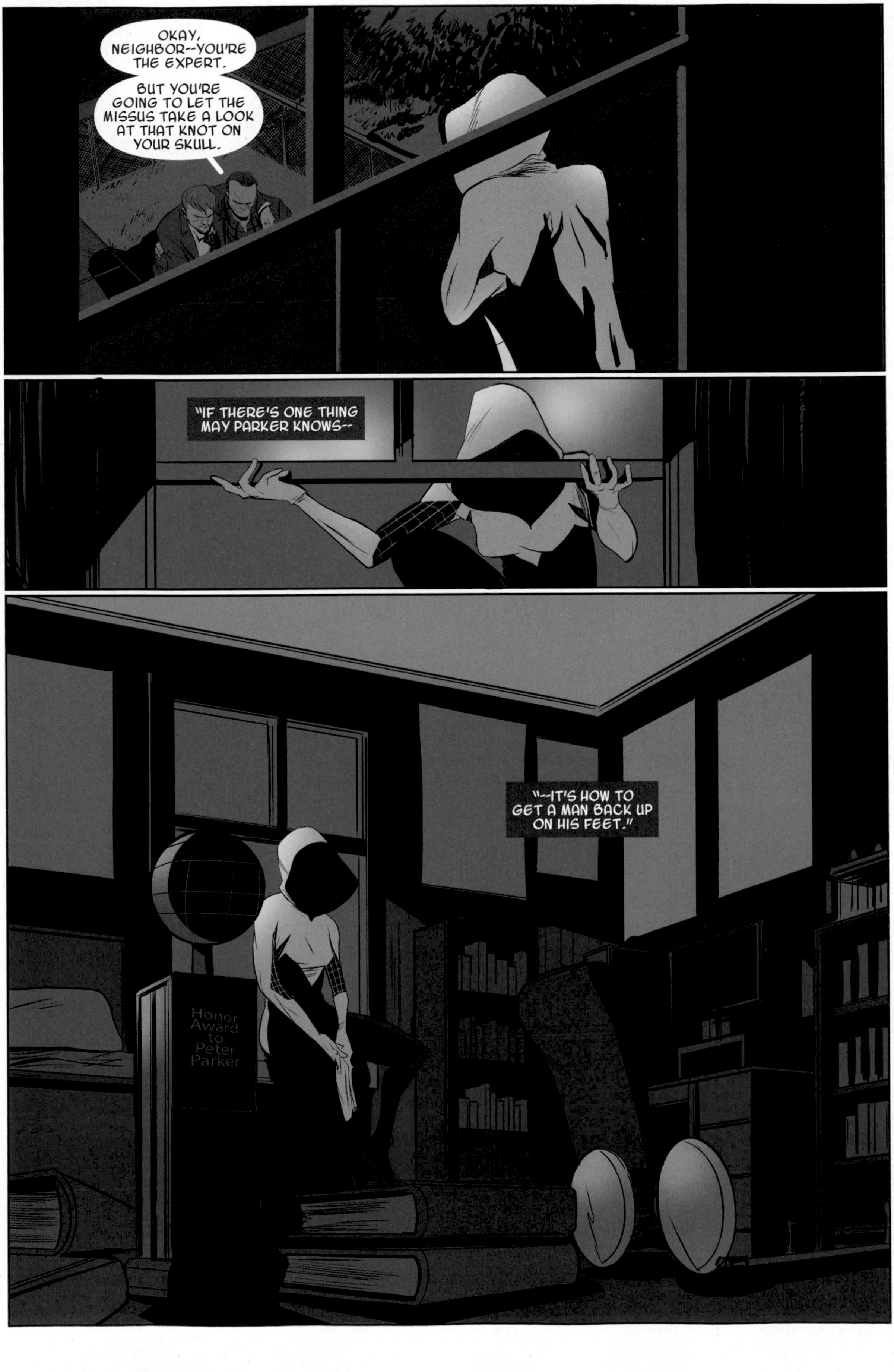
OKAY, NEIGHBOR--YOU'RE THE EXPERT.
BUT YOU'RE GOING TO LET THE MISSUS TAKE A LOOK AT THAT KNOT ON YOUR SKULL.
"IF THERE'S ONE THING MAY PARKER KNOWS--
Honor Award to Peter Parker
"--IT'S HOW TO GET A MAN BACK UP ON HIS FEET."

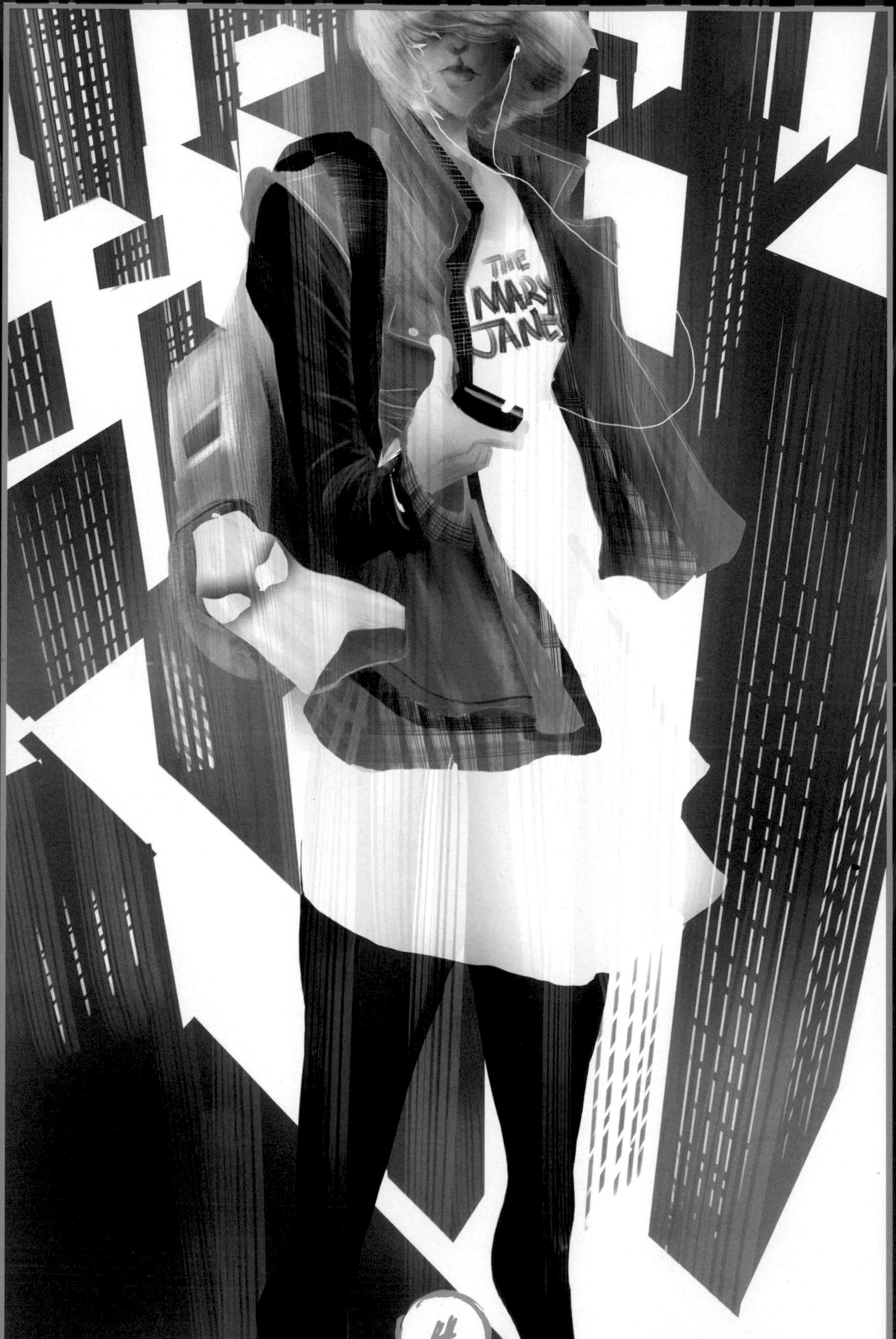
THE MARY JANES
4

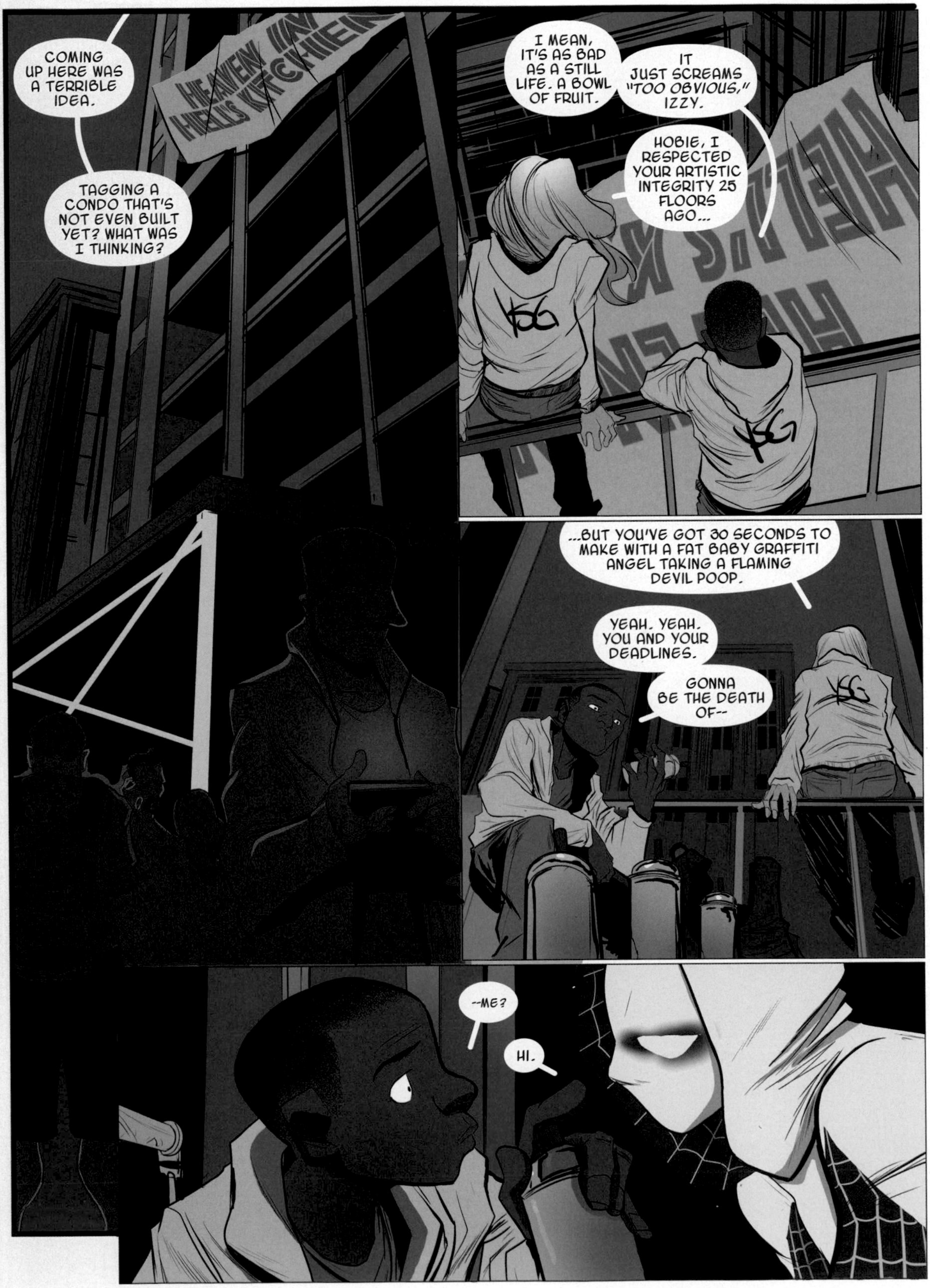

COMING UP HERE WAS A TERRIBLE IDEA.
TAGGING A CONDO THAT'S NOT EVEN BUILT YET? WHAT WAS I THINKING?
HEAVEN IN HELL'S KITCHEN
I MEAN, IT'S AS BAD AS A STILL LIFE. A BOWL OF FRUIT.
IT JUST SCREAMS "TOO OBVIOUS," IZZY.
HOBIE, I RESPECTED YOUR ARTISTIC INTEGRITY 25 FLOORS AGO...
...BUT YOU'VE GOT 30 SECONDS TO MAKE WITH A FAT BABY GRAFFITI ANGEL TAKING A FLAMING DEVIL POOP.
YEAH. YEAH. YOU AND YOUR DEADLINES.
GONNA BE THE DEATH OF--
--ME?
HI.

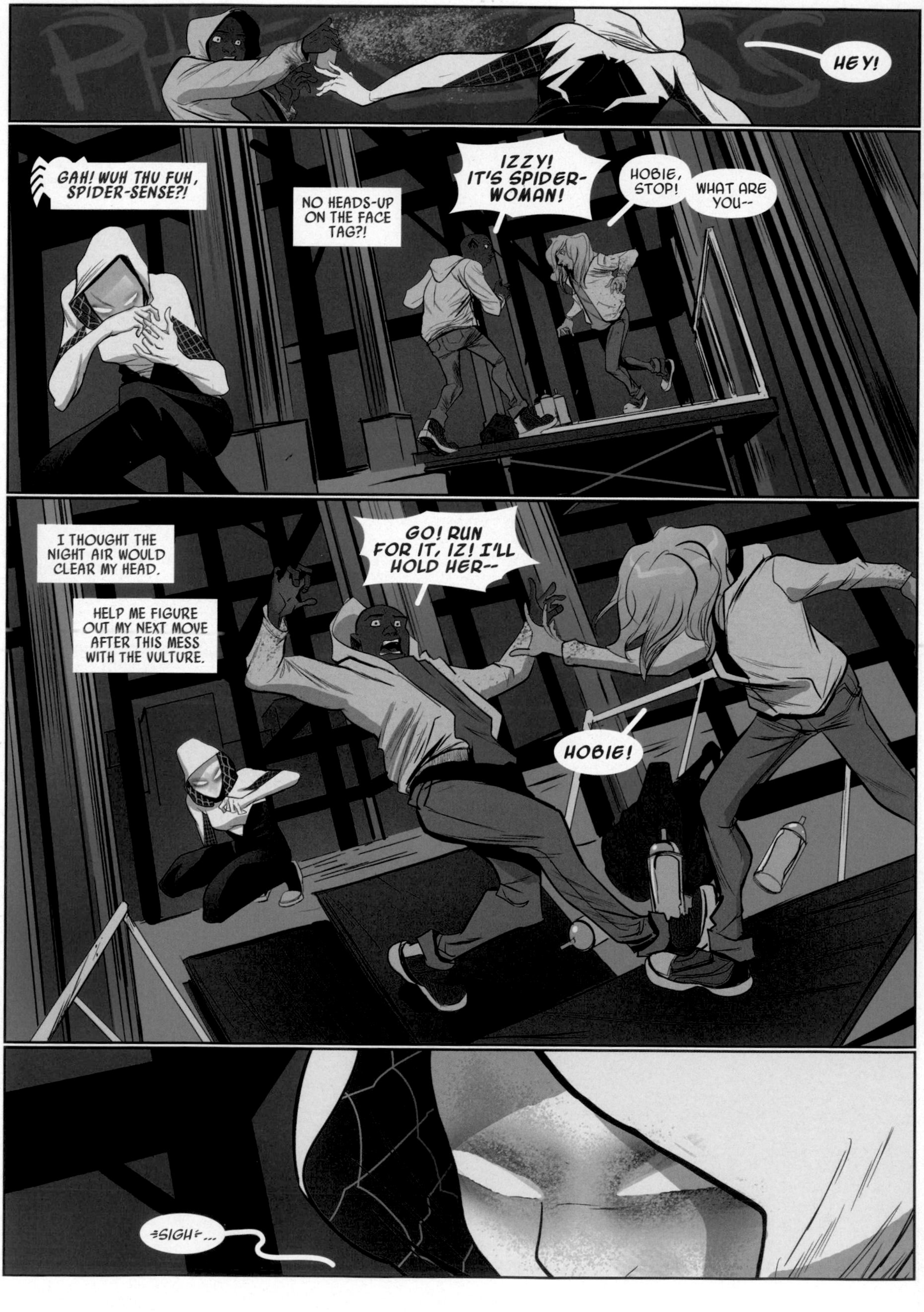
HEY!
GAH! WUH THU FUH, SPIDER-SENSE?!
NO HEADS-UP ON THE FACE TAG?!
IZZY! IT'S SPIDER-WOMAN!
HOBIE, STOP!
WHAT ARE YOU--
I THOUGHT THE NIGHT AIR WOULD CLEAR MY HEAD.
HELP ME FIGURE OUT MY NEXT MOVE AFTER THIS MESS WITH THE VULTURE.
GO! RUN FOR IT, IZ! I'LL HOLD HER--
HOBIE!
=SIGH=...

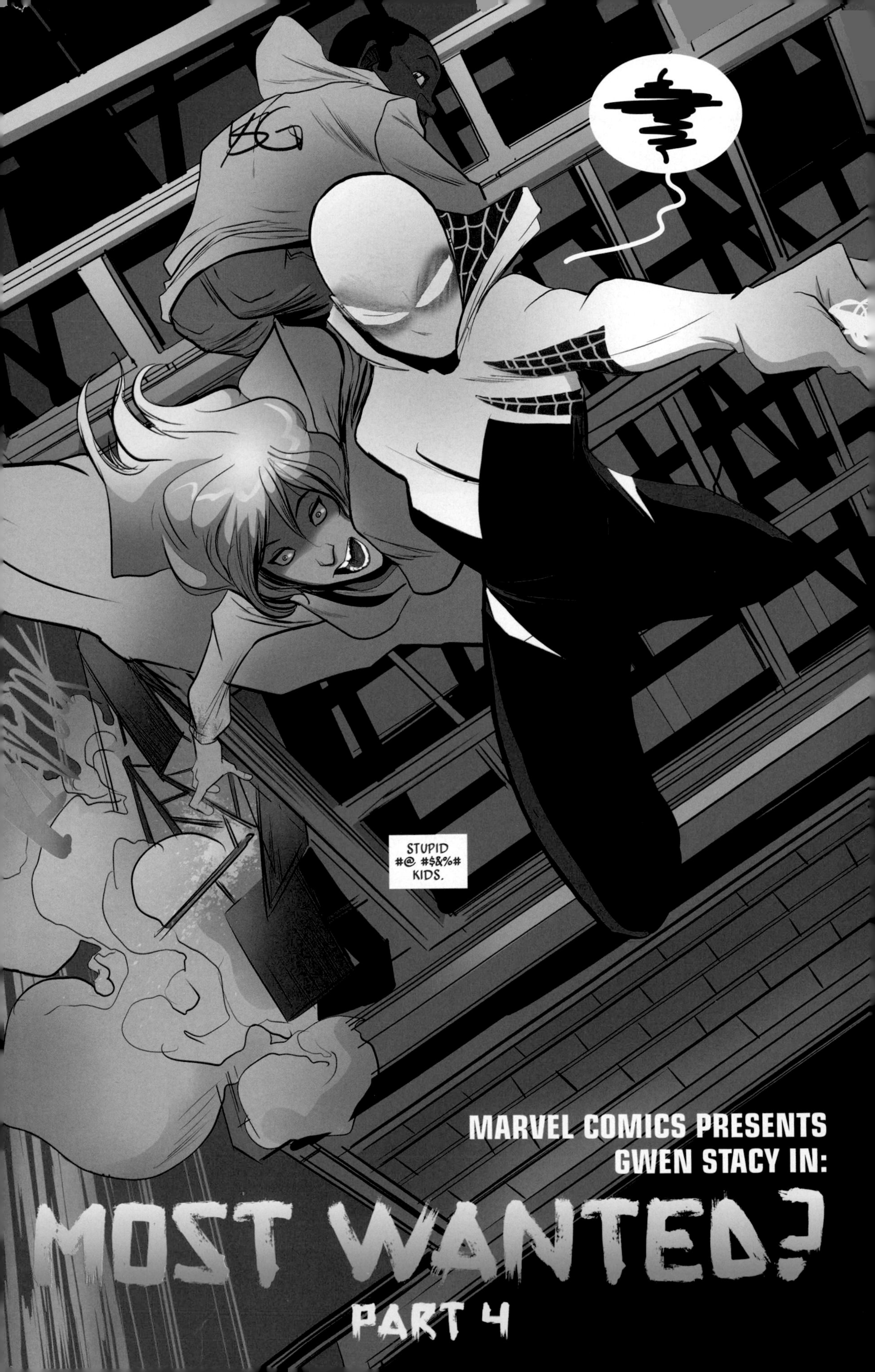
STUPID #@ #$&%# KIDS.
MARVEL COMICS PRESENTS
GWEN STACY IN:
MOST WANTED?
PART 4

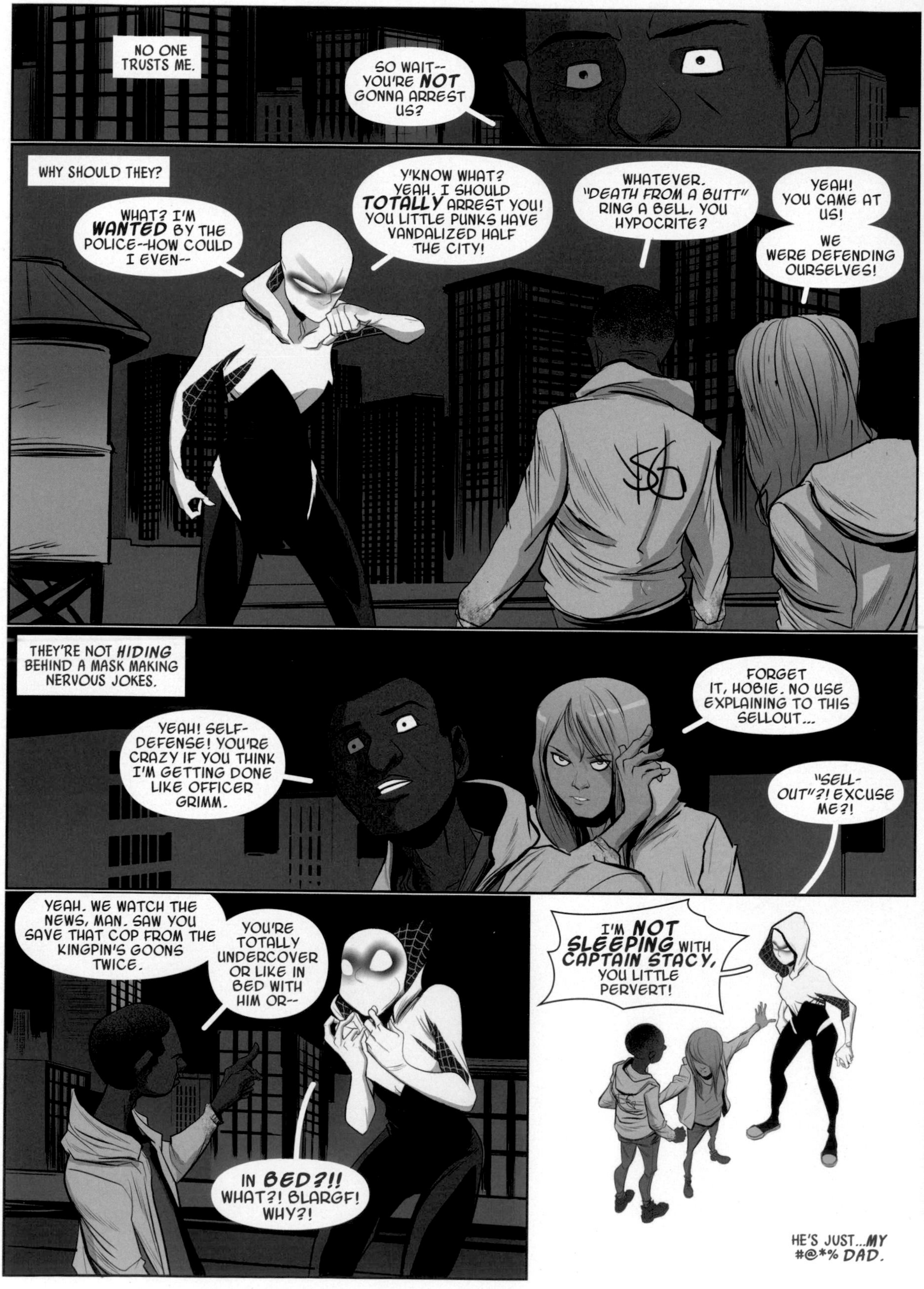
NO ONE TRUSTS ME.
SO WAIT-- YOU'RE NOT GONNA ARREST US?
WHY SHOULD THEY?
WHAT? I'M WANTED BY THE POLICE--HOW COULD I EVEN--
Y'KNOW WHAT? YEAH. I SHOULD TOTALLY ARREST YOU! YOU LITTLE PUNKS HAVE VANDALIZED HALF THE CITY!
WHATEVER. "DEATH FROM A BUTT" RING A BELL, YOU HYPOCRITE?
YEAH! YOU CAME AT US!
WE WERE DEFENDING OURSELVES!
THEY'RE NOT HIDING BEHIND A MASK MAKING NERVOUS JOKES.
YEAH! SELF-DEFENSE! YOU'RE CRAZY IF YOU THINK I'M GETTING DONE LIKE OFFICER GRIMM.
FORGET IT, HOBIE. NO USE EXPLAINING TO THIS SELLOUT...
"SELL-OUT"?! EXCUSE ME?!
YEAH. WE WATCH THE NEWS, MAN. SAW YOU SAVE THAT COP FROM THE KINGPIN'S GOONS TWICE.
YOU'RE TOTALLY UNDERCOVER OR LIKE IN BED WITH HIM OR--
IN BED?!! WHAT?! BLARGF! WHY?!
I'M NOT SLEEPING WITH CAPTAIN STACY, YOU LITTLE PERVERT!
HE'S JUST...MY #@*% DAD.

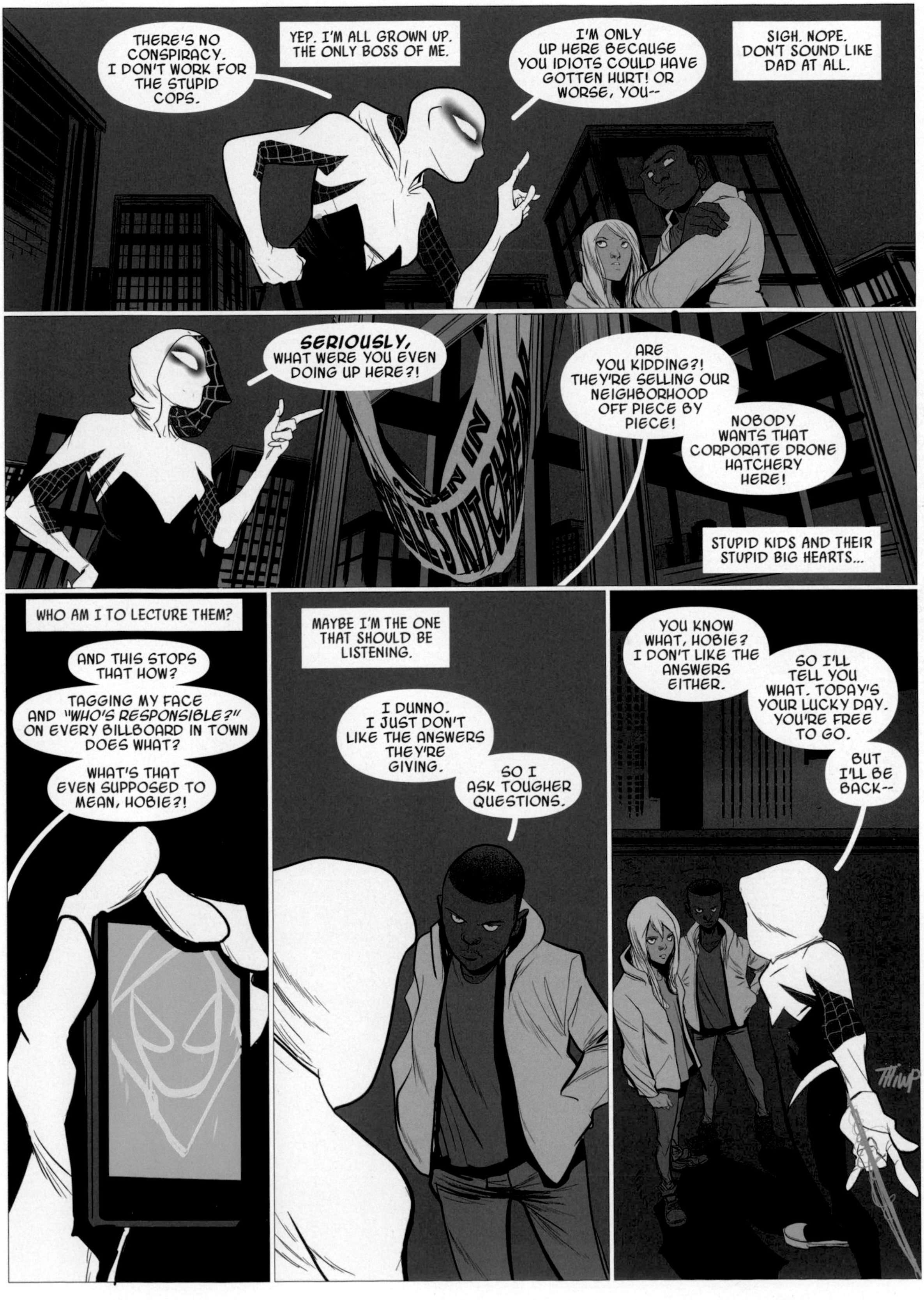
THERE'S NO CONSPIRACY. I DON'T WORK FOR THE STUPID COPS.
YEP. I'M ALL GROWN UP. THE ONLY BOSS OF ME.
I'M ONLY UP HERE BECAUSE YOU IDIOTS COULD HAVE GOTTEN HURT! OR WORSE, YOU--
SIGH. NOPE. DON'T SOUND LIKE DAD AT ALL.
SERIOUSLY, WHAT WERE YOU EVEN DOING UP HERE?!
HELL'S KITCHEN
ARE YOU KIDDING?! THEY'RE SELLING OUR NEIGHBORHOOD OFF PIECE BY PIECE!
NOBODY WANTS THAT CORPORATE DRONE HATCHERY HERE!
STUPID KIDS AND THEIR STUPID BIG HEARTS...
WHO AM I TO LECTURE THEM?
AND THIS STOPS THAT HOW?
TAGGING MY FACE AND "WHO'S RESPONSIBLE?" ON EVERY BILLBOARD IN TOWN DOES WHAT?
WHAT'S THAT EVEN SUPPOSED TO MEAN, HOBIE?!
MAYBE I'M THE ONE THAT SHOULD BE LISTENING.
I DUNNO. I JUST DON'T LIKE THE ANSWERS THEY'RE GIVING.
SO I ASK TOUGHER QUESTIONS.
YOU KNOW WHAT, HOBIE? I DON'T LIKE THE ANSWERS EITHER.
SO I'LL TELL YOU WHAT. TODAY'S YOUR LUCKY DAY. YOU'RE FREE TO GO.
BUT I'LL BE BACK--
THWP

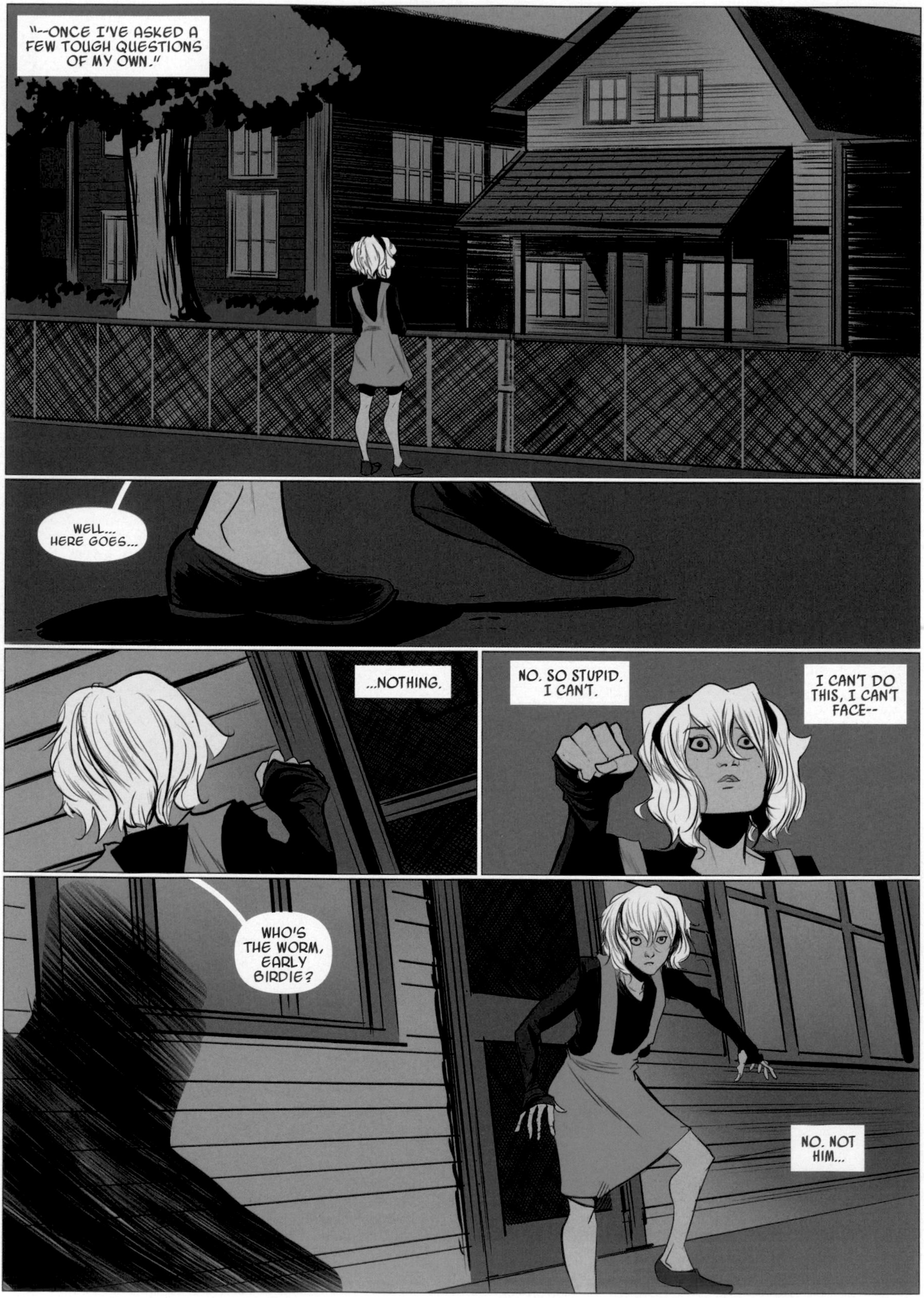
"--ONCE I'VE ASKED A FEW TOUGH QUESTIONS OF MY OWN."
WELL... HERE GOES...
...NOTHING.
NO. SO STUPID. I CAN'T.
I CAN'T DO THIS, I CAN'T FACE--
WHO'S THE WORM, EARLY BIRDIE?
NO. NOT HIM...

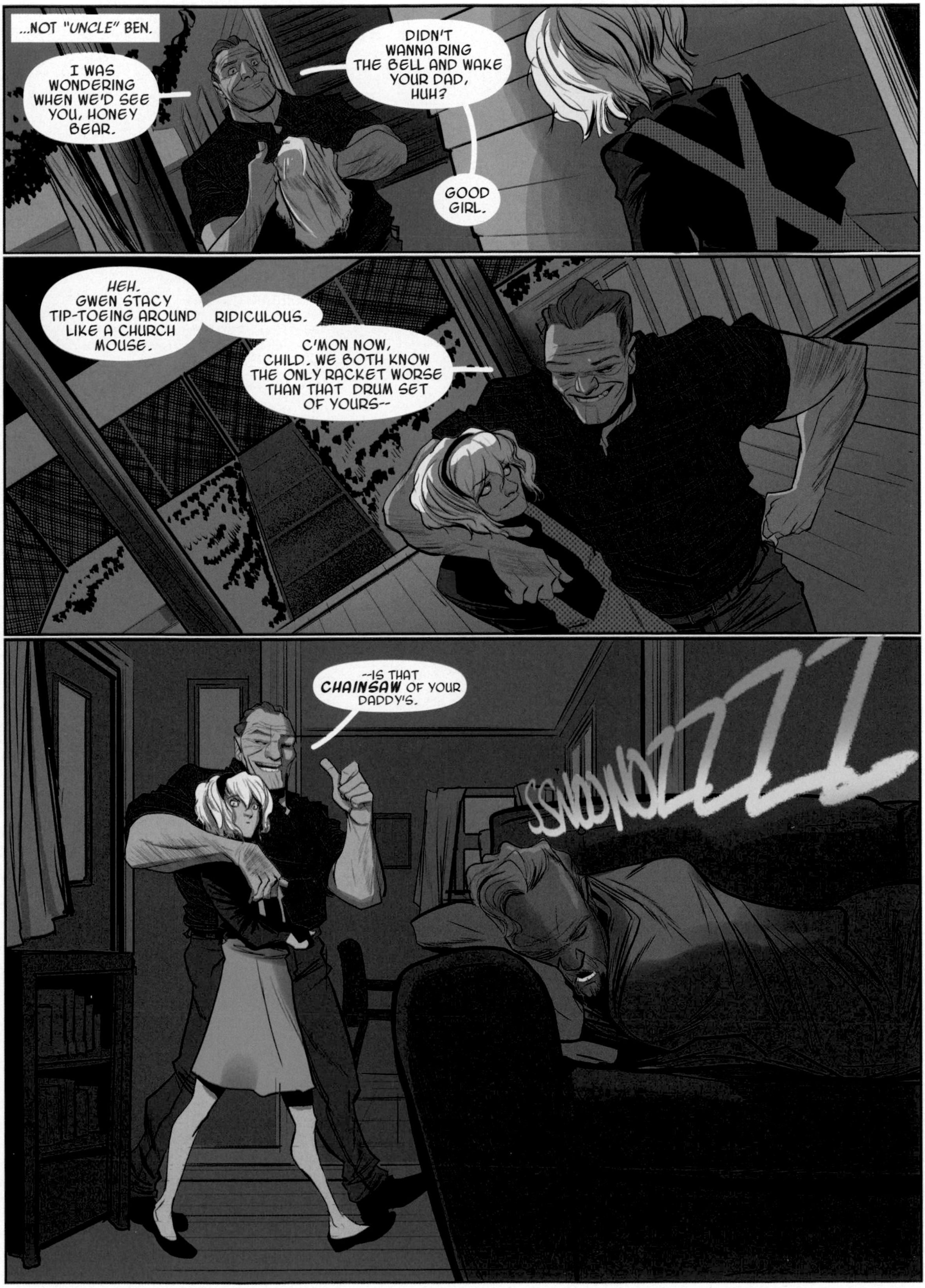
...NOT "UNCLE" BEN.
I WAS WONDERING WHEN WE'D SEE YOU, HONEY BEAR.
DIDN'T WANNA RING THE BELL AND WAKE YOUR DAD, HUH?
GOOD GIRL.
HEH. GWEN STACY TIP-TOEING AROUND LIKE A CHURCH MOUSE.
RIDICULOUS.
C'MON NOW, CHILD. WE BOTH KNOW THE ONLY RACKET WORSE THAN THAT DRUM SET OF YOURS--
--IS THAT CHAINSAW OF YOUR DADDY'S.
SSNOONOZZZZ

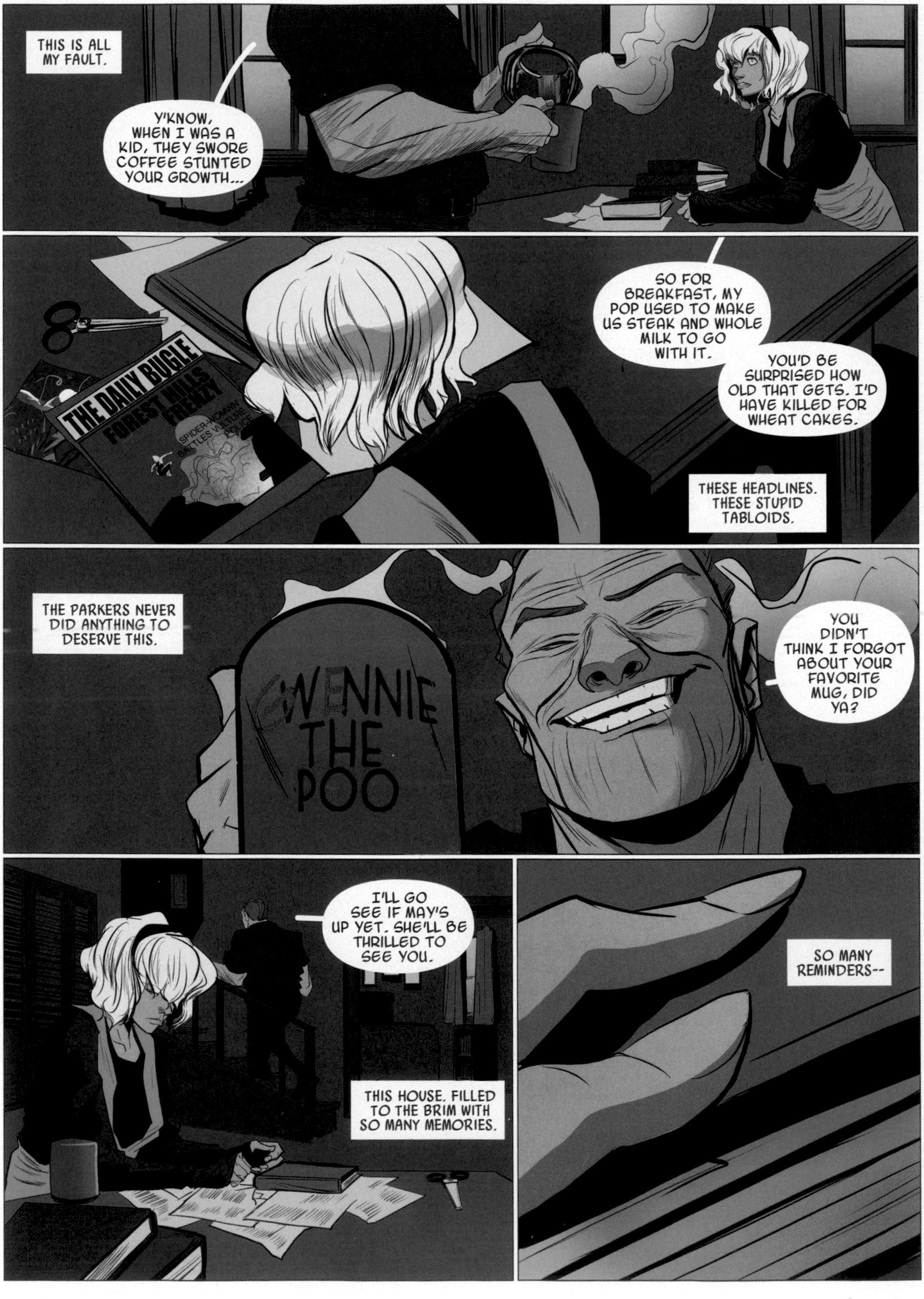
THIS IS ALL MY FAULT.
Y'KNOW, WHEN I WAS A KID, THEY SWORE COFFEE STUNTED YOUR GROWTH...
THE DAILY BUGLE
FOREST HILLS FRENZY
SPIDER-WOMAN BATTLES VULTURE POLICE
SO FOR BREAKFAST, MY POP USED TO MAKE US STEAK AND WHOLE MILK TO GO WITH IT.
YOU'D BE SURPRISED HOW OLD THAT GETS. I'D HAVE KILLED FOR WHEAT CAKES.
THESE HEADLINES. THESE STUPID TABLOIDS.
THE PARKERS NEVER DID ANYTHING TO DESERVE THIS.
WENNIE THE POO
YOU DIDN'T THINK I FORGOT ABOUT YOUR FAVORITE MUG, DID YA?
I'LL GO SEE IF MAY'S UP YET. SHE'LL BE THRILLED TO SEE YOU.
THIS HOUSE. FILLED TO THE BRIM WITH SO MANY MEMORIES.
SO MANY REMINDERS--

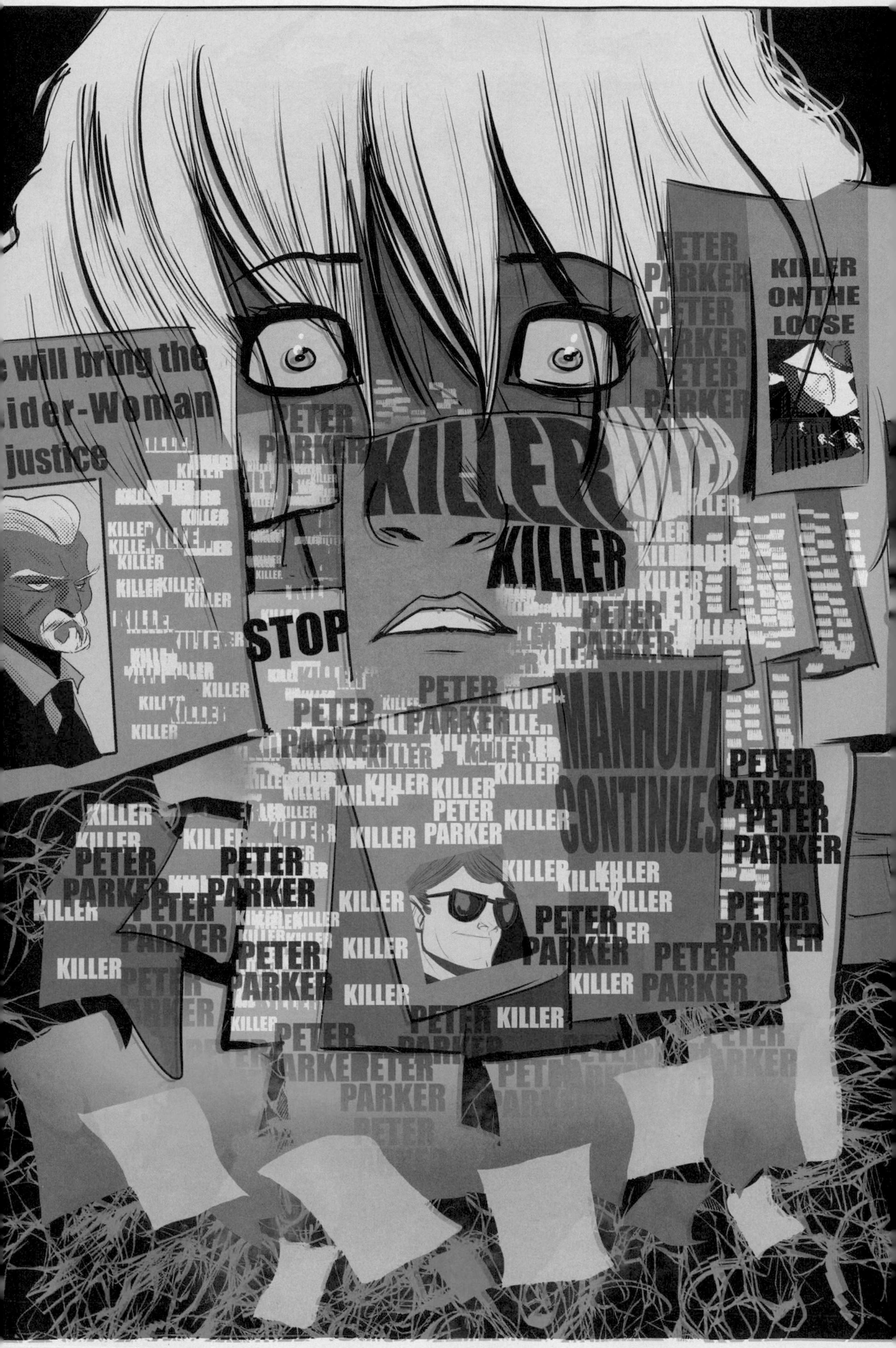
will bring the
ider-Woman
justice
KILLER
KILLER
STOP
PETER PARKER
KILLER ON THE LOOSE
MANHUNT CONTINUES
PETER PARKER
KILLER

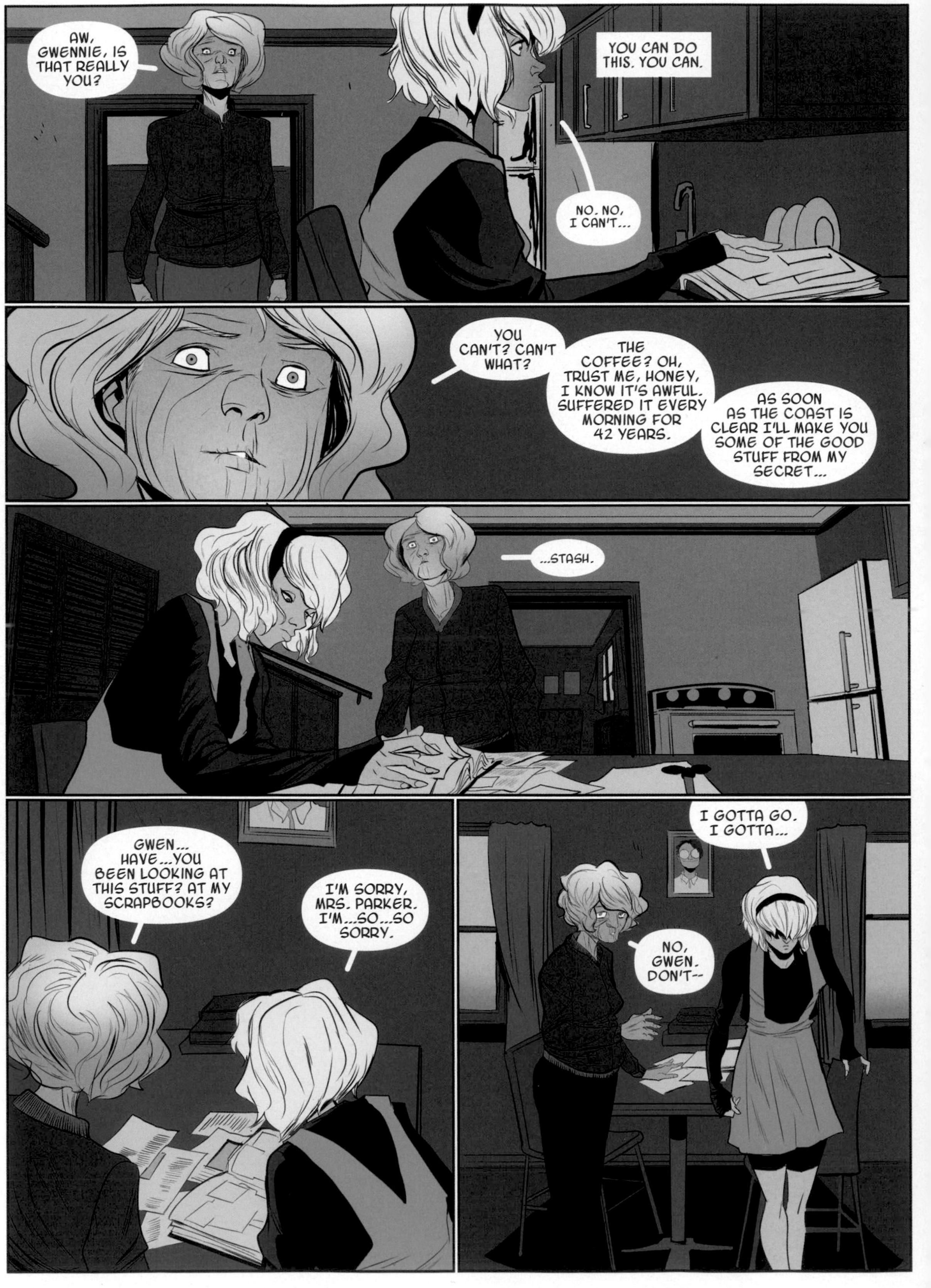
AW, GWENNIE, IS THAT REALLY YOU?
YOU CAN DO THIS. YOU CAN.
NO. NO, I CAN'T...
YOU CAN'T? CAN'T WHAT?
THE COFFEE? OH, TRUST ME, HONEY, I KNOW IT'S AWFUL. SUFFERED IT EVERY MORNING FOR 42 YEARS.
AS SOON AS THE COAST IS CLEAR I'LL MAKE YOU SOME OF THE GOOD STUFF FROM MY SECRET...
...STASH.
GWEN... HAVE...YOU BEEN LOOKING AT THIS STUFF? AT MY SCRAPBOOKS?
I'M SORRY, MRS. PARKER. I'M...SO...SO SORRY.
I GOTTA GO. I GOTTA...
NO, GWEN. DON'T--

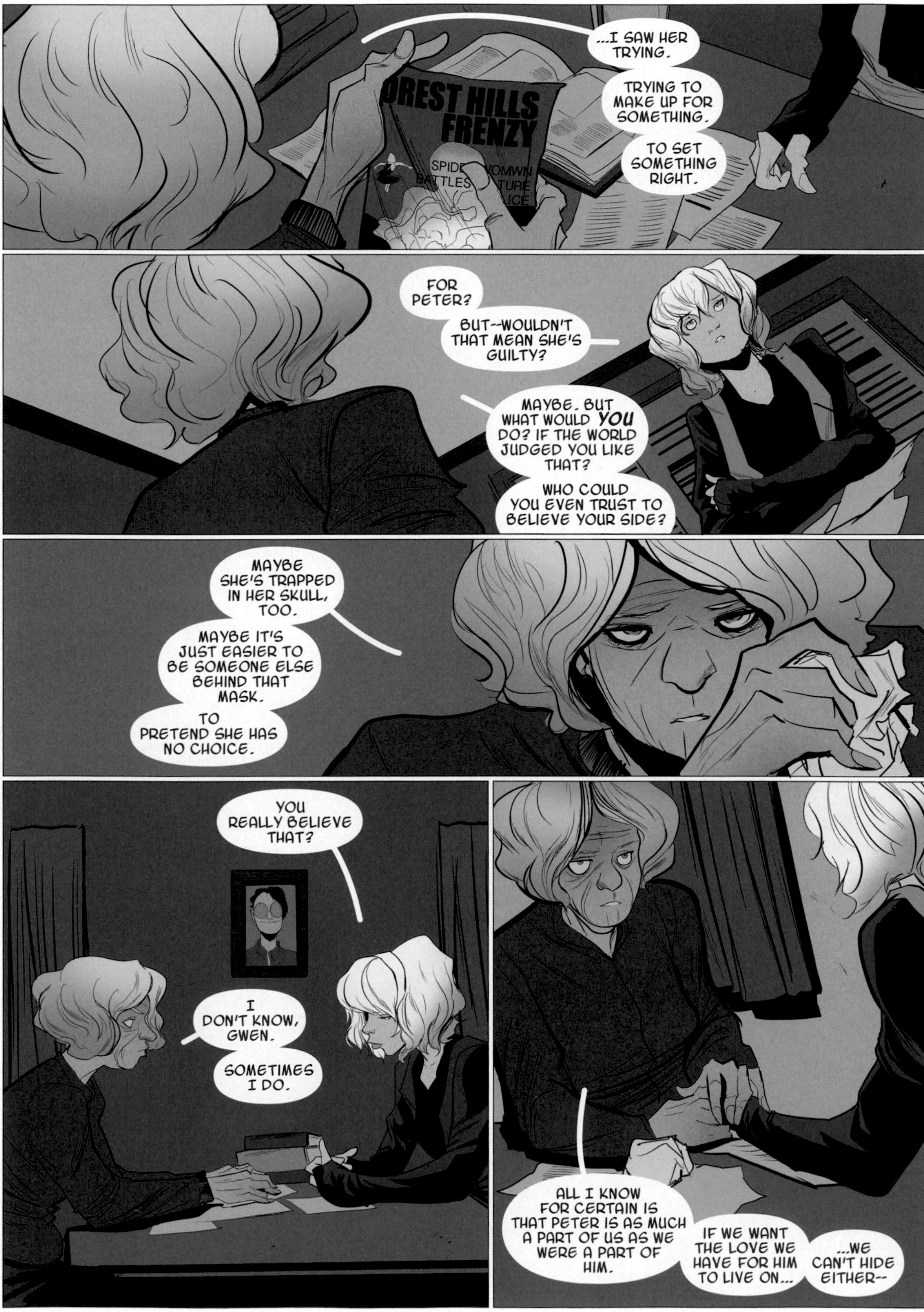
...I SAW HER TRYING.
TRYING TO MAKE UP FOR SOMETHING.
TO SET SOMETHING RIGHT.
FRENZY
FOR PETER?
BUT--WOULDN'T THAT MEAN SHE'S GUILTY?
MAYBE. BUT WHAT WOULD YOU DO? IF THE WORLD JUDGED YOU LIKE THAT?
WHO COULD YOU EVEN TRUST TO BELIEVE YOUR SIDE?
MAYBE SHE'S TRAPPED IN HER SKULL, TOO.
MAYBE IT'S JUST EASIER TO BE SOMEONE ELSE BEHIND THAT MASK.
TO PRETEND SHE HAS NO CHOICE.
YOU REALLY BELIEVE THAT?
I DON'T KNOW, GWEN.
SOMETIMES I DO.
ALL I KNOW FOR CERTAIN IS THAT PETER IS AS MUCH A PART OF US AS WE WERE A PART OF HIM.
IF WE WANT THE LOVE WE HAVE FOR HIM TO LIVE ON...
...WE CAN'T HIDE EITHER--

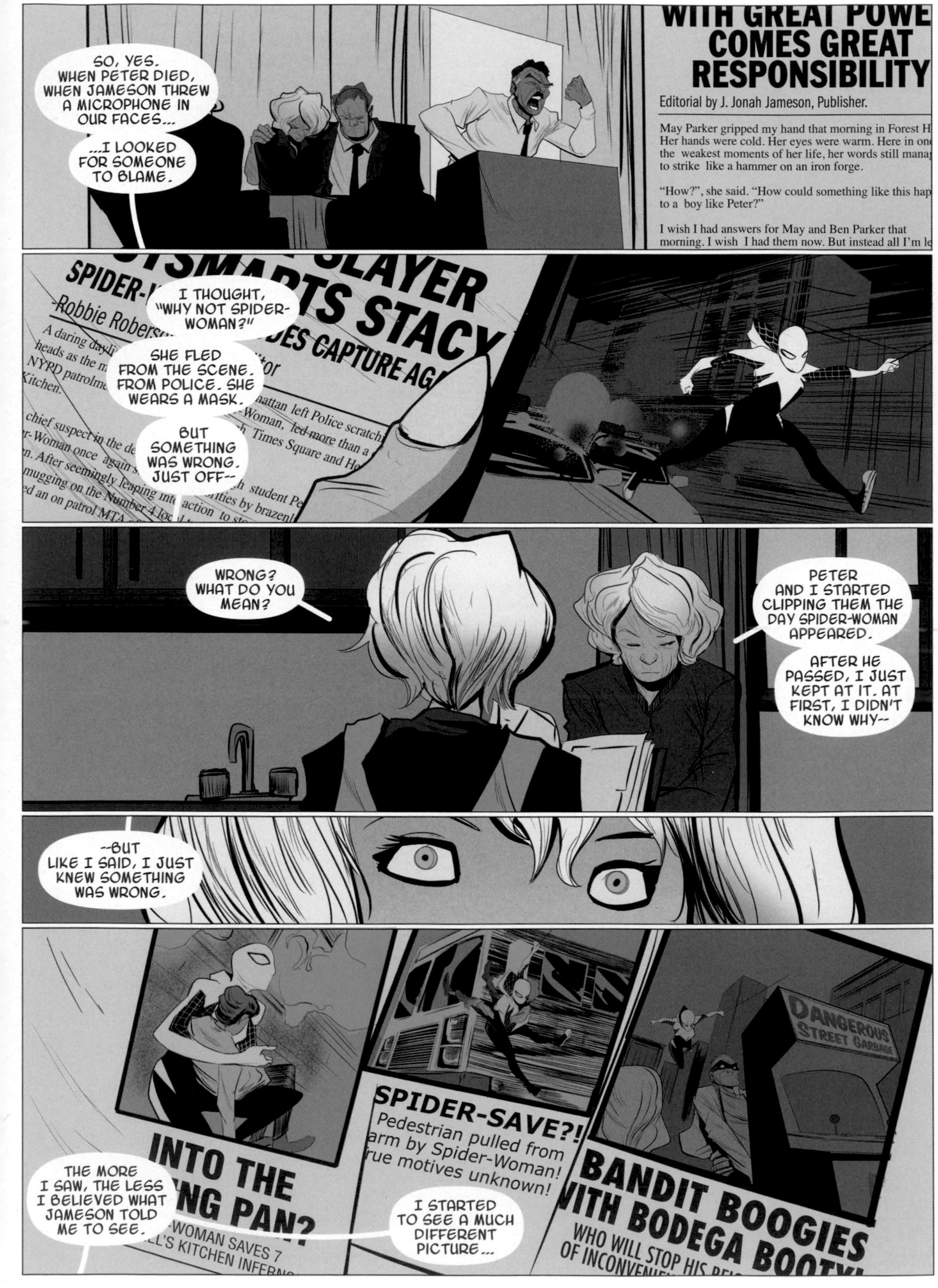
SO, YES. WHEN PETER DIED, WHEN JAMESON THREW A MICROPHONE IN OUR FACES...
...I LOOKED FOR SOMEONE TO BLAME.
COMES GREAT
RESPONSIBILITY
Editorial by J. Jonah Jameson, Publisher.
May Parker gripped my hand that morning in Forest H
Her hands were cold. Her eyes were warm. Here in on
the weakest moments of her life, her words still manag
to strike like a hammer on an iron forge.
"How?", she said. "How could something like this hap
to a boy like Peter?"
I wish I had answers for May and Ben Parker that
morning. I wish I had them now. But instead all I'm le
I THOUGHT, "WHY NOT SPIDER-WOMAN?"
SHE FLED FROM THE SCENE. FROM POLICE. SHE WEARS A MASK.
BUT SOMETHING WAS WRONG. JUST OFF--
WRONG? WHAT DO YOU MEAN?
PETER AND I STARTED CLIPPING THEM THE DAY SPIDER-WOMAN APPEARED.
AFTER HE PASSED, I JUST KEPT AT IT. AT FIRST, I DIDN'T KNOW WHY--
--BUT LIKE I SAID, I JUST KNEW SOMETHING WAS WRONG.
DANGEROUS STREET GARBAGE
SPIDER-SAVE?!
Pedestrian pulled from
arm by Spider-Woman!
rue motives unknown!
INTO THE
NG PAN?
BANDIT BOOGIES
WITH BODEGA BOOTY
THE MORE I SAW, THE LESS I BELIEVED WHAT JAMESON TOLD ME TO SEE.
I STARTED TO SEE A MUCH DIFFERENT PICTURE...

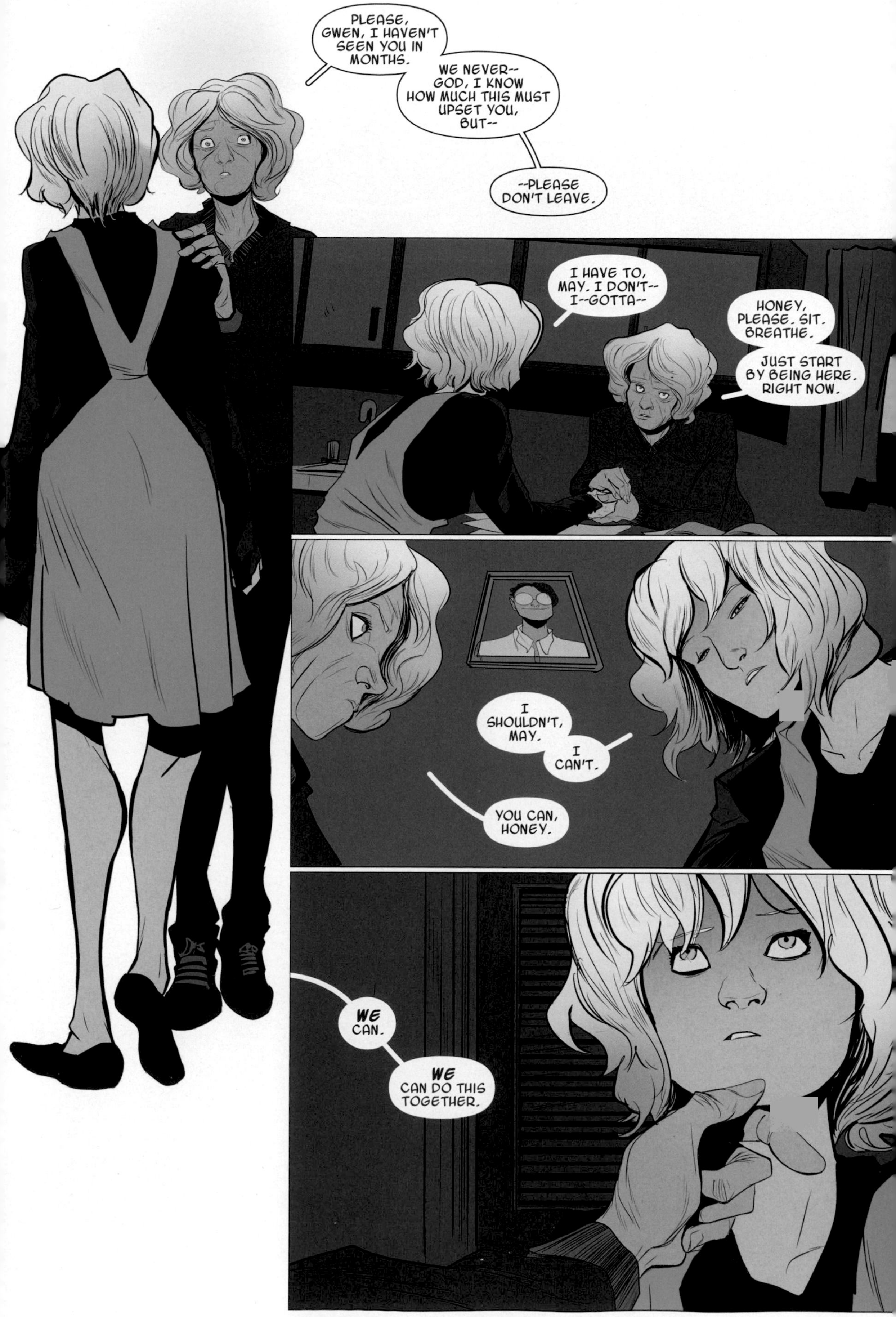
PLEASE, GWEN, I HAVEN'T SEEN YOU IN MONTHS.
WE NEVER-- GOD, I KNOW HOW MUCH THIS MUST UPSET YOU, BUT--
--PLEASE DON'T LEAVE.
I HAVE TO, MAY. I DON'T-- I--GOTTA--
HONEY, PLEASE. SIT. BREATHE.
JUST START BY BEING HERE. RIGHT NOW.
I SHOULDN'T, MAY.
I CAN'T.
YOU CAN, HONEY.
WE CAN.
WE CAN DO THIS TOGETHER.

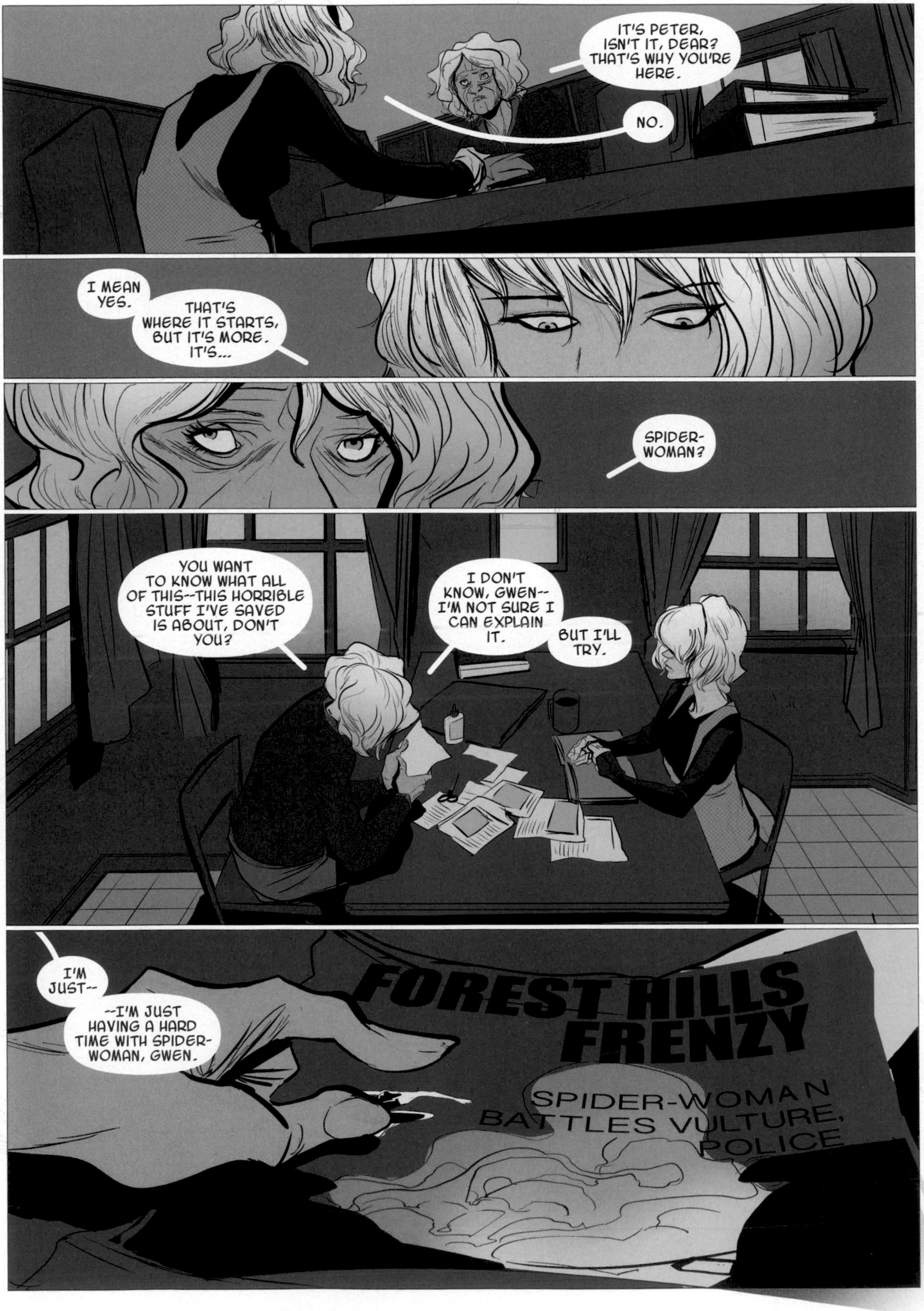
IT'S PETER, ISN'T IT, DEAR? THAT'S WHY YOU'RE HERE.
NO.
I MEAN YES.
THAT'S WHERE IT STARTS, BUT IT'S MORE. IT'S...
SPIDER-WOMAN?
YOU WANT TO KNOW WHAT ALL OF THIS--THIS HORRIBLE STUFF I'VE SAVED IS ABOUT, DON'T YOU?
I DON'T KNOW, GWEN-- I'M NOT SURE I CAN EXPLAIN IT.
BUT I'LL TRY.
I'M JUST--
--I'M JUST HAVING A HARD TIME WITH SPIDER-WOMAN, GWEN.
FOREST HILLS FRENZY
SPIDER-WOMAN BATTLES VULTURE, POLICE

A HARD TIME?

WHAT-- WHAT DO YOU MEAN?

**MYSTERIOUS FIGURE WEAVES WEB OF INTRIGUE**

**FRIEND TO CITY OR MENACE TO SOCIETY?**

**CRIME AT RECO LOW**

SPIDE STILL A

BY BEN URICH,

According to report-- major f crimes historic borough months in spite of u authorities have faile to bring their most igh profile target, The Spider-Woman, to jus ice.

"Crime is down and own dramatically in many areas," Captain eorge Stacy said at a rooklyn news confere ce to

I...I'M NOT SURE I KNOW WHERE TO BEGIN--

I DON'T KNOW HOW IT BEGAN. BUT I ALWAYS KNEW--

--FROM THE MOMENT SHE SHOWED UP, I KNEW.

I KNEW PETER WAS IN LOVE.

IN LOVE? WITH **SPIDER-WOMAN?** WHAT? BUT--

HE WAS IN LOVE WITH THE IDEA OF HER, GWEN.

WITH THE POWER OF IT. THE FREEDOM.

WITH THE FANTASY.

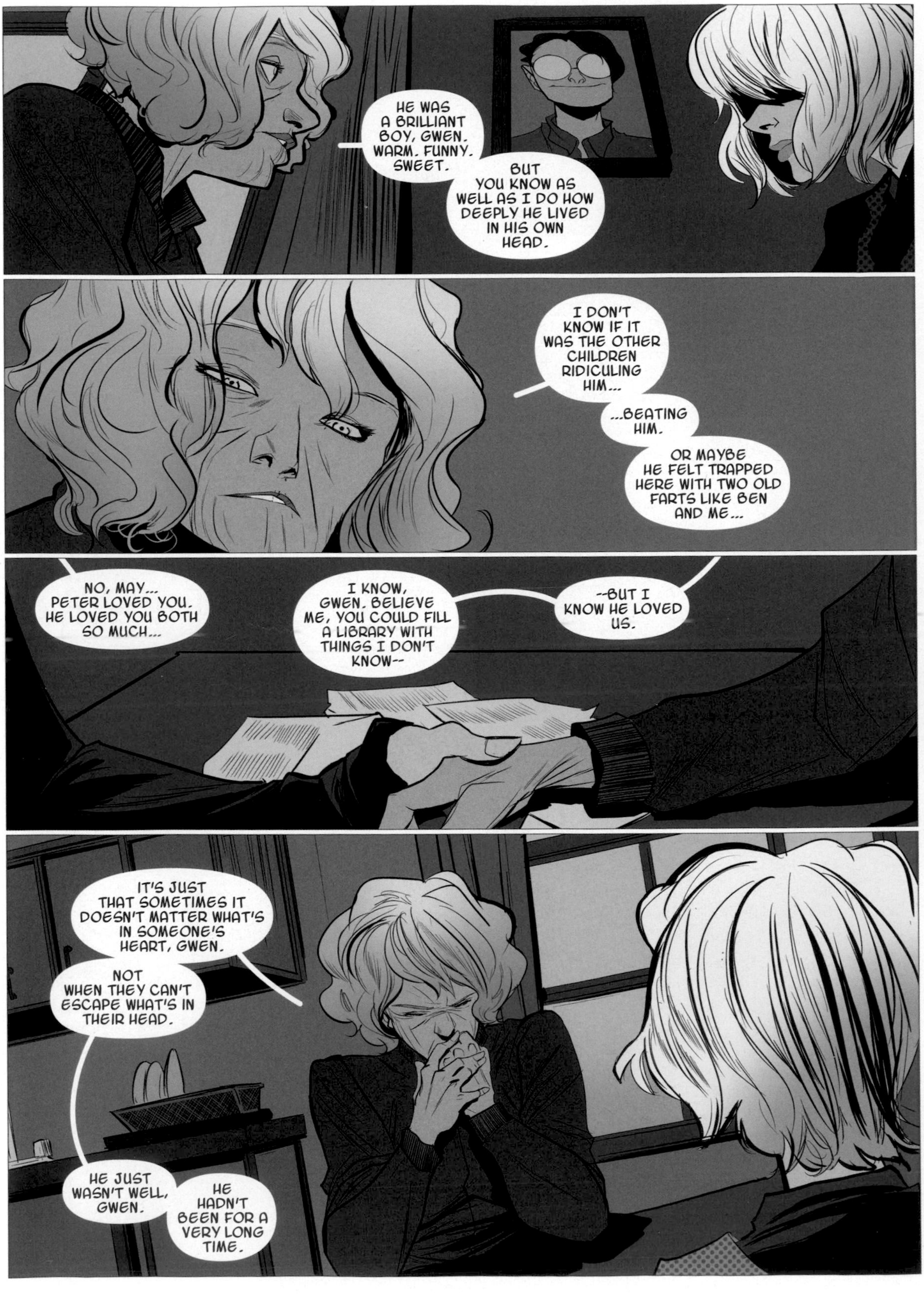
HE WAS A BRILLIANT BOY, GWEN. WARM. FUNNY. SWEET.
BUT YOU KNOW AS WELL AS I DO HOW DEEPLY HE LIVED IN HIS OWN HEAD.
I DON'T KNOW IF IT WAS THE OTHER CHILDREN RIDICULING HIM...
...BEATING HIM.
OR MAYBE HE FELT TRAPPED HERE WITH TWO OLD FARTS LIKE BEN AND ME...
NO, MAY... PETER LOVED YOU. HE LOVED YOU BOTH SO MUCH...
I KNOW, GWEN. BELIEVE ME, YOU COULD FILL A LIBRARY WITH THINGS I DON'T KNOW--
--BUT I KNOW HE LOVED US.
IT'S JUST THAT SOMETIMES IT DOESN'T MATTER WHAT'S IN SOMEONE'S HEART, GWEN.
NOT WHEN THEY CAN'T ESCAPE WHAT'S IN THEIR HEAD.
HE JUST WASN'T WELL, GWEN.
HE HADN'T BEEN FOR A VERY LONG TIME.

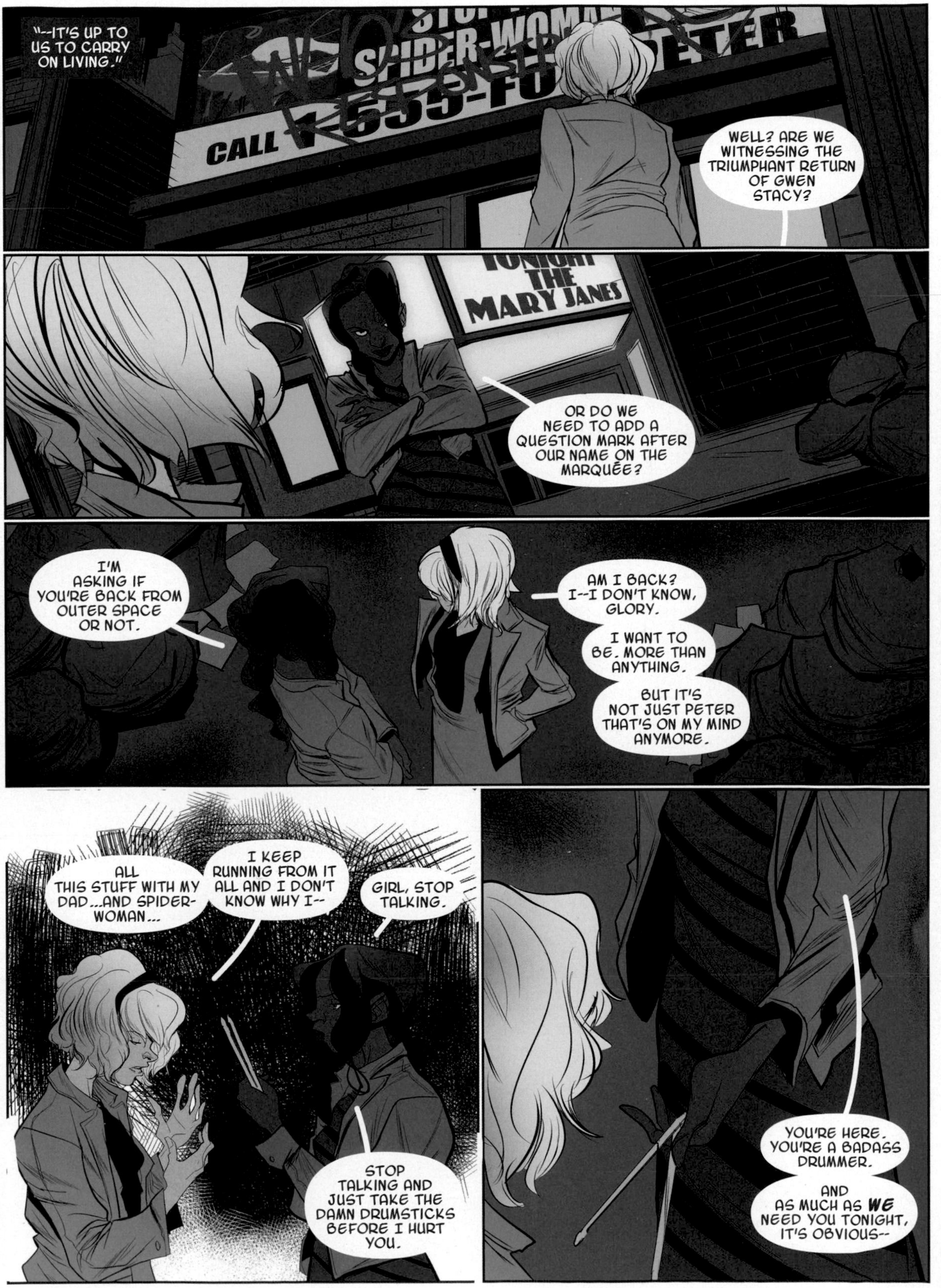
"--IT'S UP TO US TO CARRY ON LIVING."
SPIDER-WOMAN
CALL
WELL? ARE WE WITNESSING THE TRIUMPHANT RETURN OF GWEN STACY?
THE MARY JANES
OR DO WE NEED TO ADD A QUESTION MARK AFTER OUR NAME ON THE MARQUÉE?
I'M ASKING IF YOU'RE BACK FROM OUTER SPACE OR NOT.
AM I BACK? I--I DON'T KNOW, GLORY.
I WANT TO BE. MORE THAN ANYTHING.
BUT IT'S NOT JUST PETER THAT'S ON MY MIND ANYMORE.
ALL THIS STUFF WITH MY DAD...AND SPIDER-WOMAN...
I KEEP RUNNING FROM IT ALL AND I DON'T KNOW WHY I--
GIRL, STOP TALKING.
STOP TALKING AND JUST TAKE THE DAMN DRUMSTICKS BEFORE I HURT YOU.
YOU'RE HERE. YOU'RE A BADASS DRUMMER.
AND AS MUCH AS WE NEED YOU TONIGHT, IT'S OBVIOUS--

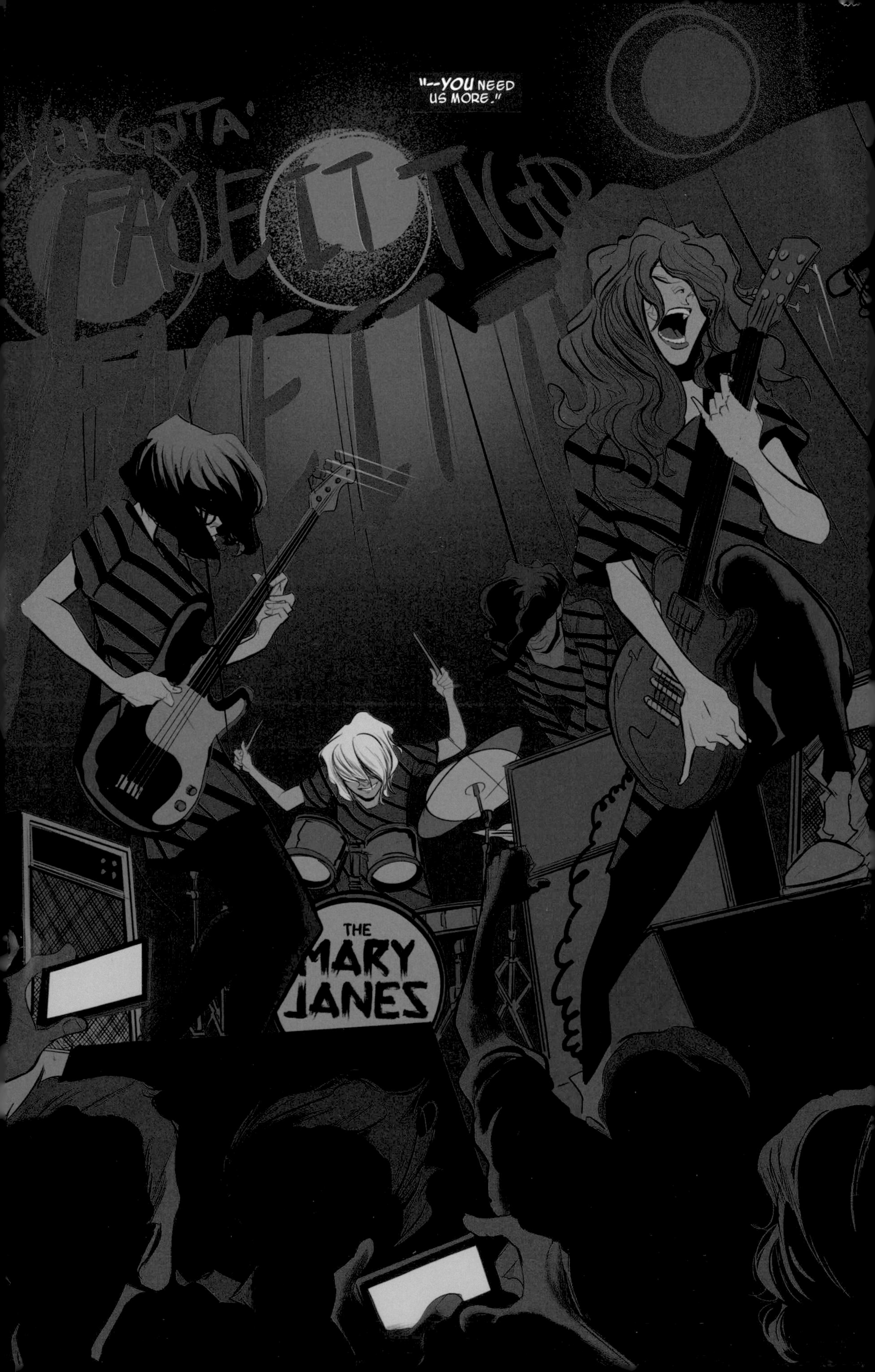
"--YOU NEED US MORE."
FACE IT
THE MARY JANES

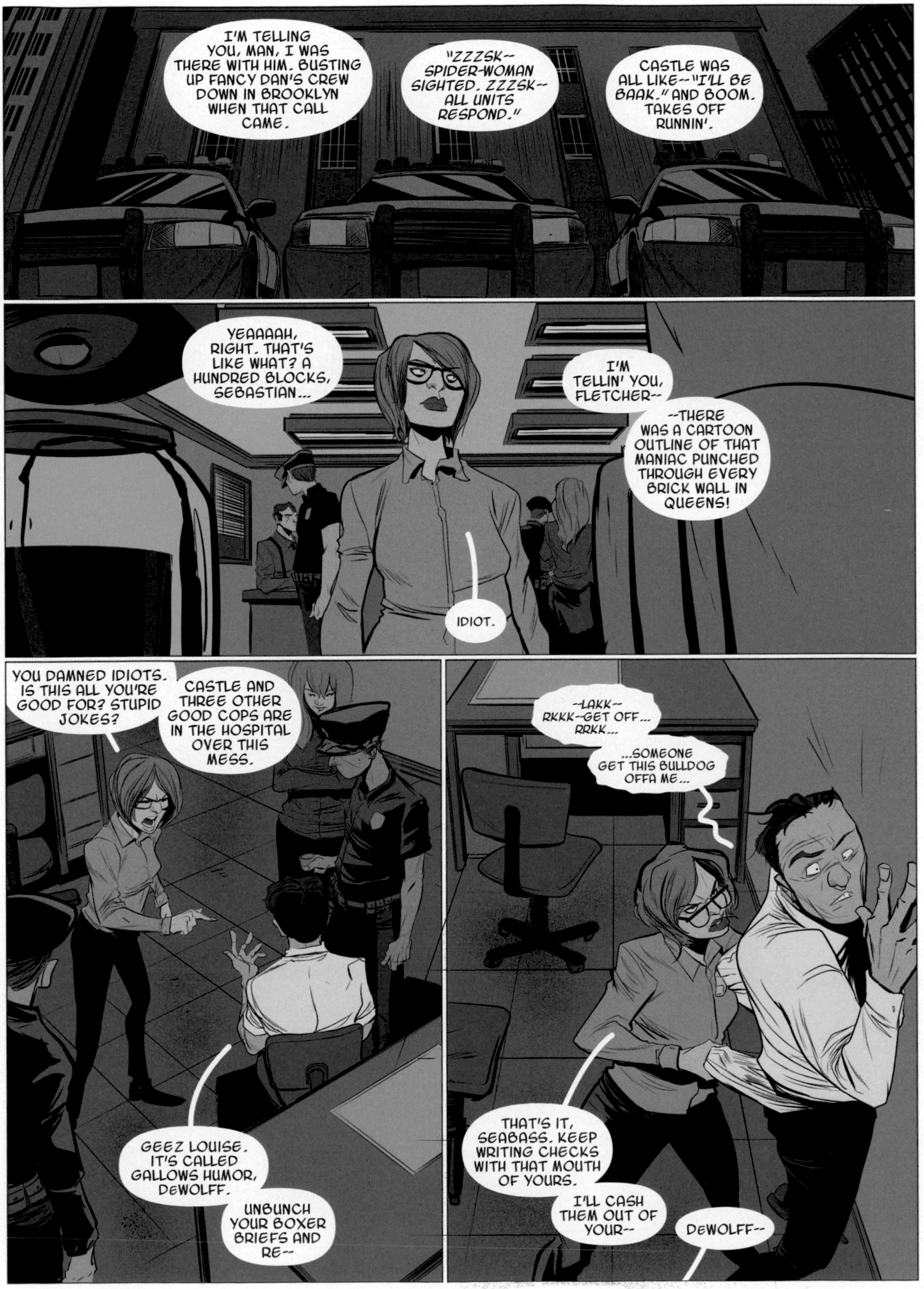
I'M TELLING YOU, MAN, I WAS THERE WITH HIM. BUSTING UP FANCY DAN'S CREW DOWN IN BROOKLYN WHEN THAT CALL CAME.
"ZZZSK--SPIDER-WOMAN SIGHTED. ZZZSK--ALL UNITS RESPOND."
CASTLE WAS ALL LIKE--"I'LL BE BAAK." AND BOOM. TAKES OFF RUNNIN'.
YEAAAAH, RIGHT. THAT'S LIKE WHAT? A HUNDRED BLOCKS, SEBASTIAN...
I'M TELLIN' YOU, FLETCHER--
--THERE WAS A CARTOON OUTLINE OF THAT MANIAC PUNCHED THROUGH EVERY BRICK WALL IN QUEENS!
IDIOT.
YOU DAMNED IDIOTS. IS THIS ALL YOU'RE GOOD FOR? STUPID JOKES?
CASTLE AND THREE OTHER GOOD COPS ARE IN THE HOSPITAL OVER THIS MESS.
GEEZ LOUISE. IT'S CALLED GALLOWS HUMOR, DeWOLFF.
UNBUNCH YOUR BOXER BRIEFS AND RE--
--LAKK--RKKK--GET OFF... RRKK...
...SOMEONE GET THIS BULLDOG OFFA ME...
THAT'S IT, SEABASS. KEEP WRITING CHECKS WITH THAT MOUTH OF YOURS.
I'LL CASH THEM OUT OF YOUR--
DeWOLFF--

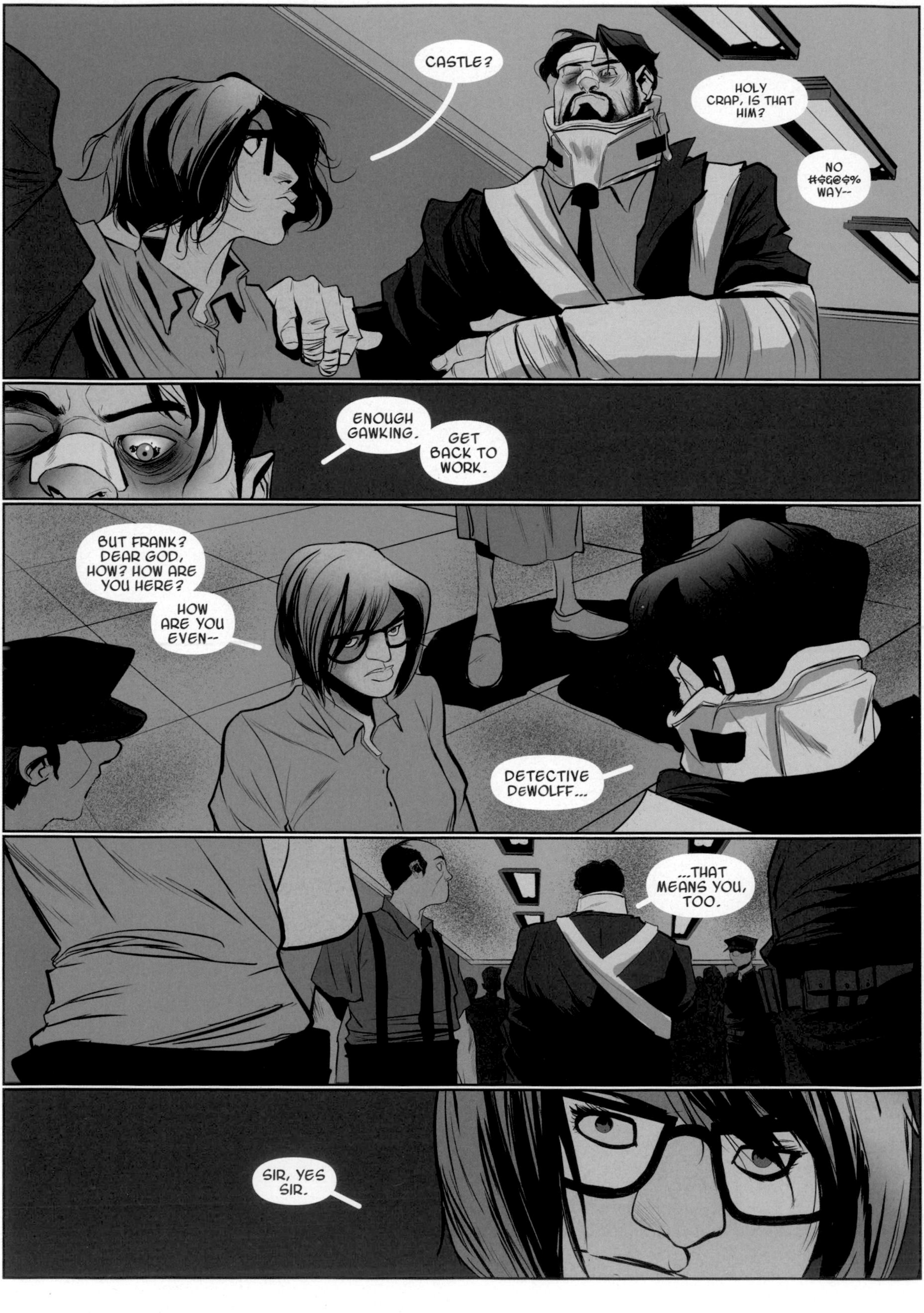
CASTLE?
HOLY CRAP, IS THAT HIM?
NO #$@@$% WAY--
ENOUGH GAWKING.
GET BACK TO WORK.
BUT FRANK? DEAR GOD, HOW? HOW ARE YOU HERE?
HOW ARE YOU EVEN--
DETECTIVE DeWOLFF...
...THAT MEANS YOU, TOO.
SIR, YES SIR.

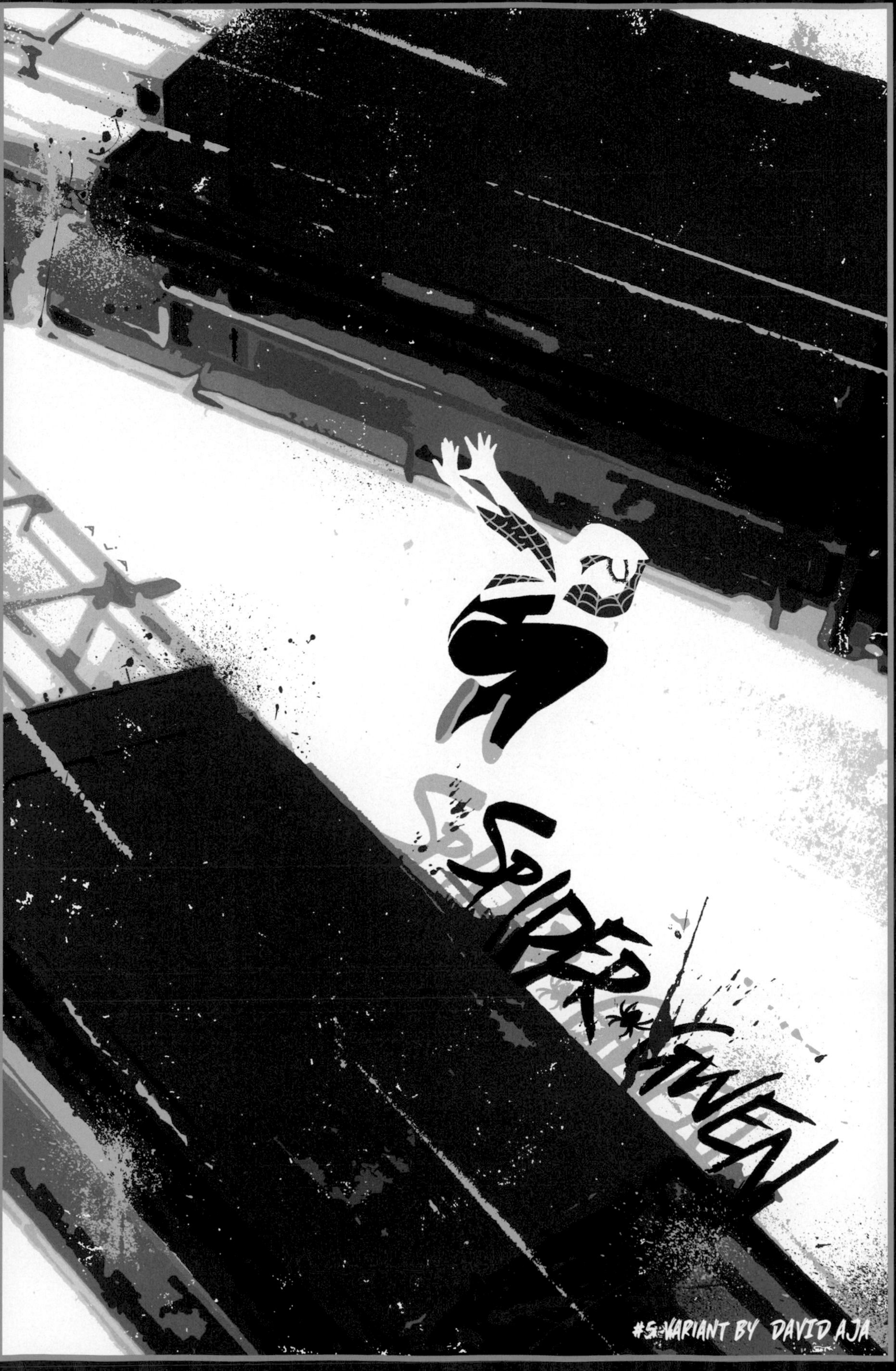
SPIDER GWEN

#5 VARIANT BY DAVID AJA

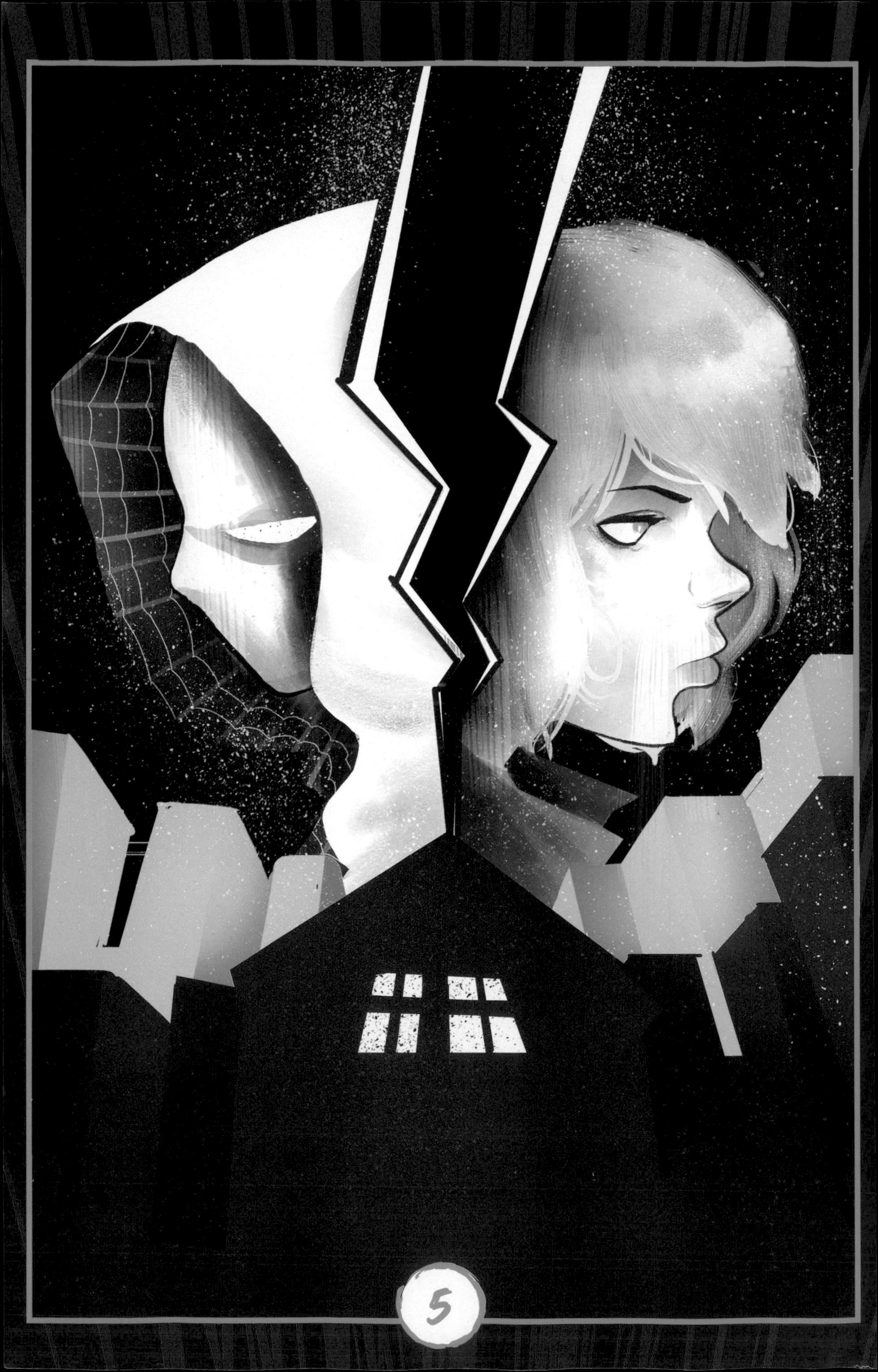
5

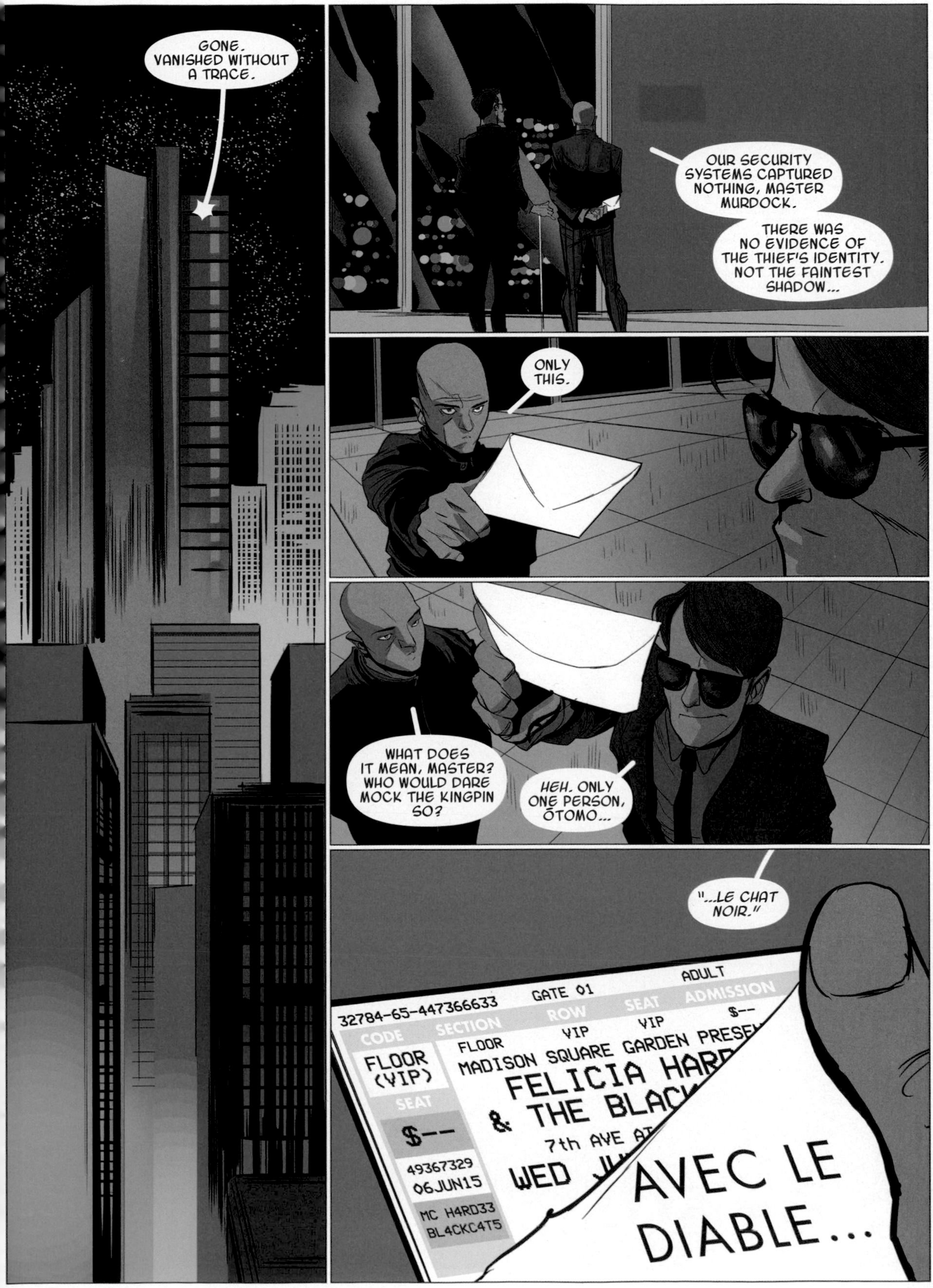
GONE. VANISHED WITHOUT A TRACE.
OUR SECURITY SYSTEMS CAPTURED NOTHING, MASTER MURDOCK.
THERE WAS NO EVIDENCE OF THE THIEF'S IDENTITY. NOT THE FAINTEST SHADOW...
ONLY THIS.
WHAT DOES IT MEAN, MASTER? WHO WOULD DARE MOCK THE KINGPIN SO?
HEH. ONLY ONE PERSON, ŌTOMO...
"...LE CHAT NOIR."
32784-65-447366633
GATE 01
ADULT
CODE
SECTION
ROW
SEAT
ADMISSION
$--
FLOOR
VIP
VIP
FLOOR (VIP)
SEAT
$--
49367329
06JUN15
MC H4RD33
BL4CKC4T5
MADISON SQUARE GARDEN PRESEN
FELICIA HAR
& THE BLAC
7th AVE AT
WED JU
AVEC LE DIABLE...

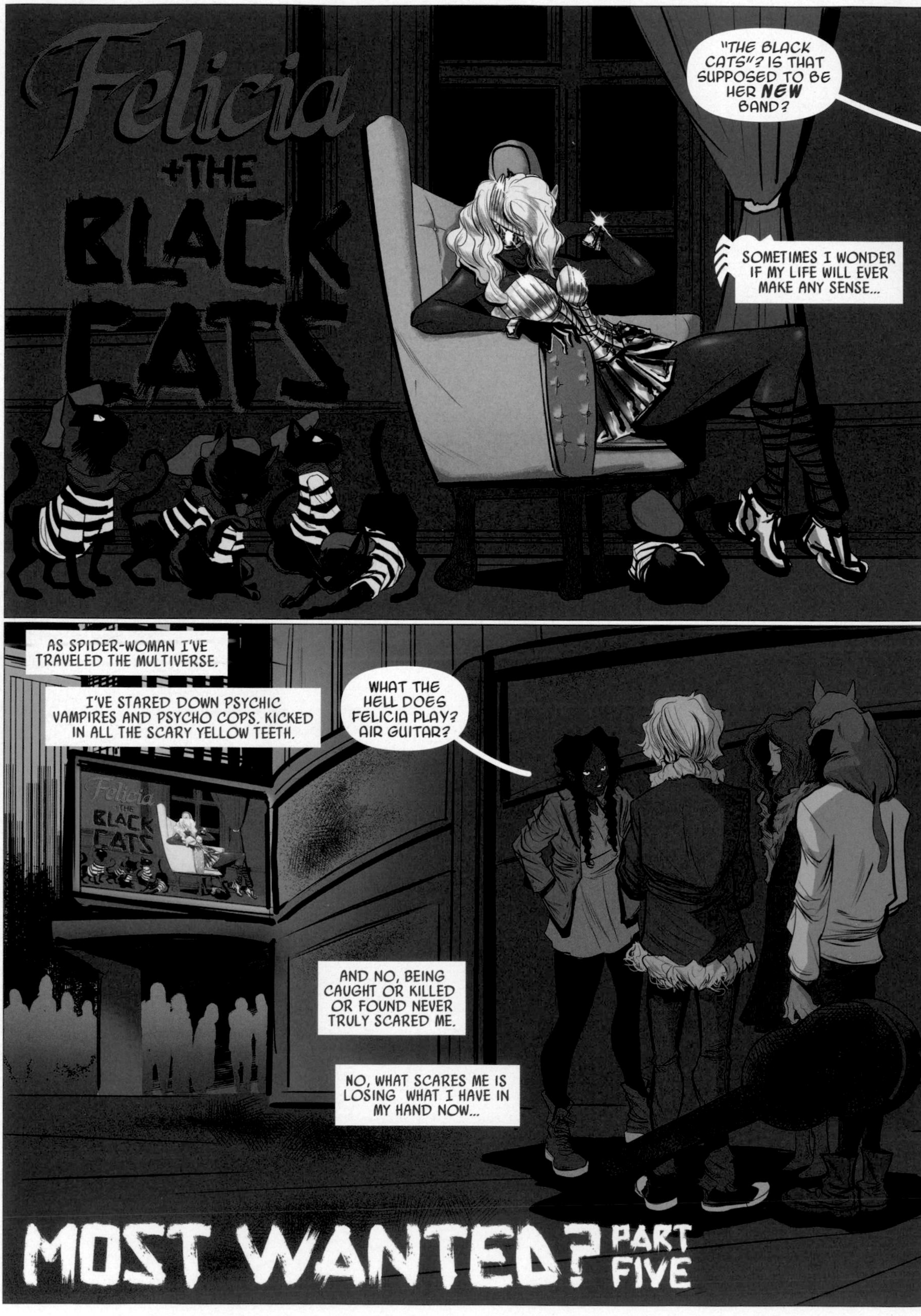
Felicia + THE BLACK CATS
"THE BLACK CATS"? IS THAT SUPPOSED TO BE HER NEW BAND?
SOMETIMES I WONDER IF MY LIFE WILL EVER MAKE ANY SENSE...
AS SPIDER-WOMAN I'VE TRAVELED THE MULTIVERSE.
I'VE STARED DOWN PSYCHIC VAMPIRES AND PSYCHO COPS. KICKED IN ALL THE SCARY YELLOW TEETH.
WHAT THE HELL DOES FELICIA PLAY? AIR GUITAR?
Felicia THE BLACK CATS
AND NO, BEING CAUGHT OR KILLED OR FOUND NEVER TRULY SCARED ME.
NO, WHAT SCARES ME IS LOSING WHAT I HAVE IN MY HAND NOW...
MOST WANTED? PART FIVE

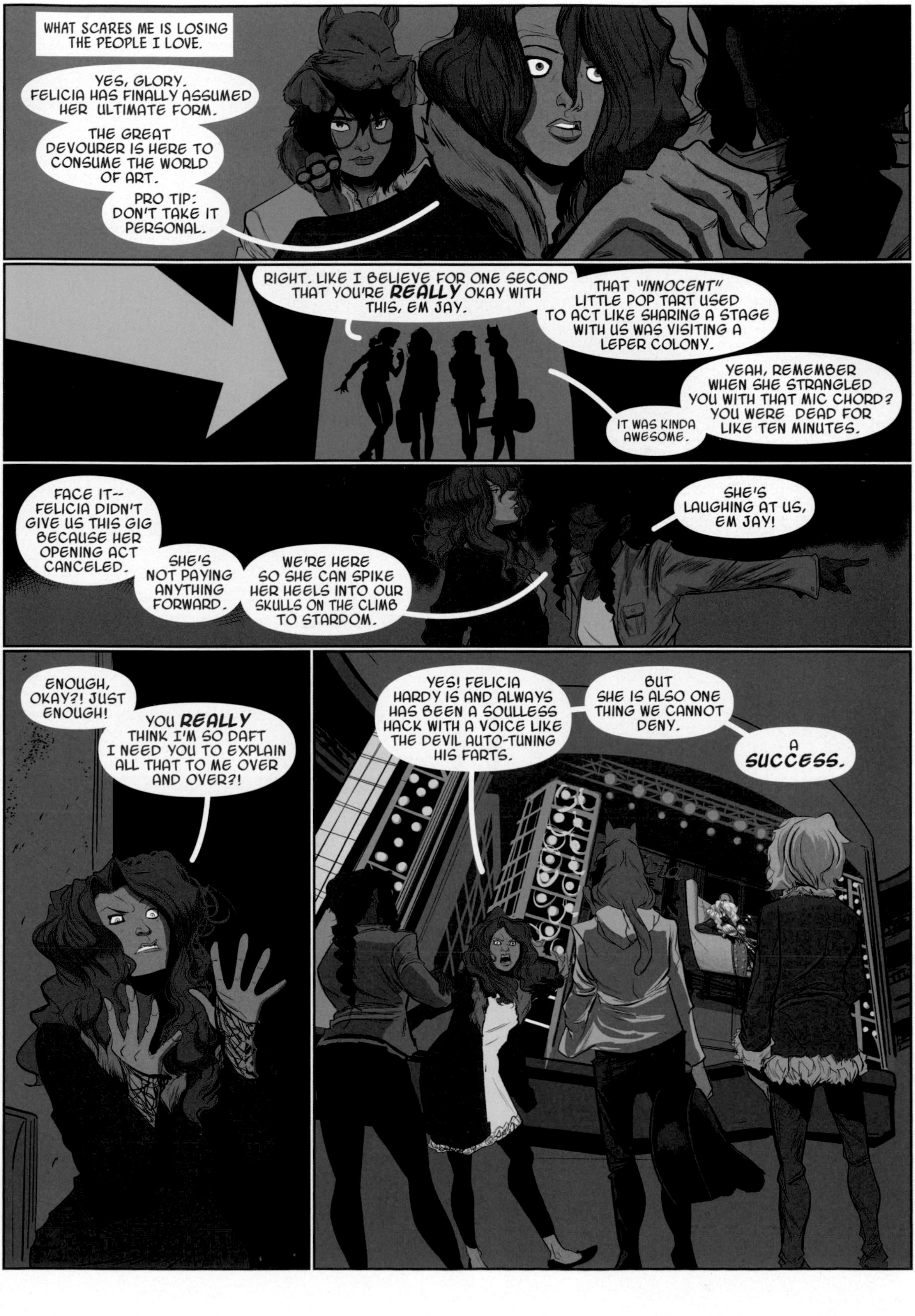
WHAT SCARES ME IS LOSING THE PEOPLE I LOVE.
YES, GLORY. FELICIA HAS FINALLY ASSUMED HER ULTIMATE FORM.
THE GREAT DEVOURER IS HERE TO CONSUME THE WORLD OF ART.
PRO TIP: DON'T TAKE IT PERSONAL.
RIGHT. LIKE I BELIEVE FOR ONE SECOND THAT YOU'RE REALLY OKAY WITH THIS, EM JAY.
THAT "INNOCENT" LITTLE POP TART USED TO ACT LIKE SHARING A STAGE WITH US WAS VISITING A LEPER COLONY.
YEAH, REMEMBER WHEN SHE STRANGLED YOU WITH THAT MIC CHORD? YOU WERE DEAD FOR LIKE TEN MINUTES.
IT WAS KINDA AWESOME.
FACE IT-- FELICIA DIDN'T GIVE US THIS GIG BECAUSE HER OPENING ACT CANCELED.
SHE'S NOT PAYING ANYTHING FORWARD.
WE'RE HERE SO SHE CAN SPIKE HER HEELS INTO OUR SKULLS ON THE CLIMB TO STARDOM.
SHE'S LAUGHING AT US, EM JAY!
ENOUGH, OKAY?! JUST ENOUGH!
YOU REALLY THINK I'M SO DAFT I NEED YOU TO EXPLAIN ALL THAT TO ME OVER AND OVER?!
YES! FELICIA HARDY IS AND ALWAYS HAS BEEN A SOULLESS HACK WITH A VOICE LIKE THE DEVIL AUTO-TUNING HIS FARTS.
BUT SHE IS ALSO ONE THING WE CANNOT DENY.
A SUCCESS.

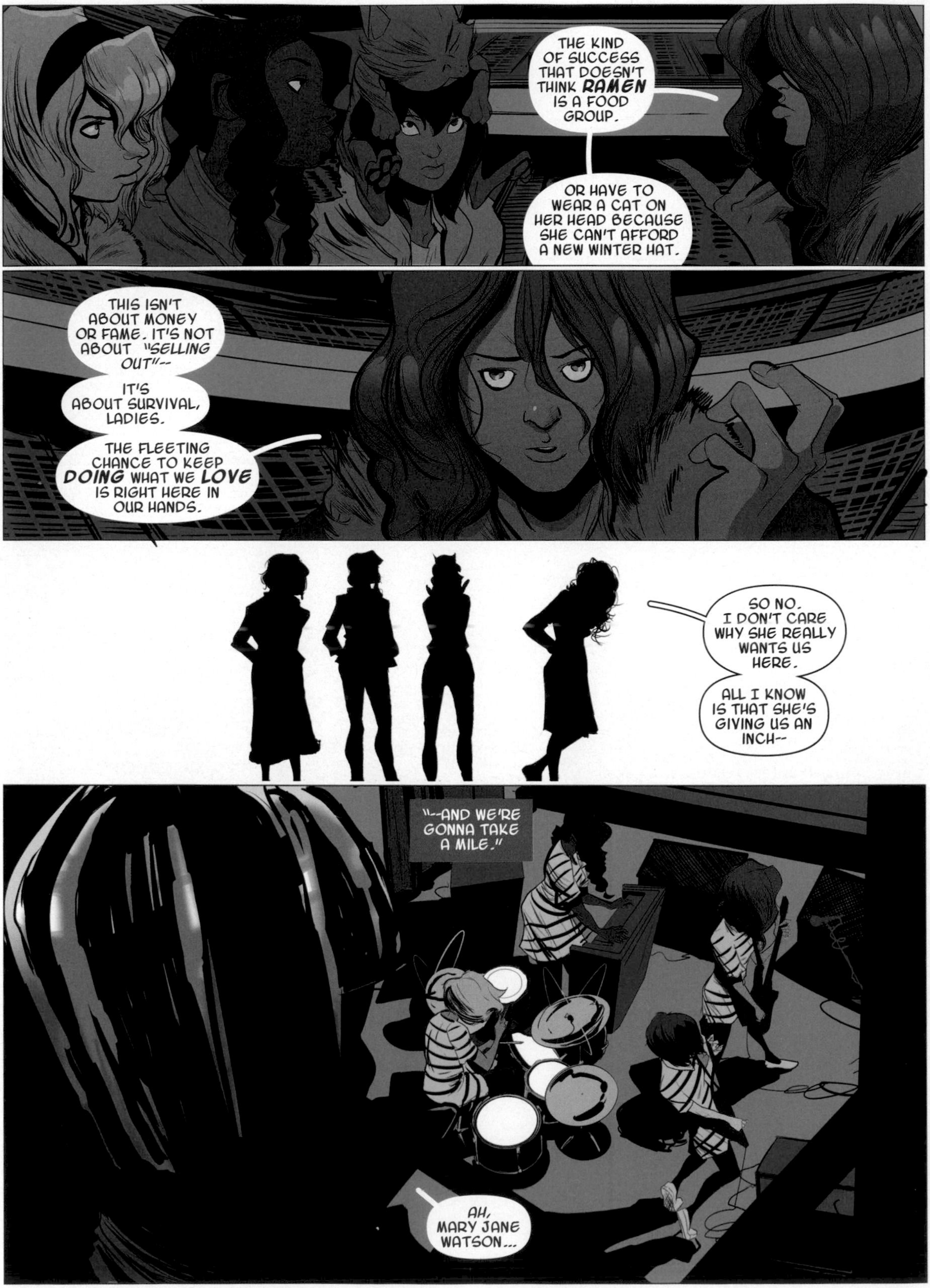
THE KIND OF SUCCESS THAT DOESN'T THINK **RAMEN** IS A FOOD GROUP.
OR HAVE TO WEAR A CAT ON HER HEAD BECAUSE SHE CAN'T AFFORD A NEW WINTER HAT.
THIS ISN'T ABOUT MONEY OR FAME. IT'S NOT ABOUT *"SELLING OUT"*--
IT'S ABOUT SURVIVAL, LADIES.
THE FLEETING CHANCE TO KEEP **DOING** WHAT WE **LOVE** IS RIGHT HERE IN OUR HANDS.
SO NO. I DON'T CARE WHY SHE REALLY WANTS US HERE.
ALL I KNOW IS THAT SHE'S GIVING US AN INCH--
"--AND WE'RE GONNA TAKE A MILE."
AH, MARY JANE WATSON...

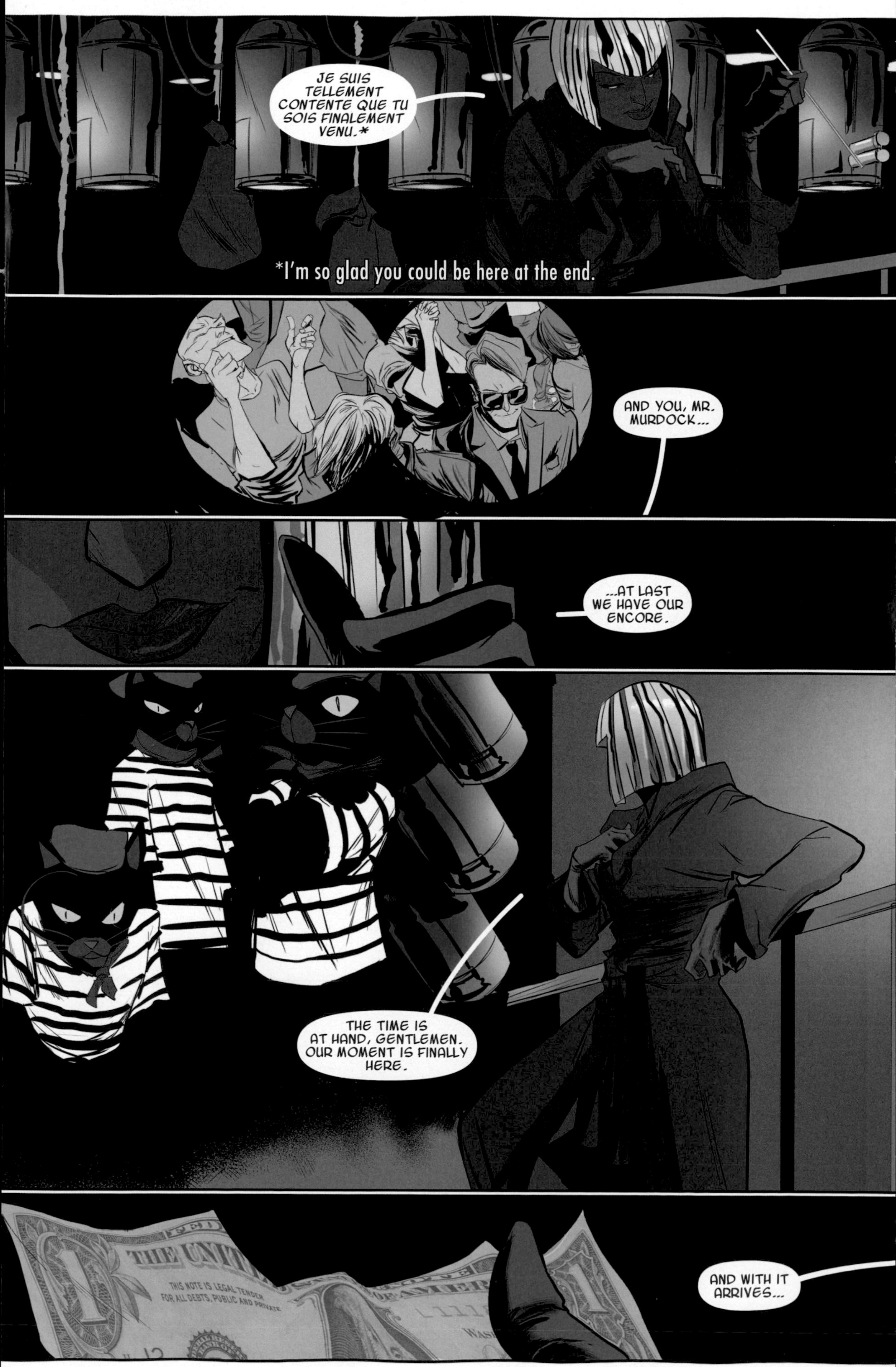
JE SUIS TELLEMENT CONTENTE QUE TU SOIS FINALEMENT VENU.*
*I'm so glad you could be here at the end.
AND YOU, MR. MURDOCK...
...AT LAST WE HAVE OUR ENCORE.
THE TIME IS AT HAND, GENTLEMEN. OUR MOMENT IS FINALLY HERE.
AND WITH IT ARRIVES...

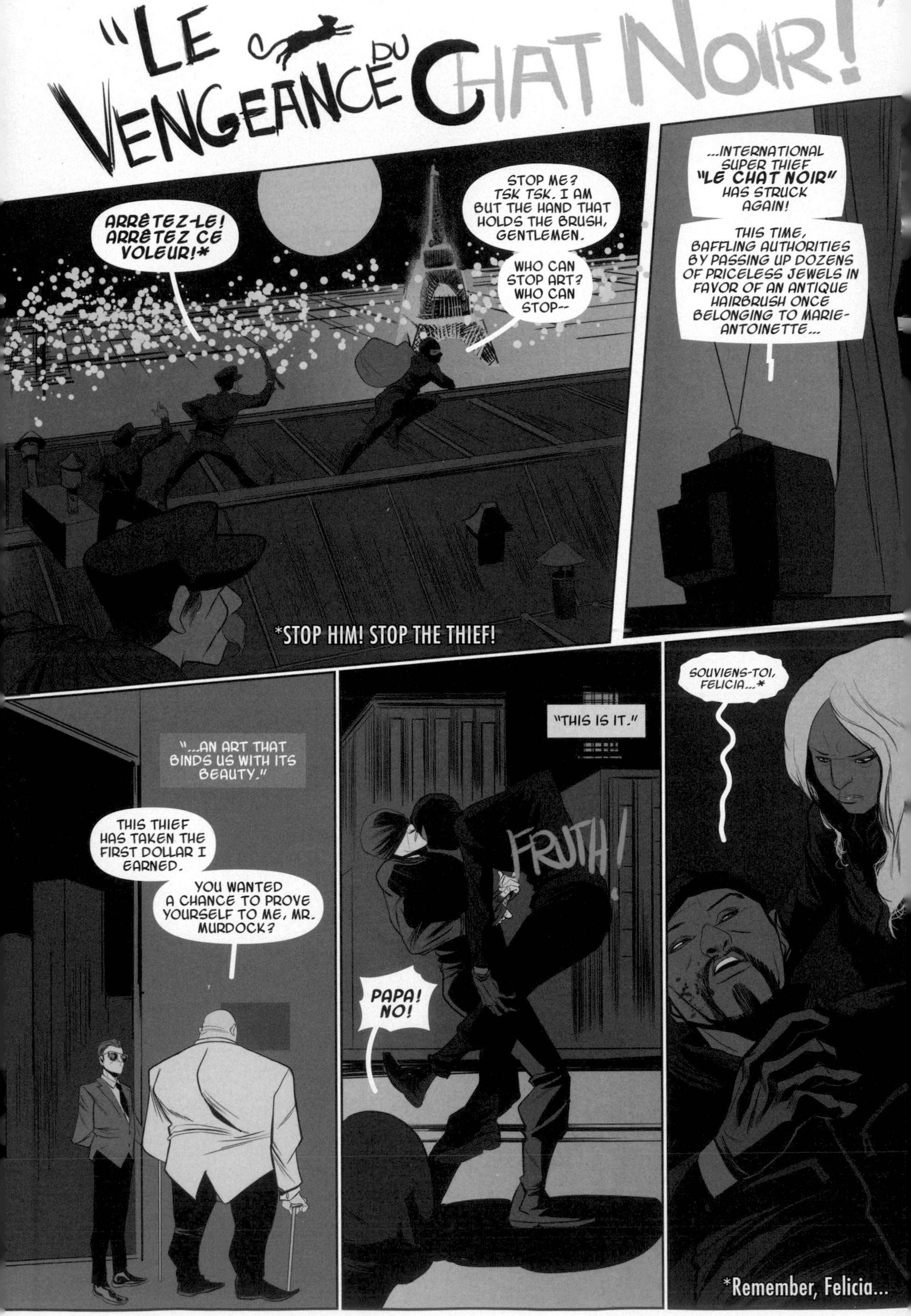
"LE VENGEANCE DU CHAT NOIR!"
ARRÊTEZ-LE! ARRÊTEZ CE VOLEUR!*
STOP ME? TSK TSK. I AM BUT THE HAND THAT HOLDS THE BRUSH, GENTLEMEN.
WHO CAN STOP ART? WHO CAN STOP--
*STOP HIM! STOP THE THIEF!
...INTERNATIONAL SUPER THIEF "LE CHAT NOIR" HAS STRUCK AGAIN!
THIS TIME, BAFFLING AUTHORITIES BY PASSING UP DOZENS OF PRICELESS JEWELS IN FAVOR OF AN ANTIQUE HAIRBRUSH ONCE BELONGING TO MARIE-ANTOINETTE...
"...AN ART THAT BINDS US WITH ITS BEAUTY."
THIS THIEF HAS TAKEN THE FIRST DOLLAR I EARNED.
YOU WANTED A CHANCE TO PROVE YOURSELF TO ME, MR. MURDOCK?
"THIS IS IT."
FRUTH!
PAPA! NO!
SOUVIENS-TOI, FELICIA...*
*Remember, Felicia...

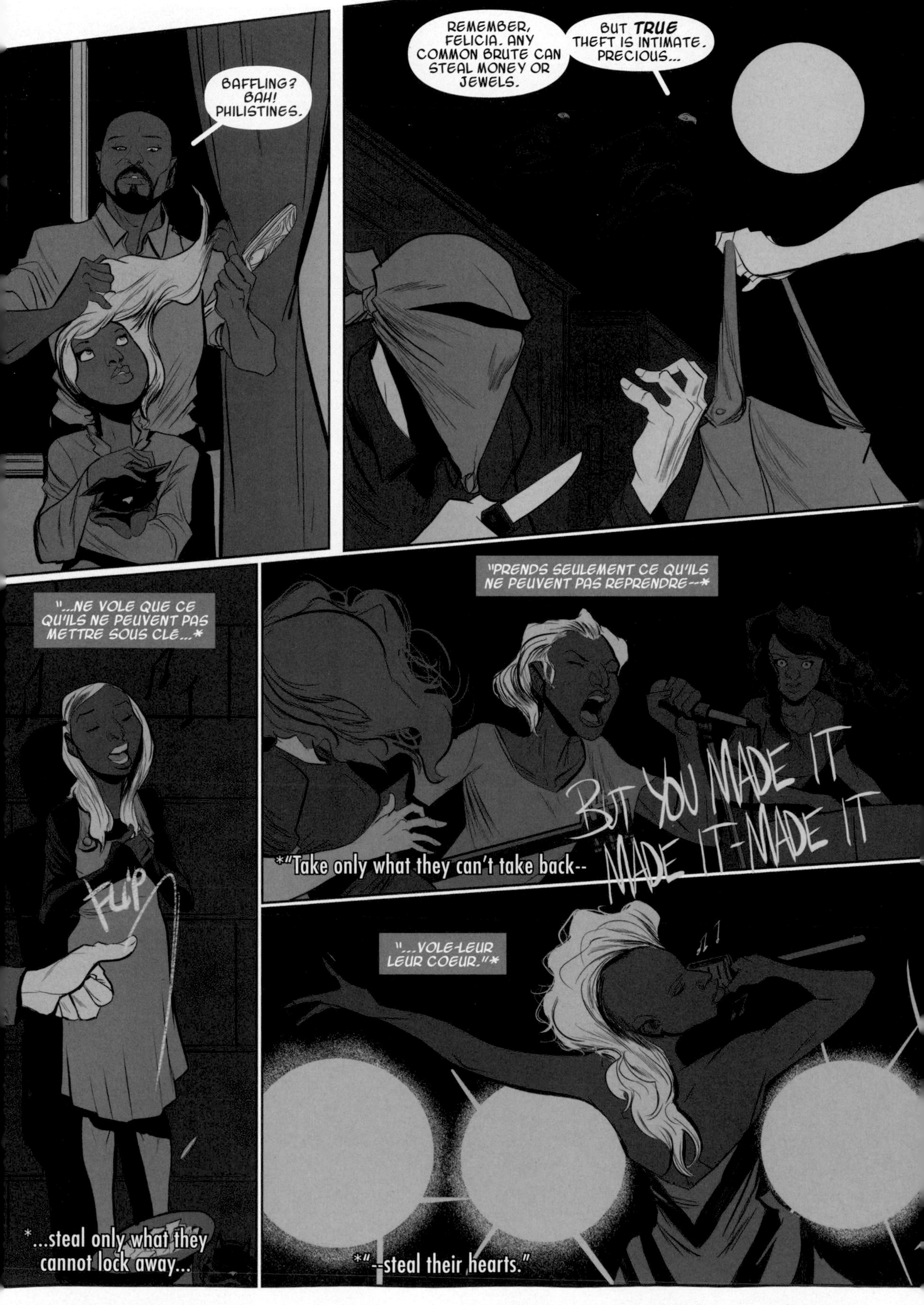
BAFFLING? BAH! PHILISTINES.
REMEMBER, FELICIA. ANY COMMON BRUTE CAN STEAL MONEY OR JEWELS.
BUT TRUE THEFT IS INTIMATE. PRECIOUS...
"...NE VOLE QUE CE QU'ILS NE PEUVENT PAS METTRE SOUS CLÉ...*
FLIP
*...steal only what they cannot lock away...
"PRENDS SEULEMENT CE QU'ILS NE PEUVENT PAS REPRENDRE--*
BUT YOU MADE IT MADE IT-MADE IT
*"Take only what they can't take back--
"...VOLE-LEUR LEUR COEUR."*
*"--steal their hearts."

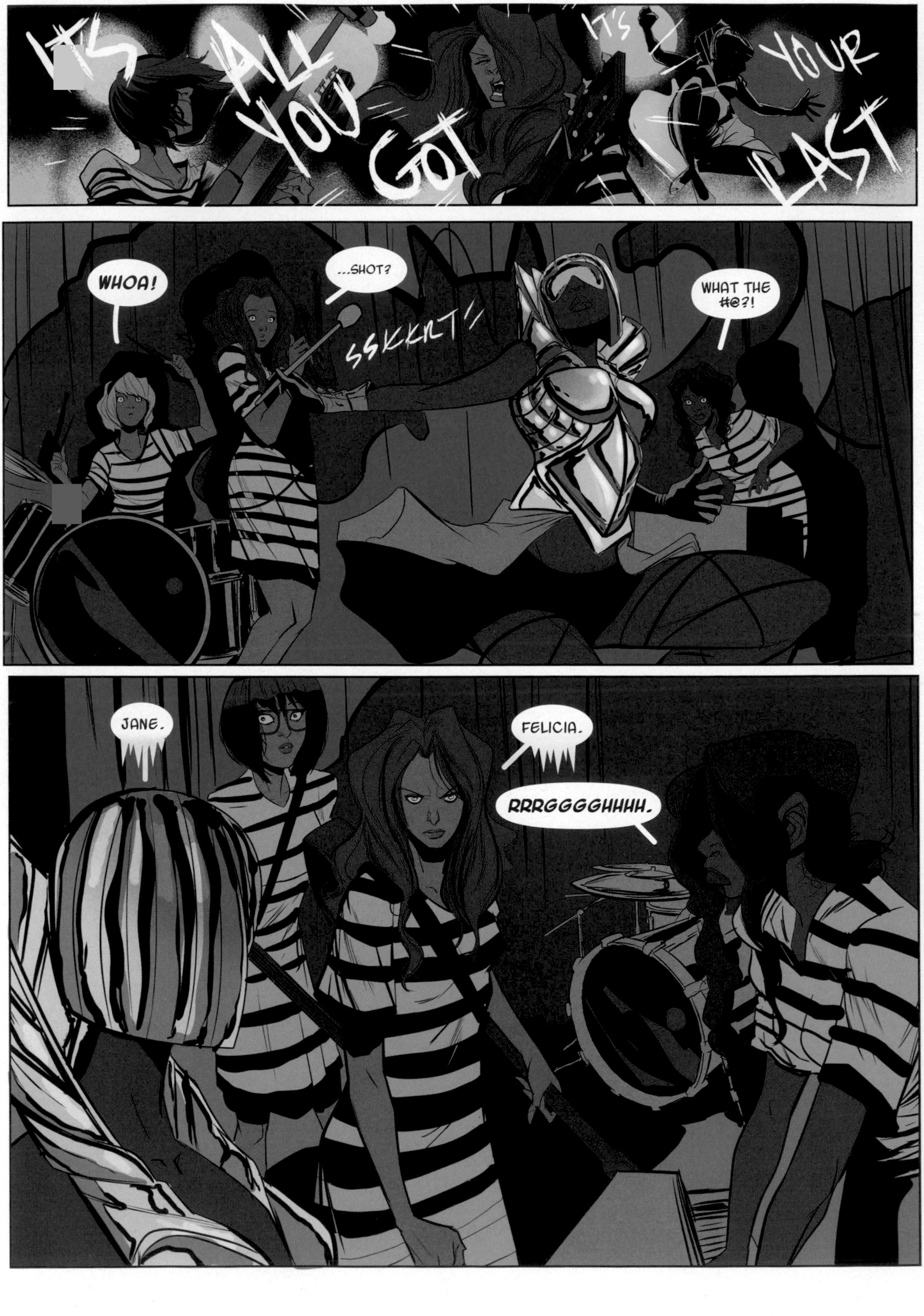
IT'S ALL YOU GOT
IT'S YOUR LAST
WHOA!
...SHOT?
SSKKRT
WHAT THE #@?!
JANE.
FELICIA.
RRRGGGGHHHH.

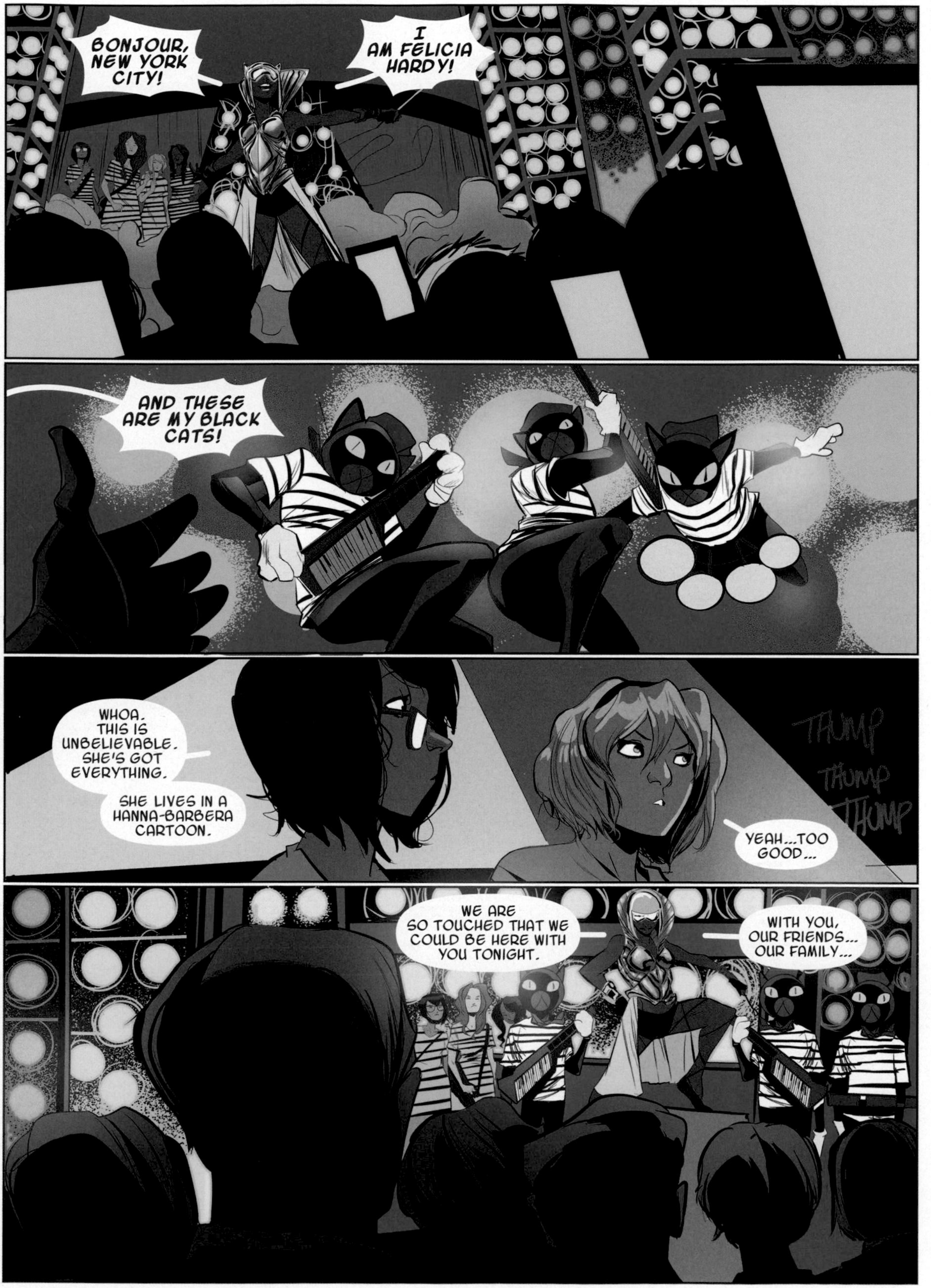

BONJOUR, NEW YORK CITY!
I AM FELICIA HARDY!
AND THESE ARE MY BLACK CATS!
WHOA. THIS IS UNBELIEVABLE. SHE'S GOT EVERYTHING.
SHE LIVES IN A HANNA-BARBERA CARTOON.
THUMP
THUMP
THUMP
YEAH...TOO GOOD...
WE ARE SO TOUCHED THAT WE COULD BE HERE WITH YOU TONIGHT.
WITH YOU, OUR FRIENDS... OUR FAMILY...

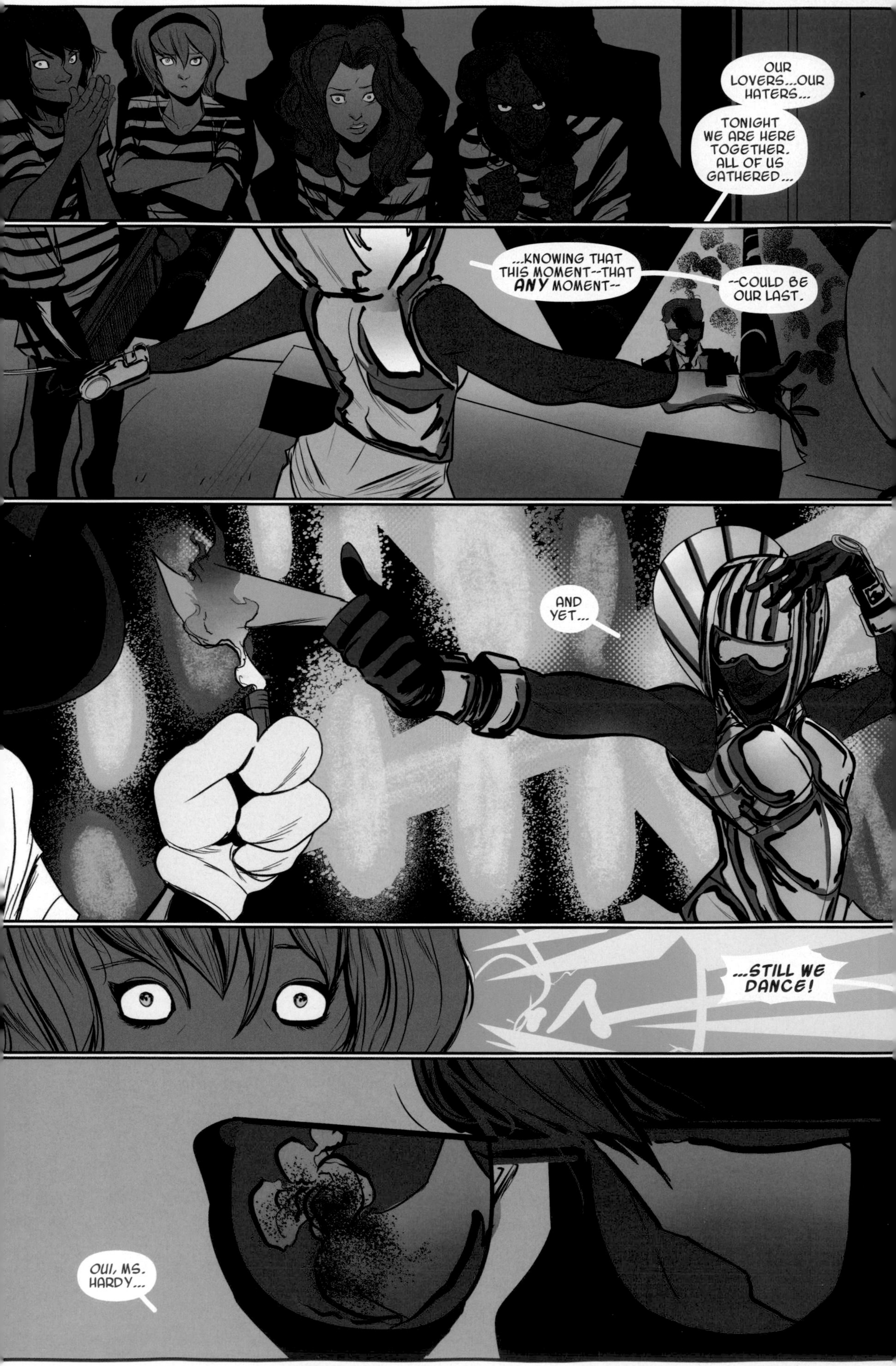
OUR LOVERS...OUR HATERS...
TONIGHT WE ARE HERE TOGETHER. ALL OF US GATHERED...
...KNOWING THAT THIS MOMENT--THAT ANY MOMENT--
--COULD BE OUR LAST.
AND YET...
...STILL WE DANCE!
OUI, MS. HARDY...

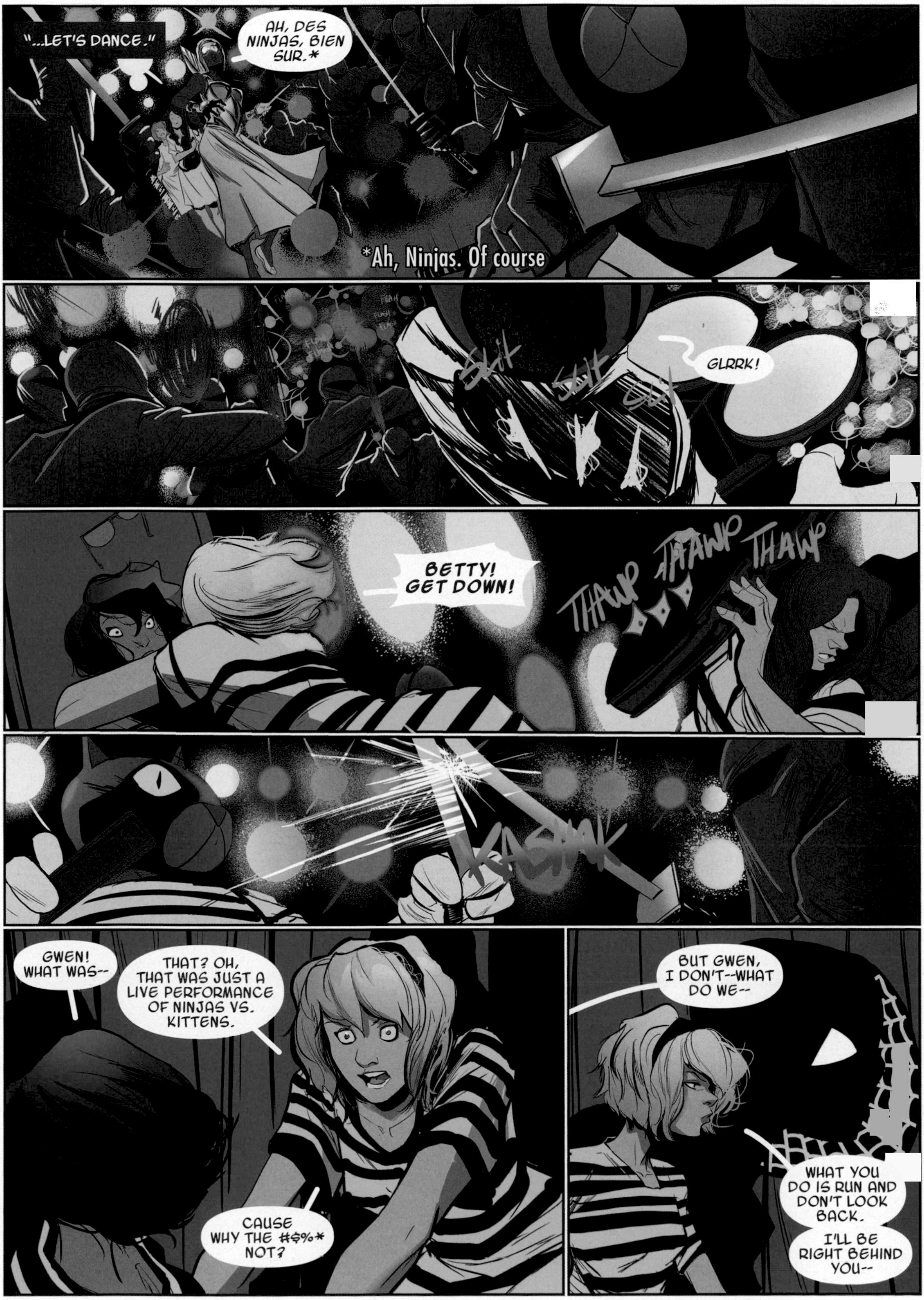
"...LET'S DANCE."
AH, DES NINJAS, BIEN SUR.*
*Ah, Ninjas. Of course
GLRRK!
BETTY! GET DOWN!
THAWP THAWP THAWP
KASHAK
GWEN! WHAT WAS--
THAT? OH, THAT WAS JUST A LIVE PERFORMANCE OF NINJAS VS. KITTENS.
CAUSE WHY THE #$%* NOT?
BUT GWEN, I DON'T--WHAT DO WE--
WHAT YOU DO IS RUN AND DON'T LOOK BACK.
I'LL BE RIGHT BEHIND YOU--

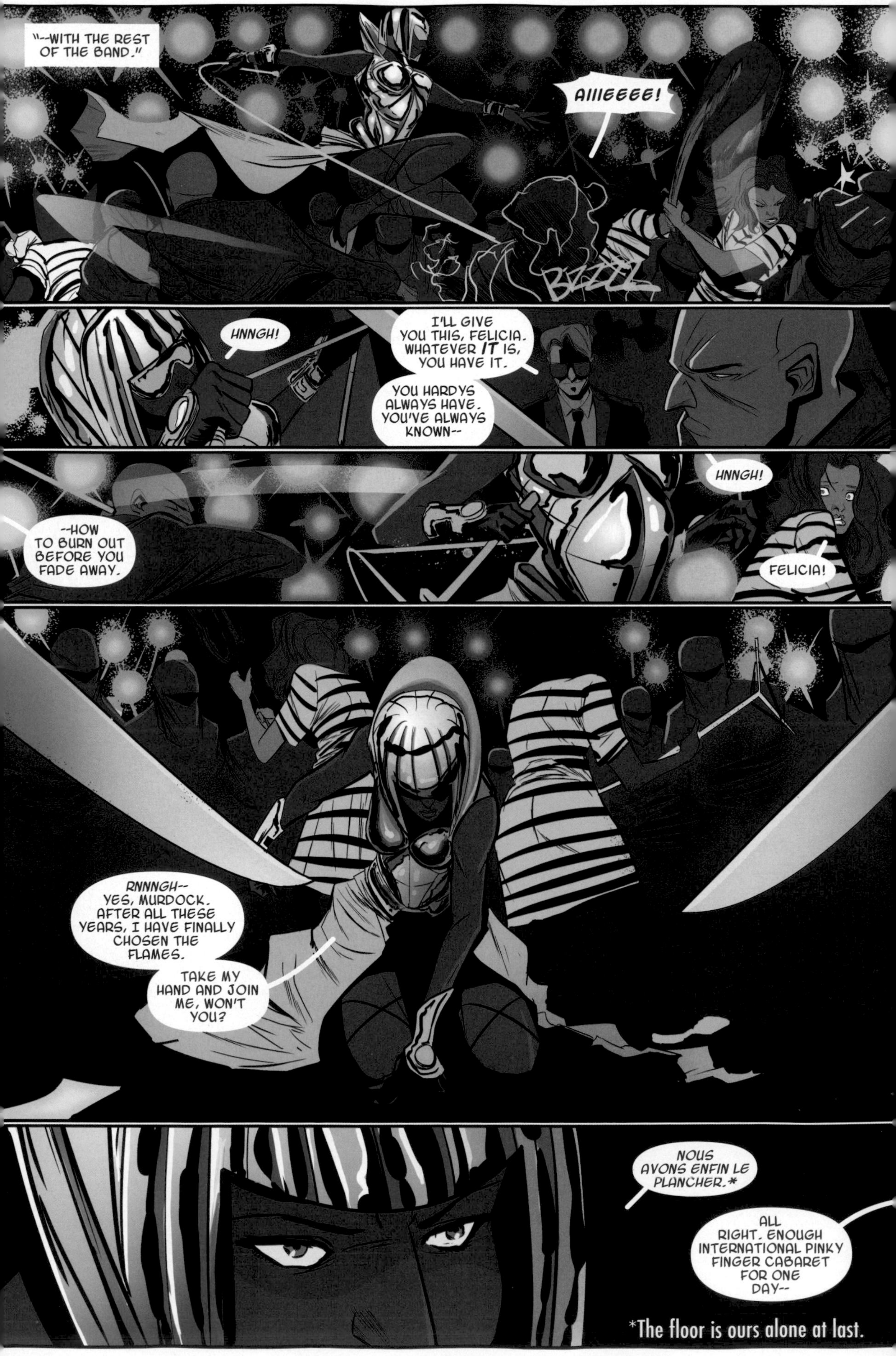
"--WITH THE REST OF THE BAND."
AIIIEEEE!
BZZZZ
HNNGH!
I'LL GIVE YOU THIS, FELICIA. WHATEVER IT IS, YOU HAVE IT.
YOU HARDYS ALWAYS HAVE. YOU'VE ALWAYS KNOWN--
--HOW TO BURN OUT BEFORE YOU FADE AWAY.
HNNGH!
FELICIA!
RNNNGH-- YES, MURDOCK. AFTER ALL THESE YEARS, I HAVE FINALLY CHOSEN THE FLAMES.
TAKE MY HAND AND JOIN ME, WON'T YOU?
NOUS AVONS ENFIN LE PLANCHER.*
ALL RIGHT. ENOUGH INTERNATIONAL PINKY FINGER CABARET FOR ONE DAY--
*The floor is ours alone at last.

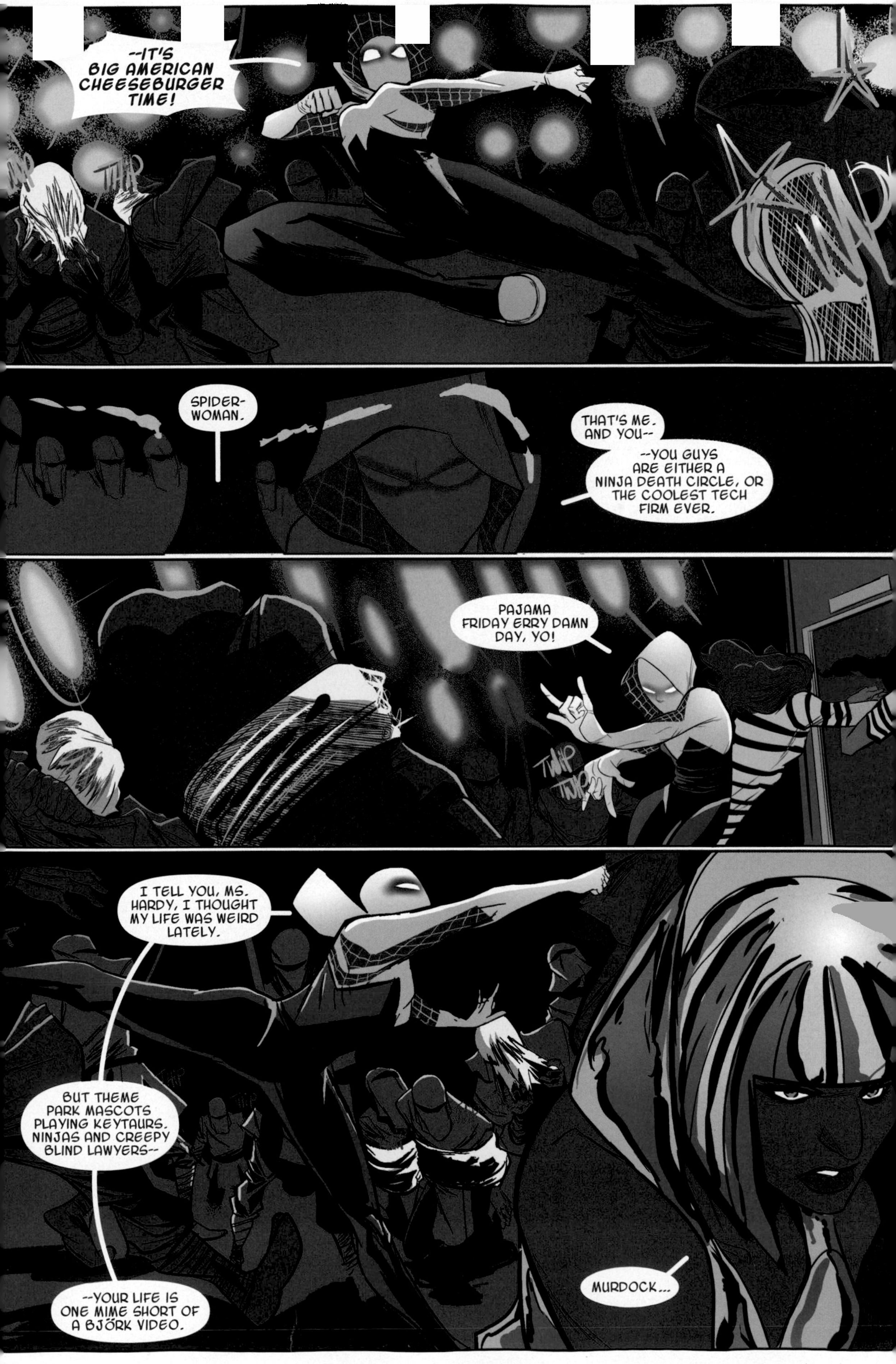
--IT'S BIG AMERICAN CHEESEBURGER TIME!
THWP
SPIDER-WOMAN.
THAT'S ME. AND YOU--
--YOU GUYS ARE EITHER A NINJA DEATH CIRCLE, OR THE COOLEST TECH FIRM EVER.
PAJAMA FRIDAY ERRY DAMN DAY, YO!
TWIP TWIP
I TELL YOU, MS. HARDY, I THOUGHT MY LIFE WAS WEIRD LATELY.
BUT THEME PARK MASCOTS PLAYING KEYTAURS. NINJAS AND CREEPY BLIND LAWYERS--
--YOUR LIFE IS ONE MIME SHORT OF A BJÖRK VIDEO.
MURDOCK...

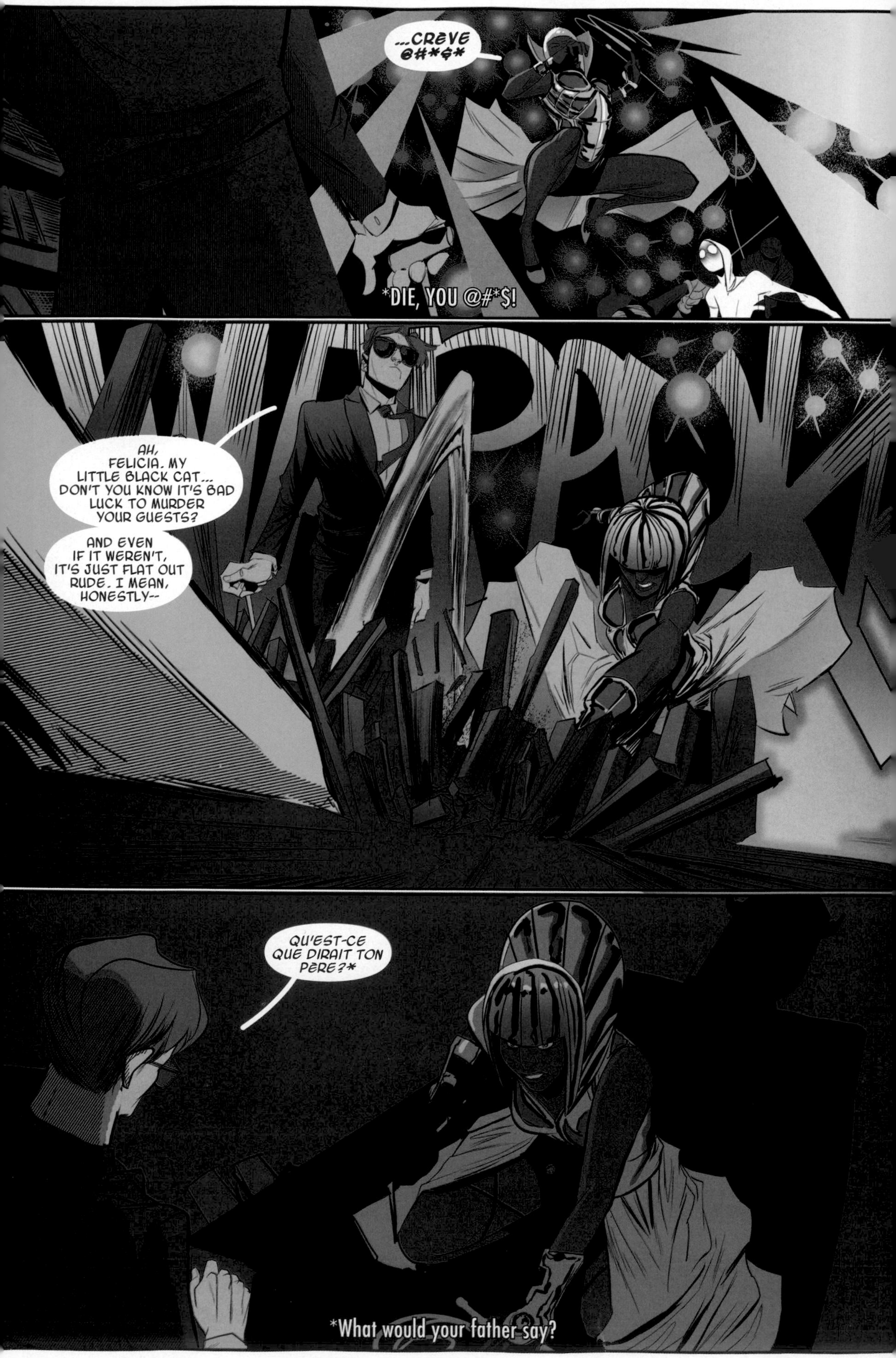

...CRÈVE @#*$*
*DIE, YOU @#*$!
AH, FELICIA. MY LITTLE BLACK CAT... DON'T YOU KNOW IT'S BAD LUCK TO MURDER YOUR GUESTS?
AND EVEN IF IT WEREN'T, IT'S JUST FLAT OUT RUDE. I MEAN, HONESTLY--
QU'EST-CE QUE DIRAIT TON PÈRE?*
*What would your father say?

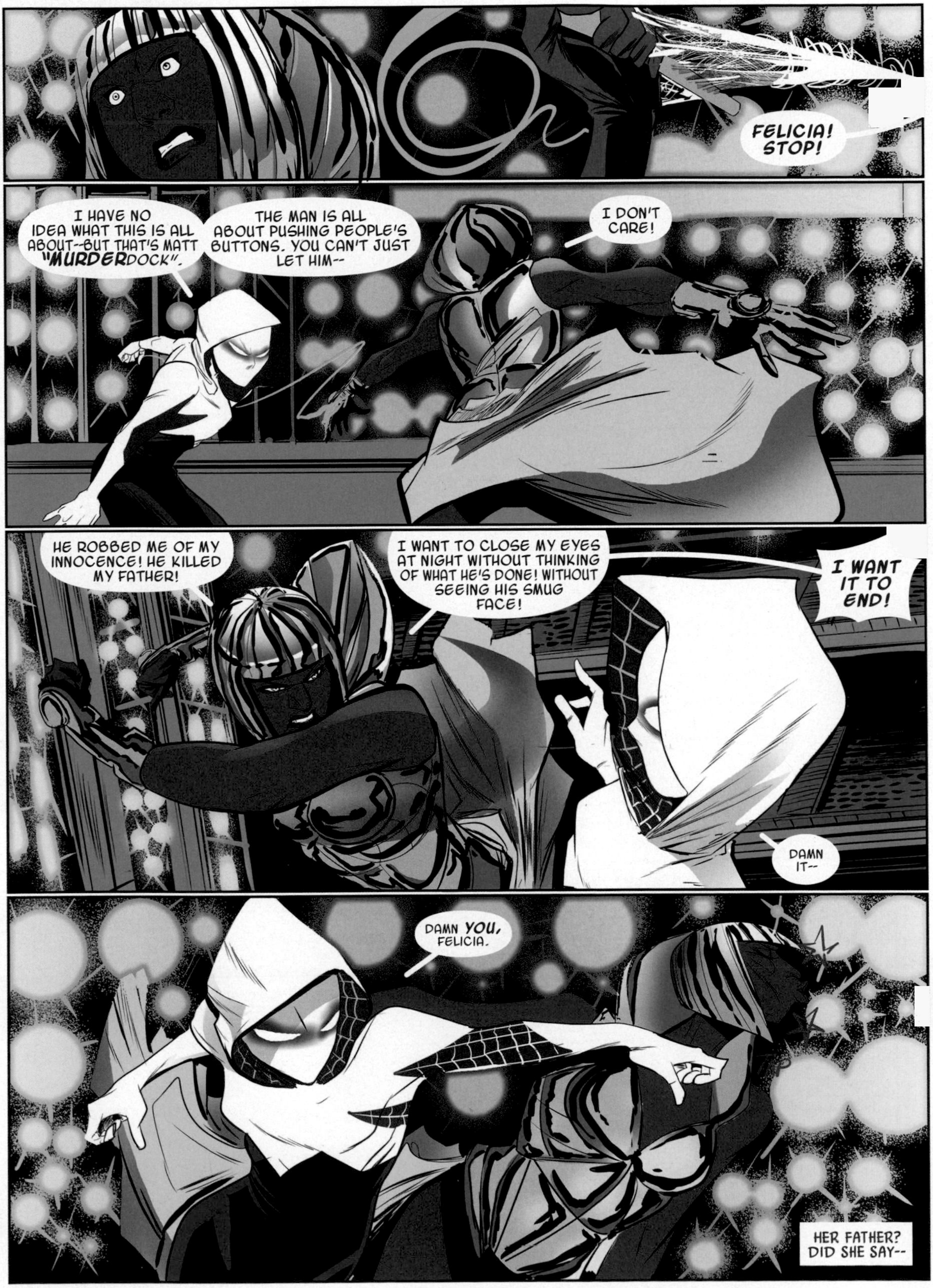
FELICIA! STOP!
I HAVE NO IDEA WHAT THIS IS ALL ABOUT--BUT THAT'S MATT "MURDERDOCK".
THE MAN IS ALL ABOUT PUSHING PEOPLE'S BUTTONS. YOU CAN'T JUST LET HIM--
I DON'T CARE!
HE ROBBED ME OF MY INNOCENCE! HE KILLED MY FATHER!
I WANT TO CLOSE MY EYES AT NIGHT WITHOUT THINKING OF WHAT HE'S DONE! WITHOUT SEEING HIS SMUG FACE!
I WANT IT TO END!
DAMN IT--
DAMN YOU, FELICIA.
HER FATHER? DID SHE SAY--

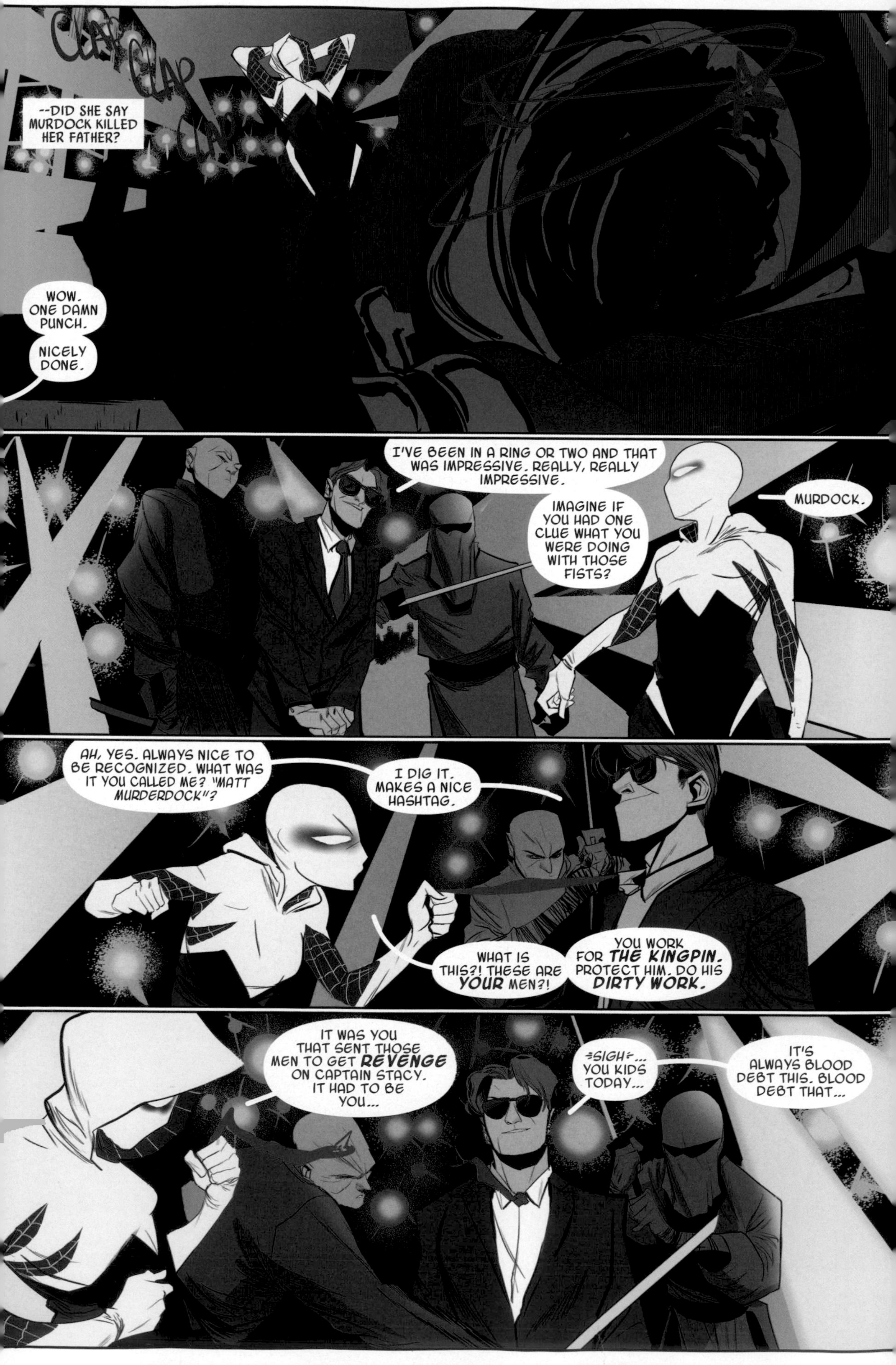
CLAP CLAP CLAP CLAP
--DID SHE SAY MURDOCK KILLED HER FATHER?
WOW. ONE DAMN PUNCH.
NICELY DONE.
I'VE BEEN IN A RING OR TWO AND THAT WAS IMPRESSIVE. REALLY, REALLY IMPRESSIVE.
IMAGINE IF YOU HAD ONE CLUE WHAT YOU WERE DOING WITH THOSE FISTS?
MURDOCK.
AH, YES. ALWAYS NICE TO BE RECOGNIZED. WHAT WAS IT YOU CALLED ME? "MATT MURDERDOCK"?
I DIG IT. MAKES A NICE HASHTAG.
WHAT IS THIS?! THESE ARE YOUR MEN?!
YOU WORK FOR THE KINGPIN. PROTECT HIM. DO HIS DIRTY WORK.
IT WAS YOU THAT SENT THOSE MEN TO GET REVENGE ON CAPTAIN STACY. IT HAD TO BE YOU...
=SIGH=... YOU KIDS TODAY...
IT'S ALWAYS BLOOD DEBT THIS. BLOOD DEBT THAT...

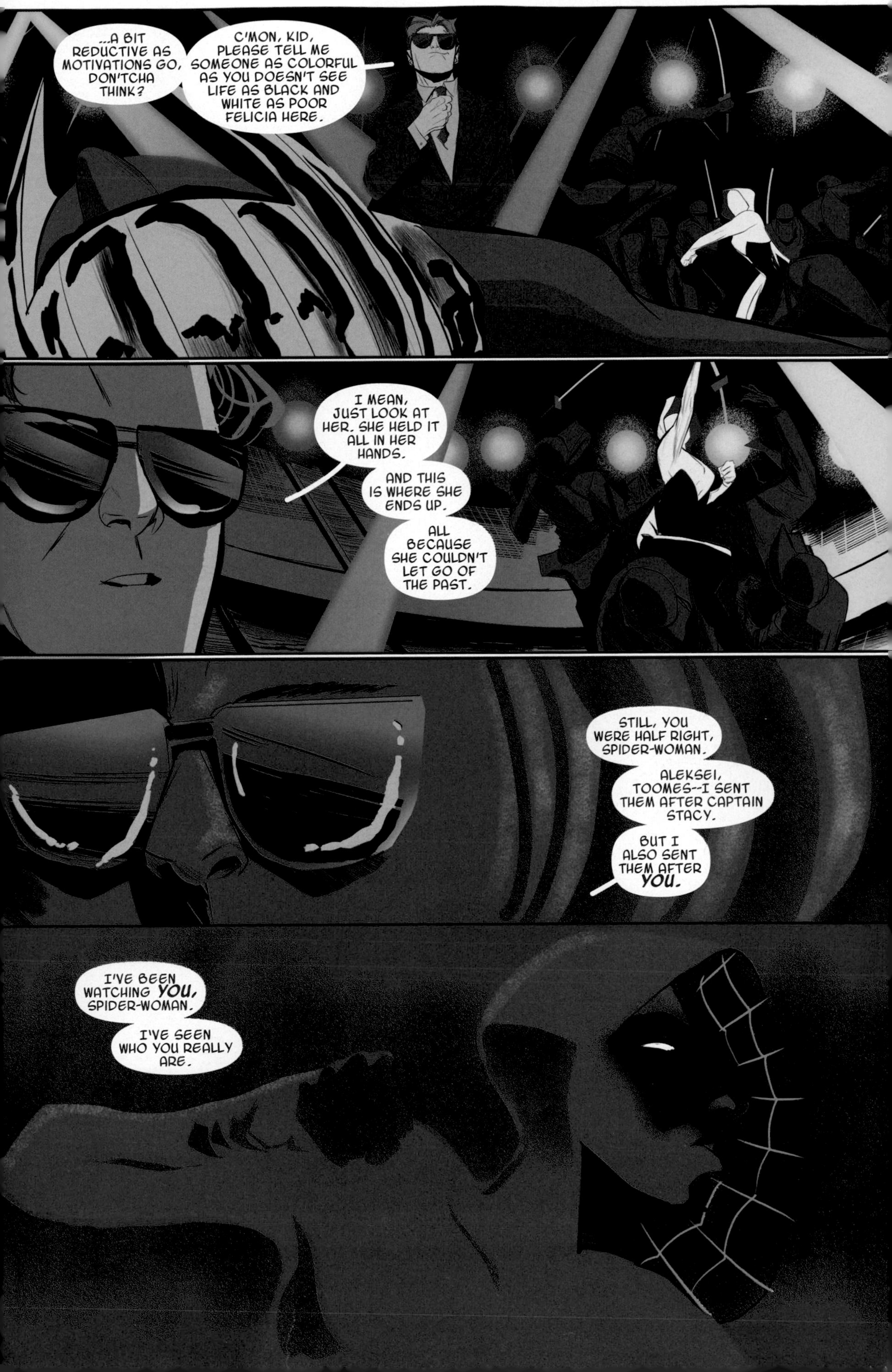
...A BIT REDUCTIVE AS MOTIVATIONS GO, DON'TCHA THINK?
C'MON, KID, PLEASE TELL ME SOMEONE AS COLORFUL AS YOU DOESN'T SEE LIFE AS BLACK AND WHITE AS POOR FELICIA HERE.
I MEAN, JUST LOOK AT HER. SHE HELD IT ALL IN HER HANDS.
AND THIS IS WHERE SHE ENDS UP.
ALL BECAUSE SHE COULDN'T LET GO OF THE PAST.
STILL, YOU WERE HALF RIGHT, SPIDER-WOMAN.
ALEKSEI, TOOMES--I SENT THEM AFTER CAPTAIN STACY.
BUT I ALSO SENT THEM AFTER YOU.
I'VE BEEN WATCHING YOU, SPIDER-WOMAN.
I'VE SEEN WHO YOU REALLY ARE.

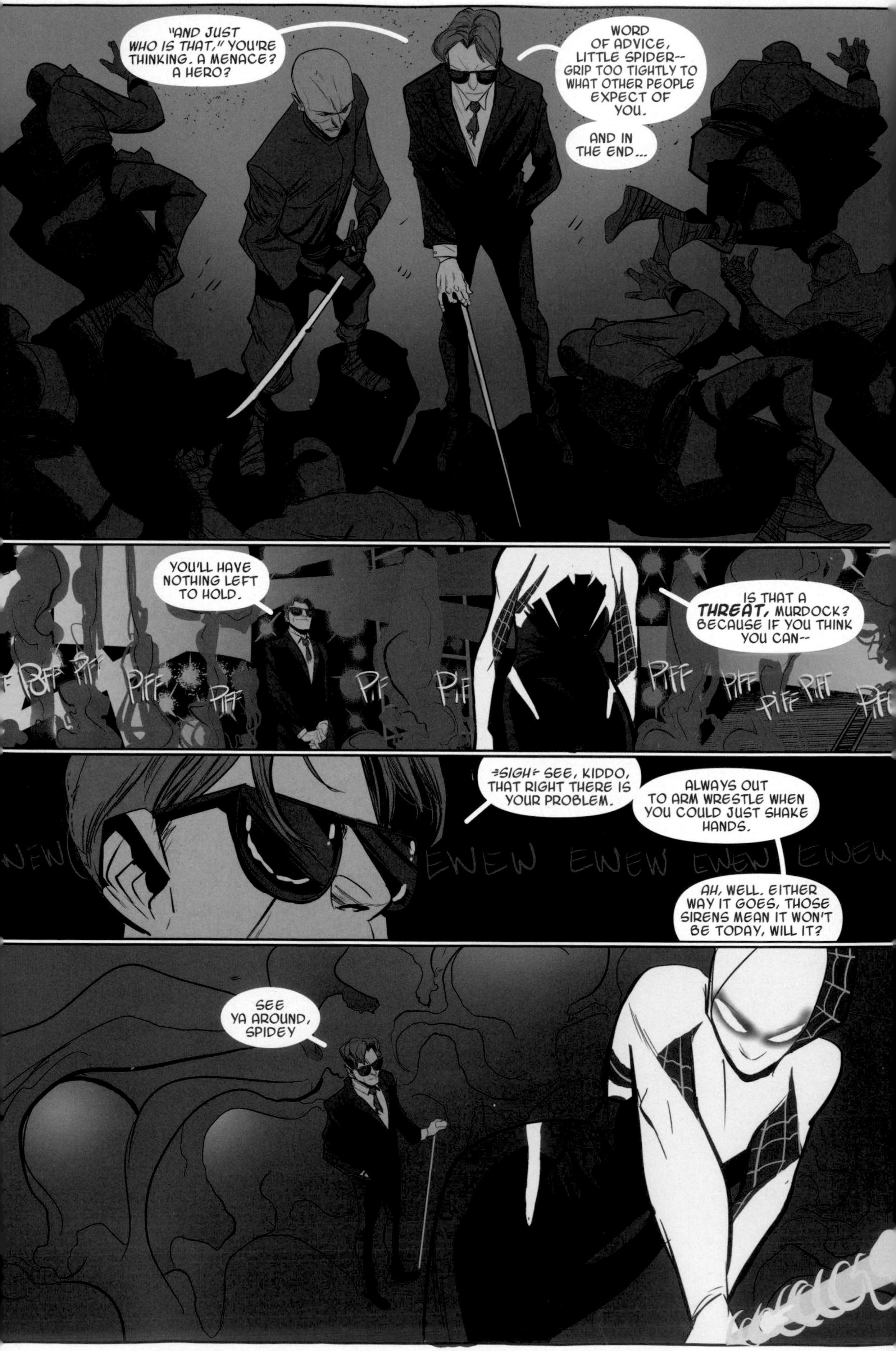
"AND JUST WHO IS THAT," YOU'RE THINKING. A MENACE? A HERO?
WORD OF ADVICE, LITTLE SPIDER-- GRIP TOO TIGHTLY TO WHAT OTHER PEOPLE EXPECT OF YOU.
AND IN THE END...
YOU'LL HAVE NOTHING LEFT TO HOLD.
IS THAT A THREAT, MURDOCK? BECAUSE IF YOU THINK YOU CAN--
PIFF PIFF PIFF PIFF PIFF PIFF PIFF PIFF PIFF PIFF
=SIGH= SEE, KIDDO, THAT RIGHT THERE IS YOUR PROBLEM.
ALWAYS OUT TO ARM WRESTLE WHEN YOU COULD JUST SHAKE HANDS.
EWEW EWEW EWEW EWEW EWEW
AH, WELL. EITHER WAY IT GOES, THOSE SIRENS MEAN IT WON'T BE TODAY, WILL IT?
SEE YA AROUND, SPIDEY

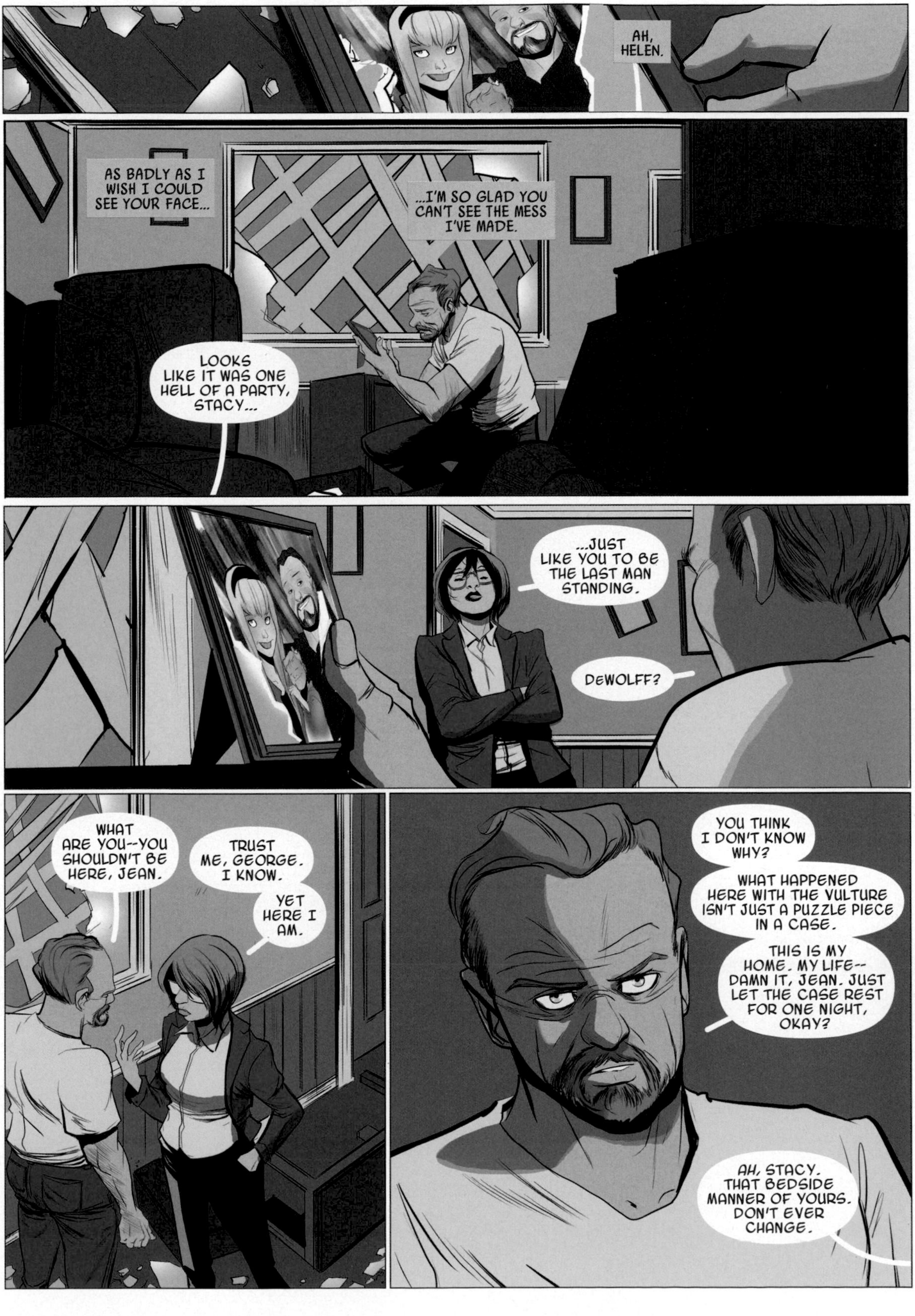
AH, HELEN.
AS BADLY AS I WISH I COULD SEE YOUR FACE...
...I'M SO GLAD YOU CAN'T SEE THE MESS I'VE MADE.
LOOKS LIKE IT WAS ONE HELL OF A PARTY, STACY...
...JUST LIKE YOU TO BE THE LAST MAN STANDING.
DEWOLFF?
WHAT ARE YOU--YOU SHOULDN'T BE HERE, JEAN.
TRUST ME, GEORGE. I KNOW.
YET HERE I AM.
YOU THINK I DON'T KNOW WHY?
WHAT HAPPENED HERE WITH THE VULTURE ISN'T JUST A PUZZLE PIECE IN A CASE.
THIS IS MY HOME. MY LIFE-- DAMN IT, JEAN. JUST LET THE CASE REST FOR ONE NIGHT, OKAY?
AH, STACY. THAT BEDSIDE MANNER OF YOURS. DON'T EVER CHANGE.

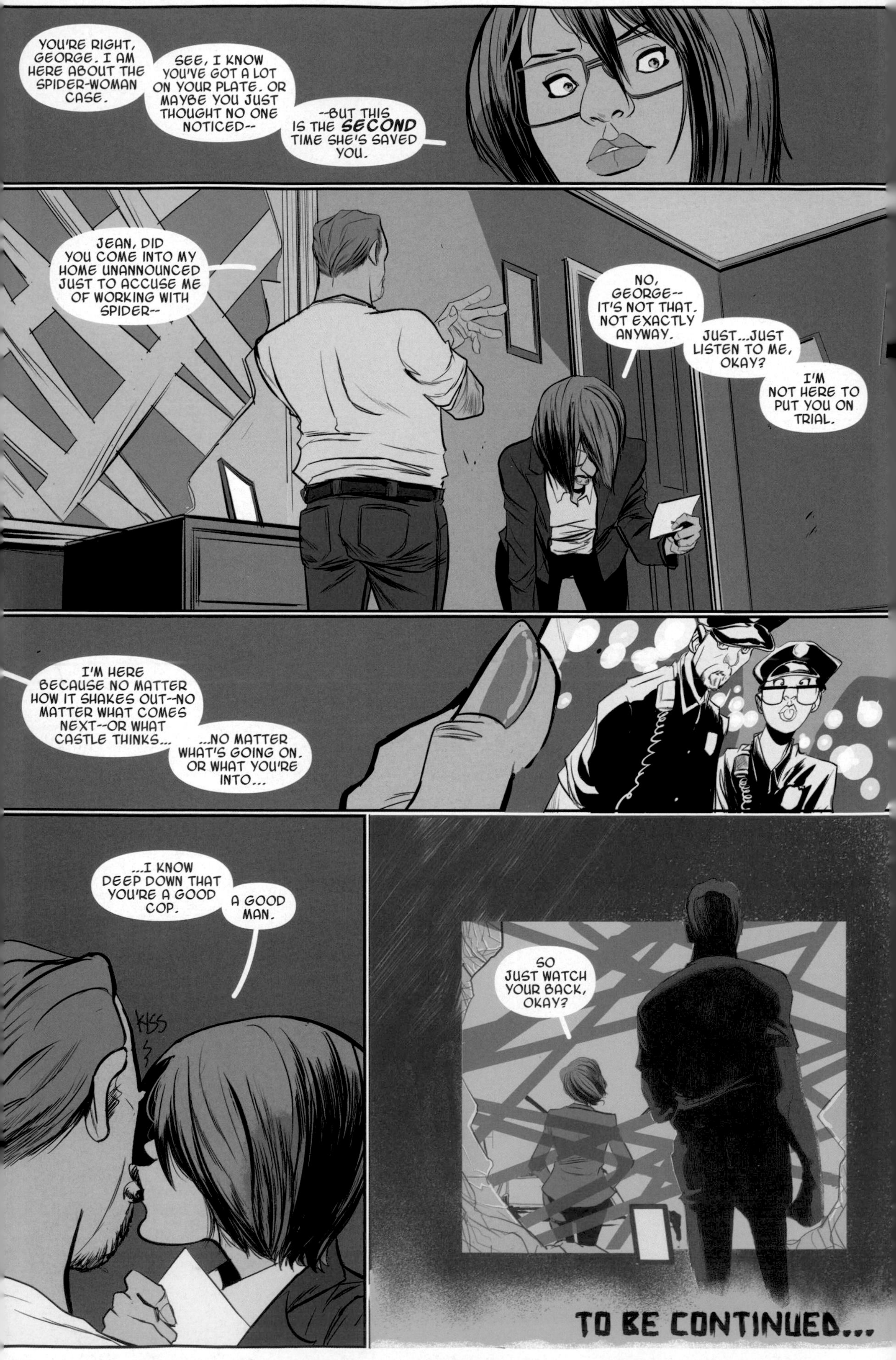
YOU'RE RIGHT, GEORGE. I AM HERE ABOUT THE SPIDER-WOMAN CASE.
SEE, I KNOW YOU'VE GOT A LOT ON YOUR PLATE. OR MAYBE YOU JUST THOUGHT NO ONE NOTICED--
--BUT THIS IS THE SECOND TIME SHE'S SAVED YOU.
JEAN, DID YOU COME INTO MY HOME UNANNOUNCED JUST TO ACCUSE ME OF WORKING WITH SPIDER--
NO, GEORGE-- IT'S NOT THAT. NOT EXACTLY ANYWAY.
JUST...JUST LISTEN TO ME, OKAY?
I'M NOT HERE TO PUT YOU ON TRIAL.
I'M HERE BECAUSE NO MATTER HOW IT SHAKES OUT--NO MATTER WHAT COMES NEXT--OR WHAT CASTLE THINKS...
...NO MATTER WHAT'S GOING ON. OR WHAT YOU'RE INTO...
...I KNOW DEEP DOWN THAT YOU'RE A GOOD COP.
A GOOD MAN.
KISS
SO JUST WATCH YOUR BACK, OKAY?
TO BE CONTINUED...

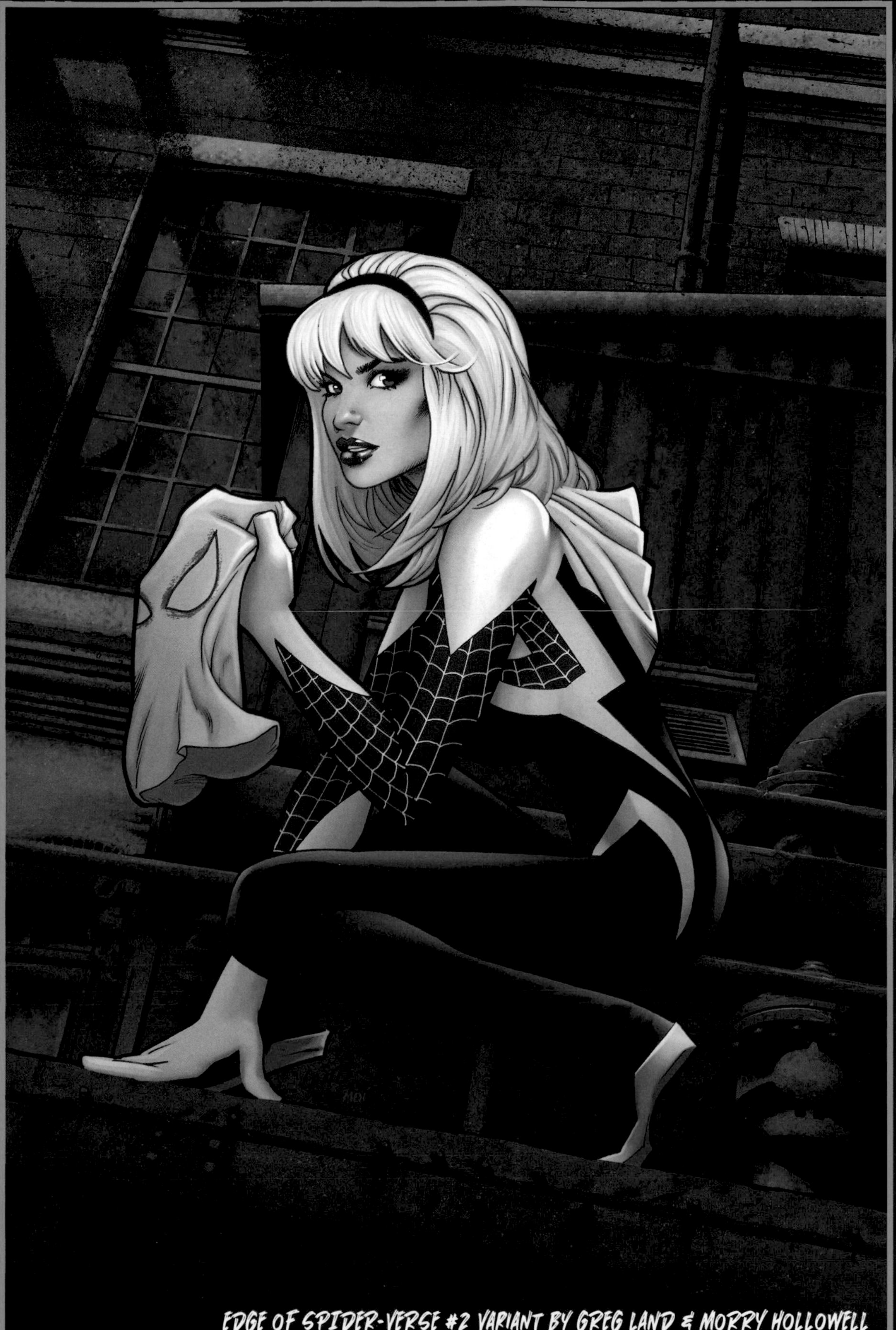

EDGE OF SPIDER-VERSE #2 VARIANT BY GREG LAND & MORRY HOLLOWELL

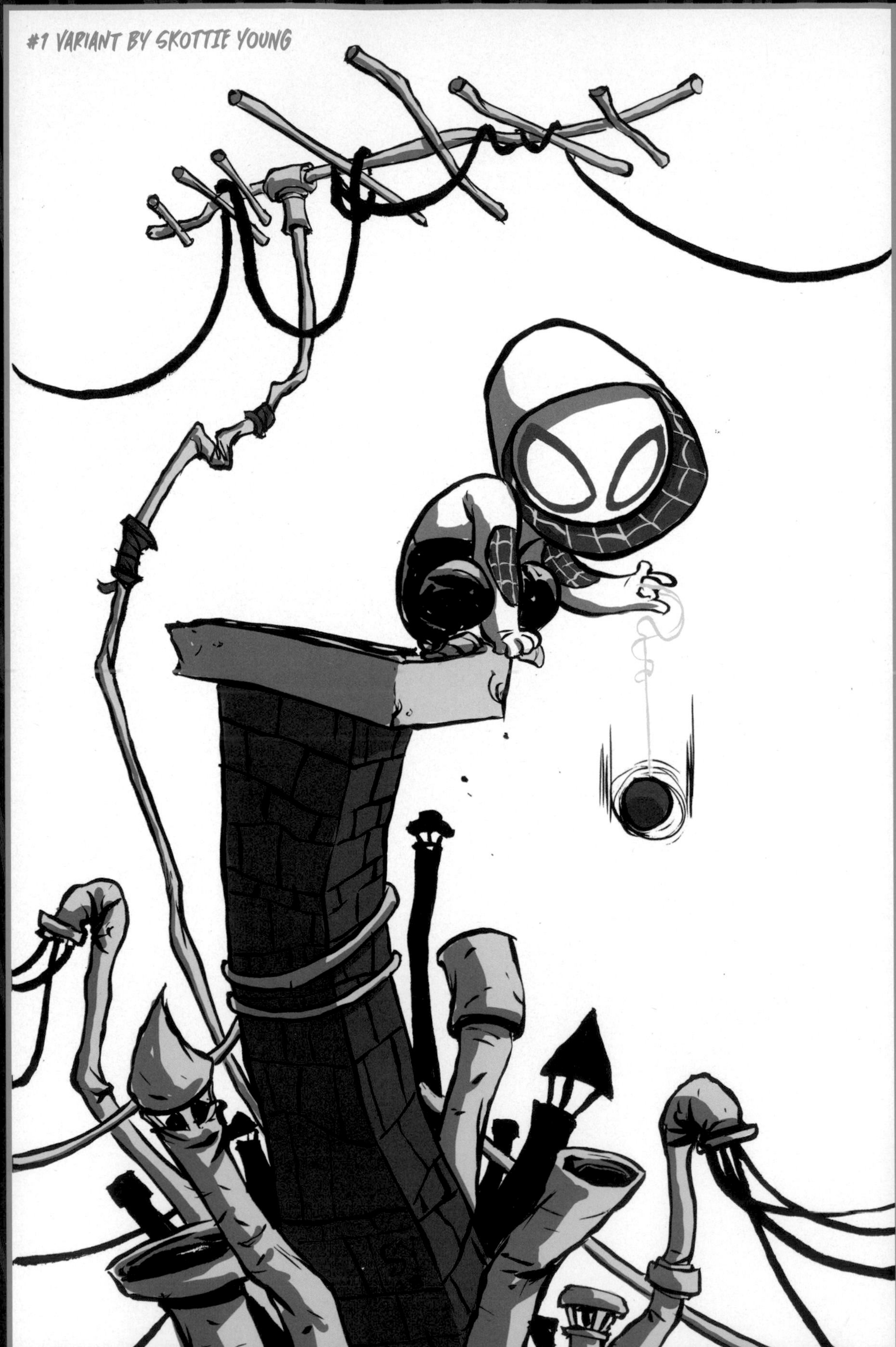
#1 VARIANT BY SKOTTIE YOUNG

#1 VARIANT BY KRIS ANKA

#2 VARIANT BY SARA PICHELLI

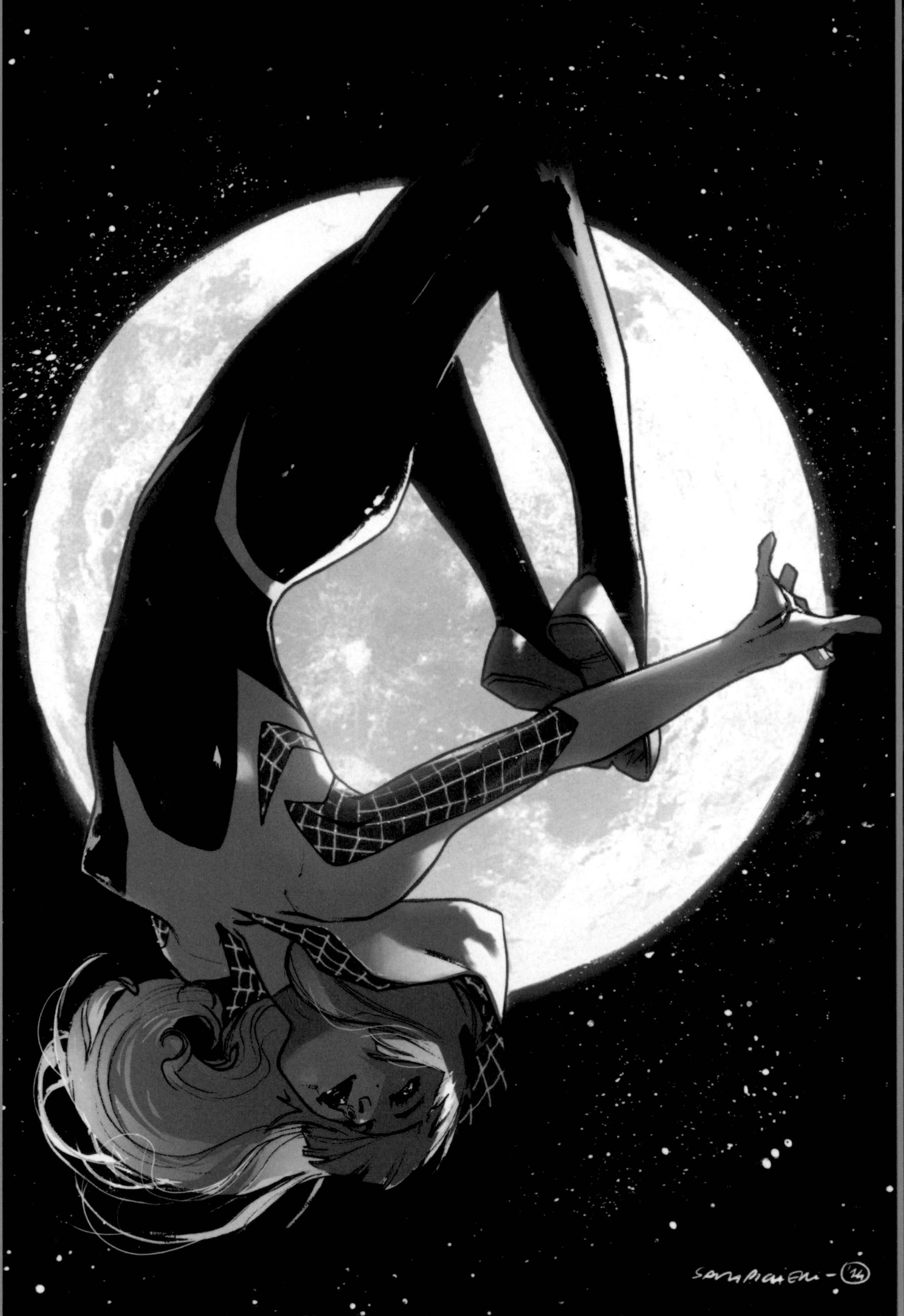

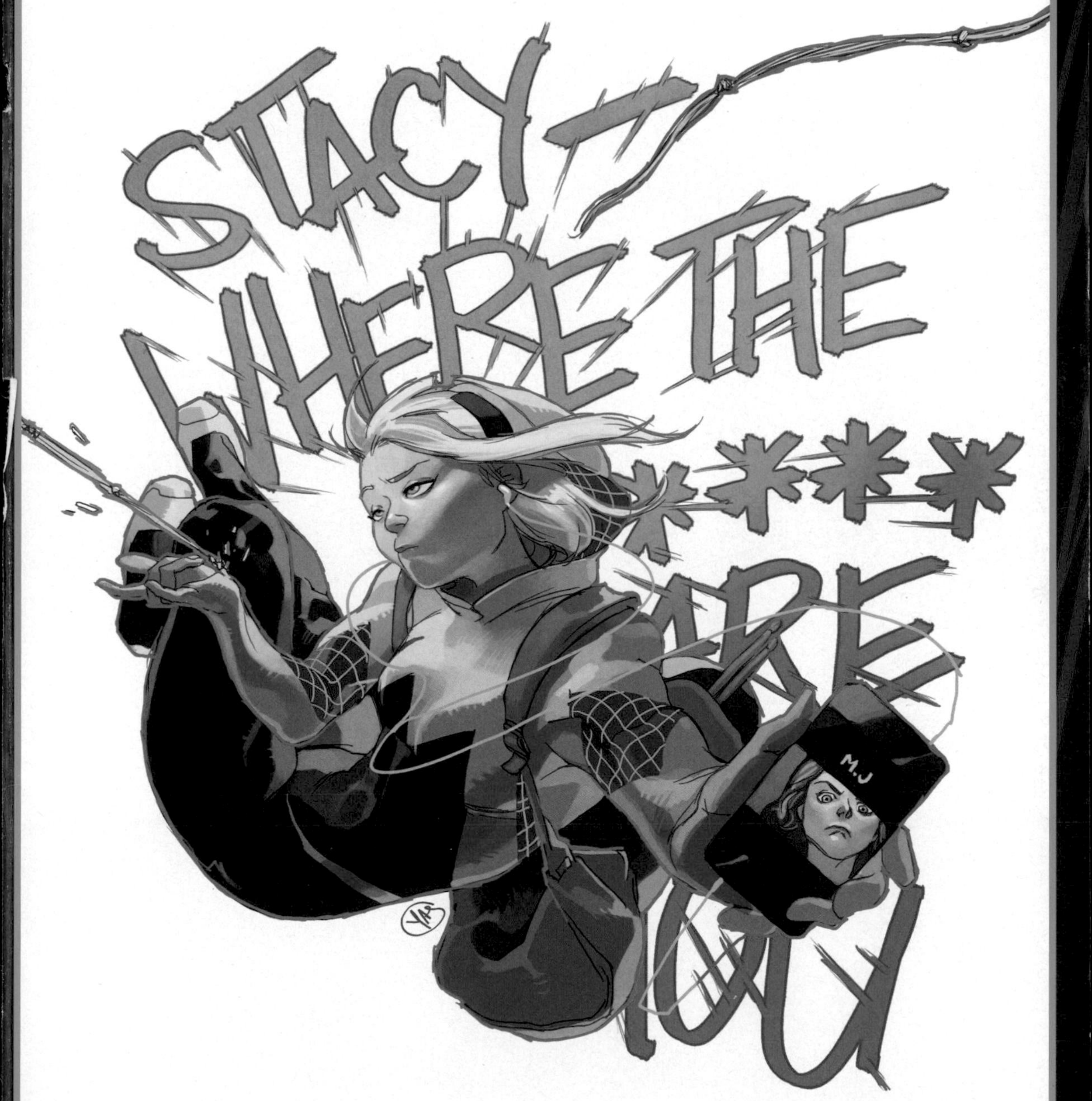
STACY—
WHERE THE
****
ARE
YOU
M.J

#3 VARIANT BY YASMINE PUTRI

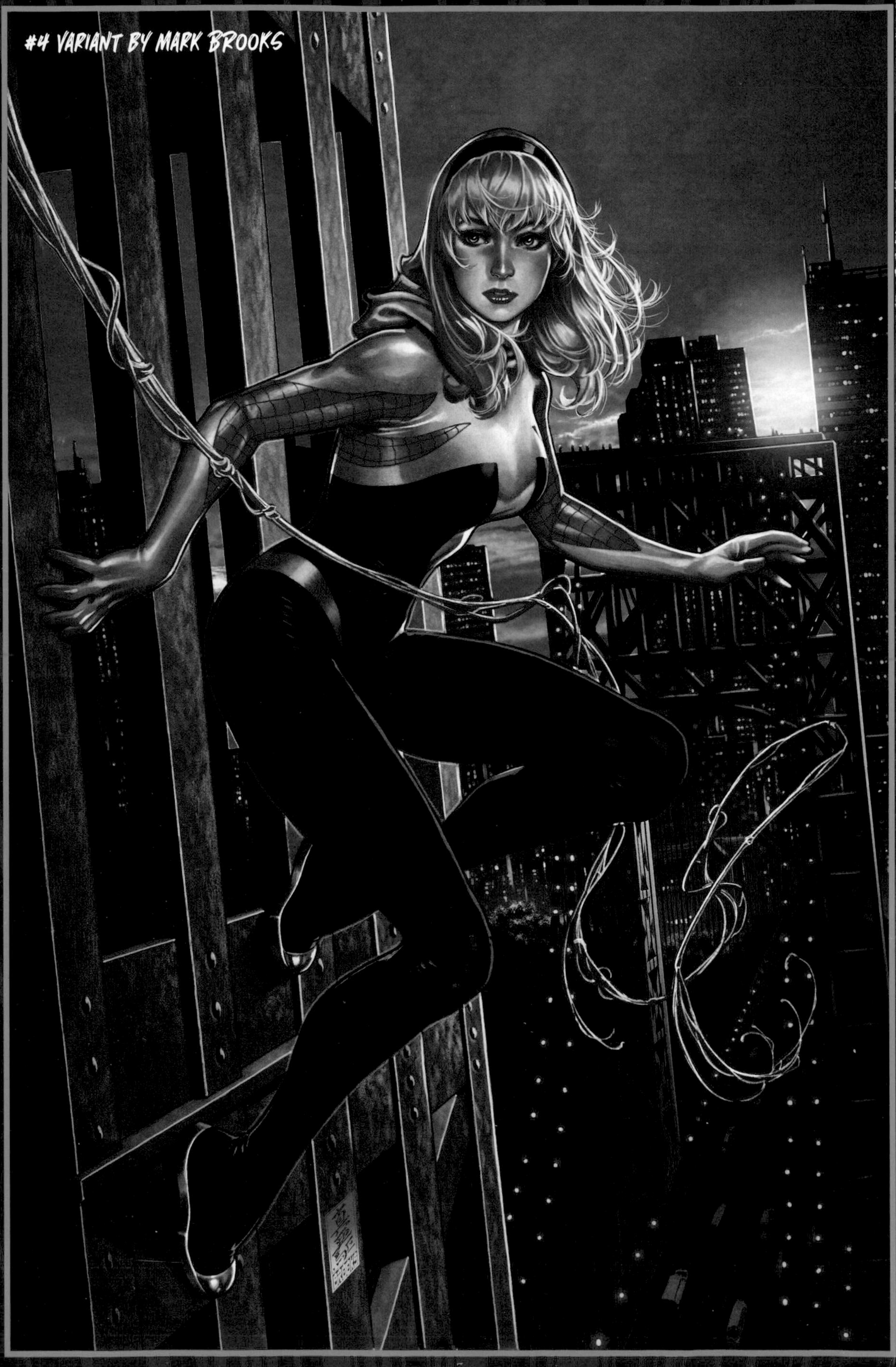
#4 VARIANT BY MARK BROOKS